SEX DETERMINATION TEST AND HUMAN RIGHTS

SEX DETERMINATION TEST AND HUMAN RIGHTS

DR. SAPNA RATHI
LL.M. Ph.D.

DEEP & DEEP PUBLICATIONS PVT. LTD.
F-159, Rajouri Garden, New Delhi - 110 027

SEX DETERMINATION TEST AND HUMAN RIGHTS

ISBN 978-81-8450-401-9

Typeset by RAHUL COMPOSERS
358, Pocket-B, Phase-2, Sector-16B, Dwarka, New Delhi - 110 075

Printed in India at MAYUR ENTERPRISES
WZ Plot No. 3, Gujjar Market, Tihar Village, New Delhi - 110 018

Published by DEEP & DEEP PUBLICATIONS PVT. LTD.
F-159, Rajouri Garden, New Delhi - 110 027 • Phone : 25435369, 25440916
E-mail : ddpubs@gmail.com • ddpubs@yahoo.com
Showroom :
2/13, Ansari Road, Daryaganj, New Delhi - 110 002 • Telefax : 23245122

Contents

Preface

Science and technology have been an integral part of Indian civilization and culture over the past several millennia. Few are aware that India was the fountainhead of important foundational scientific developments and approaches. These cover many great scientific discoveries and technological achievements in mathematics, astronomy, architecture, chemistry, metallurgy, medicine, natural philosophy and other areas.

India's traditions have been founded on the principles of universal harmony, respect for all creation and an integrated holistic approach. This background is likely to provide valuable insights for future scientific advances. During the century prior to Independence, there was an awakening of modern science in India through the efforts of a number of outstanding scientists. They were responsible for great scientific advances of the highest international caliber.

In the half century since Independence, India has been committed to the task of promoting the spread of science. The key role of technology as an important element of national development is also well recognized. The Indian policies have emphasized self-reliance, as also sustainable and equitable development. They embody a vision and strategy that are applicable today, and would continue to inspire us in our endeavours.

Science and technology have had unprecedented impact on human rights. Scientific and technological developments today also have deep ethical, legal and social implications. There are deep concerns in society about these. The ongoing globalization and the intensely competitive environment have a significant impact, both negative and positive, on human rights regime that has posed certain challenges.

Nevertheless, the development of science and technology, especially, in field of medical science, helped the human being in his development to great extent. For instance, new techniques of treatment of cancer, T.B. and other diseases saved the life of human beings. Latest technology of Sex Determination Test also made a revolutionary change in human society.

But at the same time, we observe that gifts of the science and technology have been misused by the human society which yields gross violation of the human rights and posed challenges to Human Values like—moral, social, ethical, cultural as well as the legal aspects also. As scientific advances improve our lives, they also complicate how we live and react to the new technologies. More and more, human values come into conflict with scientific advancement as we deal with important issues such as nuclear power, environmental degradation and information technology.

In these days, the advancement of medical science, especially, the Sex Determination Technology has made an adverse impact upon the progress of Human Rights. The advancement in such medical science hampered the true spirit of law, medical science and Human Rights.

With the passage of time, the technique which was developed for the noble cause for the benevolent of human beings, started to be misused by man and that has violated the human rights of the fetus even in mother's womb. In present scenario, this is one of the burning issues and it puts a question mark on the human rights of the fetus in the mother's womb.

The scientific and technological development is one of the emerging areas, which has attracted the attention of legislatures, judges, jurists, etc. and puzzled them in tracing out the solution of various ethical and legal problems, especially, related to Sex Determination Test.

So far as the constructive side of development of science is concerned, it is of great significance, but we can not ignore the other destructive side also. In fact, there is nothing wrong in science itself, but it is there in human being, who has exploited scientific developments for his vested interests. He has forgotten that scientific developments are not only meant for him, but also for the common good of the society.

The objective of present study is to examine the present legal provisions relating to sex determination test and to point out flaws in them. I have not only examined the problem in national and international perspectives but also tried to point out the weaknesses of existing laws and probable consequences of latest developments of science and technology, i.e. sex determination test.

Collection of legal facts and comparison of laws of different countries has also become a part of this study. I have thoroughly examined the subject to find out truth of hypothesis made at the time of undertaking the present work.

The present study would be helpful in understanding the real cause of the problems pertaining to the impact of science and technology on human rights and finding out the probable solution of problems arising out of it.

The study on this topic would certainly contribute in present legal literature. This study would be proved useful not only for students, and teachers but also to every one who have some interest in the subject.

DR. SAPNA RATHI

Acknowledgements

I consider it my profound privilege of having worked under the dynamic guidance and positive supervision of Revered Professor S.S. Sharma, Former Dean and Head, Faculty of Law, JNV University, Jodhpur, for his full cooperation, valuable suggestions and support in completing this present work.

I wish to express my deepest and profound gratitude to him, who despite his preoccupation, took unfailing interest, gave encouragement, wise and sound consultation in completion of this study.

I would also like to express my deep respect to Professor R.N. Sharma, Dean and Head, Faculty of Law, JNV University, Jodhpur, who has provided his guidance and constant encouragement in conducting my present work.

I am also thankful to all members of the Faculty of Law, especially Professor M.K. Vyas, Professor M.K. Bhandari, Associate Professor R.K. Sinha, Associate Professor Vijaya Sharma, Associate Professor Chandan Bala for extending their constant guidance and encouragement in accomplishing this task.

I have taken the benefit of the services of the staff and officials of the library, Faculty of Law. I am thankful to them for their valuable services and assistance.

I thank Shri Nirmal Tak, who has taken in hand the task of typing the present work and executed it with indefatigable spirit and I would like to convey my thanks to all those who helped me directly and indirectly in completion of this work.

Finally and most importantly, I am grateful to my parents Executive Engineer I.P.S. Rathi and S. Lata Rathi (M.A.), brother and bhabhi Ashwani Rathi (M.B.A.) and Anita Rathi (M.A. Economics), twin sister Dr. Seema Rathi (LL.M., Ph.D.) and younger sister Er. Sonika (B.Tech., LL.B., M.B.A.) without whose cooperation, it would have been difficult.

DR. SAPNA RATHI

Introduction

The present generation is highly indebted to modern science that has provided the human society a variety of facilities in all spheres of life. By virtue of scientific developments, a man is living in such a comfortable way as he never thought of or expected two centuries ago.

Man is the most intellectual creature in the universe; he always endeavored to bring out changes for development and betterment of his life. He continued to discover something new in every walk of life so that he can make his life more convenient and comfortable. The scientific and technological development is the result of the mental potentials of man, which has made tremendous impact on human life and human rights.

The invention of new medical tools and techniques has made the complicated operations/surgery easier. Today, due to new medicines, the normal span of human life has been increased and death ratio had been decreased. In this way, the medical science has also contributed a lot in human life and improved the human health to a great extent.

Science and technology have profoundly influenced the course of human civilization. Science has provided us remarkable insights into the world we live in. As we stand today at the beginning of a new century, we have to ensure fullest use of these developments for the well-being of our people. Science and technology have been an integral part of Indian civilization and culture over the past several millennia. During the century prior to Independence, there was an awakening of modern science in India through the efforts of a number of outstanding scientists. They were responsible for great scientific advances of the highest international caliber.

Since Independence, India is making constant endeavors in promoting the cause of science and technology. The key role of technology as an important element of national development is also well recognized. The Scientific Policy Resolution of 1958 and the Technology Policy Statement of 1983 enunciated the principles on which the growth of science and technology in India has been based over the past several decades. These policies have emphasized self-reliance, as also sustainable and equitable development. They embody a vision and strategy that are applicable today, and would continue to inspire us in our endeavors.

With the encouragement and support that has been provided, today there is a sound infrastructural base for science and technology. These include research laboratories, higher educational institutions and highly skilled human resource. Indian capabilities in science and technology cover an impressive range of diverse disciplines, areas of competence and of applications.

India's strength in basic research is recognized internationally. Successes in agriculture, health care, chemicals and pharmaceuticals, nuclear energy, astronomy and astrophysics, space technology and applications, defense research, biotechnology, electronics, information technology and oceanography are widely acknowledged. Major national achievements include very significant increase in food production, eradication or control of several diseases and increased life expectancy of our citizens.

Science and technology are closely intertwined and that any policy pertaining to them is to be considered together.

Scientific and technological developments today also have deep ethical, legal and social implications. There is a deep concern in society about science and technology. The ongoing globalization and the intensive competitive environment have further made a significant impact on the development of science and technology.

The nation continues to be firm in its resolve to support science and technology in all its facets. It recognizes its central role in raising the quality of life of the people of the country, particularly of the disadvantaged sections of society, in creating wealth for all, in making India globally competitive, in utilizing natural resources in a sustainable manner, in protecting the environment and ensuring national security.

We are in the phase of the twenty-first century and witnessing that technology is playing an increasingly important role in every facet of the international and national lives of the people at every corner of the globe. We must therefore, also anticipate some of the grave problems that may emerge in the disciplines of law and human rights.

In fact, law has to cope with the development of science and technology. Indeed, law moves very slowly, while technology moves rapidly. The result is that technology is racing out of legal control. In consequence, there can be grave damage to human rights as well.

Science is thus progressing in its technical ability, its physical power and its political influence, the law, which should be the sentinel or the watchdog protecting the rights of the public, is often outstripped and unprepared to meet these new challengeable responsibilities.

It is true that legal systems are adaptable to changing circumstances but there are number of inherent weaknesses that must be pointed out in this regard. Industrialization leads to pollution, as in certain towns of our country where the pollution is so bad that people suffer permanent health damage for every day that they work or stay in the industrialized centre.

Advances in information technology benefit human rights movements by enabling rapid transmission of information to monitor and respond to human rights violations. The internet is gaining a significant role in aiding in the understanding of human rights and other important global issues. Throughout time, people have sought out newer, faster, and more modern ways of transmitting information across nations. The internet is now the best way to do so. Using the internet, human rights organizations are able to have the world view their cause with just the click of a mouse.

The fact is that popular organizations can use the internet and are using it as a powerful instrument for democratization of information and exchange of common plans, policies and strategies. And while they are surfing the net, they can also receive information on human rights issues, causes, and movements. With such an open forum on human rights, some countries are worried. The internet could be used to communicate human rights violations that would reflect badly on that country. The internet provides a new avenue of communication that was not previously available to many.

As more people access the internet, more information gets out, and it is passed to millions each day. For human rights causes, this is a wonderful wave of the future. Persecuted and imprisoned scholars are being aided by human-rights groups innovative use of the Internet. Information technologies are an excellent means of organizing people globally and distributing petitions on behalf of scientists and scholars.

The faster information is transmitted, and faster people become aware of human rights violations and causes all across the world. The faster they learn, the faster they will react, and then, they will act. The internet has become the world's library. It is accessible to almost everyone all over the world, and its use is increasing day-by-day. For human rights organizations, the internet provides a bridge to parts of the world that cannot be reached by telephone or fax. It works to close the gap between peoples of every country so that we all may be closer. Even though technology can be frightening, it can also be a blessing.

Nevertheless, the development of science and technology, especially, in field of Medical science, helped the human being in his development to great extent. For instance, new techniques of treatment of cancer, T.B. and other diseases saved the life of human beings. Latest technology of Sex

Determination Test also made a revolutionary change in human society.

But at the same time, we observe that gifts of the science and technology have been misused by the human society which yields gross violation of the human rights and posed challenges to Human Values like—moral, social, ethical, cultural as well as the legal aspects also. As scientific advances improve our lives, they also complicate how we live and react to the new technologies. More and more, human values come into conflict with scientific advancement as we deal with important issues such as nuclear power, environmental degradation and information technology.

In these days, the advancement of medical science, especially, the Sex Determination Technology has made an adverse impact upon the progress of Human Rights. The advancement of Medical Science hampered the true spirit of law, medical science and Human Rights.

With the passage of time, the technique which was developed for the noble cause for the benevolent of human beings, started to be misused by man and that has violated the human rights of the fetus even in mother's womb. In present scenario, this is one of the burning issues and it puts a question mark on the human rights of the fetus in the mother's womb.

The Scientific and Technological development is one of the emerging areas, which has attracted the attention of legislatures, judges, jurists, etc. and puzzled them in tracing out the solution of various ethical and legal problems, especially, related to Sex Determination Test. The proposed study would be helpful in understanding the real cause of the problems and finding out the probable solution of them.

So far as the constructive side of development of science is concerned, it is of great significance, but we can not ignore the other destructive side also. In fact, there is nothing wrong in science itself, but it is there in human being, who has exploited scientific developments for his vested interests. He has forgotten that scientific developments are not only meant for him, but also for the common good of the society.

Undoubtedly, the development in the field of science and technology has brought a great revolution and social transformation in every sphere of human life but at the same time it has adversely affected the human rights jurisprudence all over the globe. Though the progress of the science and technology had upgraded the quality of human life yet it has degraded the dignity of human beings in certain spheres of life.

Every coin has two sides, on one hand the progress of science and technology strengthened the human rights movement but on another hand the blind race of science and technology affected the human life adversely. It has become a major destructive tool for the human dignity. The excessive exploitation of natural resources and technological development has polluted the environment, created danger to public health and imbalanced the ecological balance in the world.

Progress of science and technology is mandatory for the progress of a nation. So technological advancements should not be criticized, as what matters most is its manifestation and beneficial application. If doctors stop sex selection and sex determination, the dwindling sex ratio would be stabilized.

Law is one of the means to regulate the human behavior. It permits legal activities and provides punishments for unwanted or illegal actions in our society. But, law breakers are always engaged in searching new scientific devices of committing offences. The increasing trend of using scientific devices in committing offences has posed new challenges in the field of Human Rights.

Concept of protection of Human Rights has a great significance for the betterment of human life in a civil society. Human Rights are essential not merely to fulfil the metaphysical needs, but also to save the dignity of the individual. Without recognizing the Human Rights no citizen can survive a human being and the State can not achieve the purposes of welfare and democratic State. Every democratic Constitution has recognized the concept of Human rights in one or other way through out the globe.

Human rights are natural rights for every individual and they protect the human dignity. These are in-alienable rights and are free from the boundaries continents. There is no exaggeration in saying that without human rights, it is not possible to protect the human dignity. But, with the invention of sex determination test the dignity of woman is at stake.

Women are the integral part of our society and have an important role not only for rearing a child from its birth but development of man's personality, for instance; the personality of Chatrapati Shivaji was developed by his mother Jijabai. Manu, the law giver, has prescribed that a woman should not remain independent but under the control of men throughout her life–under the dominance of her father during her childhood, husband during her youth and son in advanced age. This advice by the ancient law giver is aimed at providing protection to a woman, if so required.

Our ancient scriptures have always worshipped woman as Goddess for instance 'Lakshmi' as controller of wealth; 'Saraswati' the goddess of knowledge; 'Parvati', 'Kali' or 'Durga' the Goddess of power and strength, etc. This country has seen many women occupying dominate positions in discharging their obligations very successfully. In our country, a girl is worshiped as a Devi on one hand and denied her existence on the other as if; she has no right to live.

The concept of sex determination was also existed in the primitive societies. The sex of the unborn child in the womb of the mother was being determined by the "Dai" and by the behavior of the mother (in whose womb the child is developing). Now, due to advanced scientific technology, the same is being determined by new technology like—ultra sound, sonography, Sex Determination Test (commonly called SDT), etc.

The SDT means to know the sex of the fetus, that is, whether that is male or female in prenatal stage. It is very difficult to determine the sex of the fetus in early stage. Ordinarily, every child in womb contains some characteristics of both sexes. Major determination is to see that whether the child has male organism or ovary, which is found in female.

But the development of sex organs in womb as a distinctive feature occurs at later stage. Females have functional, well-developed mammary glands. Males also have mammary glands but they are undeveloped and nonfunctional though equipped with nipples. Males have sperms, but females have ovaries. These are some secondary sexual features. The difference between the sexes is in the degree of their development and not a matter of absolute presence or absence.

The primary objective of developing the technique to check the conditions of the foetus in womb was purely humanity oriented. But, in order to serve his own interest the man began to misuse the technique and violated the human rights. The basic objectives of the above techniques were:

- to know about the health of fetus in womb of mother.
- to treat the fetus, if suffering from any deformity.
- to help the mother in case of negative effect on her health due to development of the fetus.
- to detect and treat other pregnancy related problems.
- to assess the normal development of fetus.

Sex Determination Test is a reflection of the social psyche in India. The devaluation of the Indian women and the girl child on account of inheritance/property rights, dowry, etc. has resulted in their becoming scapegoats or victims of violence.

There are several critical issues and factors which underlie and influence the problem of female foeticide and infanticide viz. state liability and apathy, governmental policies (family planning, abortion), medical ethics, laws and their implementation, criminalization of sex-selective abortion, pro-life *versus* pro-choice debate (reproductive freedom *versus* social good), impact of reproductive technologies, failure of education and socio-economic development to charge the mindset, regional variations in the sex ratio patterns, etc.

The law can compel reluctant parents to bring a female child into the world but cannot guarantee her a life of dignity and safety. The law can only facilitate an environment, but it is public awareness which is most important. We need attitudinal changes as well as laws. What is needed is a structural overhaul of society—from existing regimes of property rights and wages to the ideology of son preference. Radical economic reforms are needed to make women more beneficial to the family and society. A comprehensive action plan should be launched throughout the country to educate people about the value of the girl child.

Besides economic empowerment, curbing of dowry and strengthening of social security measures, the government should provide incentives for having a girl child through free education, subsidized ration, and tax concession for parents of girl children.

In India however, pregnancy is too often followed by the question of whether the unborn child is a girl or a boy. One son is a cause for joy while two are seen as a lifetime for celebration, the traditional thinking being that of one dies; at least the other will live to take care of the parents. In the bargain, pressures on the woman to produce a son are unending. The girl child is seen as an economic drain as her marriage and dowry crushes her family under huge burden of debts. Despite the legal emancipation of women in India, their education and employment in modern occupations, the traditional bias regarding female children has not undergone a change.

The practice of female infanticide has been supplemented or rather aggravated in recent times by the practice of female foeticide or sex selective abortions with the advent of new technology, i.e. Sex Determination Test. Female foeticide is the result of an unholy alliance between the traditional preference for sons and modern medical technology, increasing greed of doctors, rising, demand for dowry that makes daughters financial burdens, the ineffectiveness of the relevant legislation, and the lack of any serious involvement of the civil society in fighting this social menace. The issue of sex determination and sex selective abortion was initially an ethical issue.

Although there have been prevalence of gender selective abortions in many cultures over the globe, but the extent of this problem have alarming proportions in the countries of the Asian region like China and India. The phenomenon of son preference and gender discrimination is not confined to India alone, but there have been instances of millions of gender selective deaths throughout the history world over.

Thus, India is not the only country with a strong preference for sons; but it was the only country using pre-natal diagnosis frequently for this purpose. The 2001 Census highlighted the drastic disparity between the sex ratios in several states in north and west India and continued decline in major southern States.

According to the 2001 Census, there were less than 93 women for every 100 men in the Indian population. The prevailing concept that the birth of a female child can signal the beginning of financial ruin and extreme hardship for a poor Indian family is understandable. What is surprising is that even high-income families do not want a female child. The Government of India in its 10th Plan recognized the rights of the female child to equal opportunity, to be free from hunger, illiteracy, ignorance and exploitation.

The emergence and spread of prenatal sex determination clinics are the early warning signals on the imbalance of sex ratios at birth in the coming decade following selective abortion of female fetuses. The recently available urban-rural figures for 2001 on child sex ratio provide further confirmation that these declines are caused by the relative availability of sex determination facilities.

What can be the long-term implications if amniocentesis continues? Will it not aggravate the already uneven sex ratio? Sycophants of population control advocate this test because they think that the government can achieve Net Reproduction Rate (NRR) that is replacement of a mother by only one daughter, with the help of sex determination tests. The government and private medical practitioners justify sex determination test as a measure of population control.

Another economic theory is that if supply of women reduces, their demand as well as status will be enhanced. The scarcity of women will only increase their value. According to this logic, women would not be easily replaceable commodities. But how does the economist forget the socio-cultural milieu in which women live? The society that treats women as mere sex objects will not treat women in a more humane way, if they are scare of supply.

Some people think that it is better to kill a female foetus than give birth to an unwanted female child is very fatalistic. By this logic, it is better to kill poor people or third world masses, rather than let them suffer poverty and deprivation.

Another argument is that in cases where women have one or more daughters, amniocentesis can help them balance a family by having a son. Would couples with one or more sons undergo amniocentesis to get rid of a male foetus and have a daughter for balancing their family? How many abortions can a woman bear without jeopardizing her health? A complicated sex pre-selection technique, PGD (also called Ericsson's technique) involves the identification and discarding of the female embryo.

The popularity of sex selection can be more dangerous than that of sex determination tests because the former does not involve ethical issues related to abortion. It shows that male preference is not limited to the third world country like India, but that it is a universal phenomenon. Sex selection could lead to a violent social disaster, through the social consequences of sex selection and sex determination tests.

In the National Policy for the Empowerment of Women 2001, a policy framework was laid down for the elimination of discrimination against, and violation of, the rights of the female child. However, the situation continues to worsen, and studies have revealed that sex-selected abortions are practiced among all communities despite enactment of laws prohibiting prenatal sex determination. Thus, we examine the functioning and consequences of the misuse of this technology.

Abortion was legalized in India in 1971 when the UN mission to India recommended this step to strengthen the population policy. Although the stated reasons for passing the Medical Termination of Pregnancy (MTP) Act were humanitarian (to 'help' victims of sexual assault), health-related (to provide an alternative to those whose contraceptive measures failed) and eugenic (to reduce the number of 'abnormal' children born), there was a strong population control motivation underlying the passage of the Act.

In 1975, amniocentesis techniques for detecting foetal abnormalities began to be developed in India, at the All India Institute of Medical Sciences (AIIMS), New Delhi. It was soon known that these tests could detect the sex of the foetus also, and doctors at the Institute noted that most of the 11,000 couples who volunteered for the test wanted to know the sex of the child and were not interested in the possibility of genetic abnormalities. Most women who already had two or more daughters and who learnt that their expected child was female went for an abortion.

Sex-selective abortion and female infanticide are methods of sex-selection, which are practiced in areas where male children are valued over female children. Sex-selective abortion refers to the targeted abortion of female fetuses; the fetus sex may be identified by ultrasound but also rarely by amniocentesis or another procedure. Female infanticide is the practice of selective infanticide of female infants; one common method is child abandonment. Abandoning a child of the undesired sex outside legal adoption is called sex selective abandonment. Placing a child of the undesired sex for adoption is called sex selective adoption.

Sex selection and sex selective abortion is a form of discrimination faced by women in India today, which has been indicated as a major reason for a decline in the sex ratios. Declining numbers of women in the population brings in its wake a rise in violence against women and severely impinges their autonomy. It sets back all the successes that were achieved by the women's movement. What sets this form of discrimination apart from other forms of discrimination is that it requires the active intervention by the medical personnel and the misuse of medical technology.

The practice of female deselection in India could be attributed to socio-economic reasons. There is a belief by certain people in India that female children are inherently less worthy because they leave home and family when they marry, a system known to anthropologists as patri locality. There is also a clear link in modern day India with the success of Family planning, where by couples only have 1 or 2 children, and wish to ensure that they have a male child as opposed to older times when they could consider having several children in the hopes of a male child.

Studies in India have indicated three factors of female deselection in India, which are economic utility, socio cultural utility, and religious functions. The factor as to economic utility is that studies indicate that sons are more likely than daughters to provide family farm labor or provide in or for a family business, earn wages, and give old-age support for parents.

In some countries, including India, it is currently illegal to determine the sex of a child during pregnancy using ultra-sound scans. Laboratories are prohibited to reveal the fetus's sex during such scans. While most established labs comply with the law, determined persons can find a cheaper lab that would tell them.

In India, since 1978 the SDT is being used as a sex determination or sex pre-selection test. Since then the test has become extremely popular and has led to a mushrooming of private clinics which perform the test all over the country. Earlier doctors employed the controversial amniocentesis test done between 14-18 weeks to determine the sex of the foetus. The ultrasound technique has also been improved. The sex of a foetus can be determined by more sophisticated machines within 13-14 weeks of pregnancy by trans-vaginal sonography and by 14 to 16 weeks through abdominal ultrasound.

These methods have rendered sex determination cheap and easy. Some sophisticated method like Ericsson method which separates the X and Y Chromos from the sperm and then Injects back only Y chromos into the womb to ensure a boy have also been developed and that cost around Rupees 15,000 to 25,000.

Today female foeticide is no more an urban phenomenon, rural people are also getting more and more involved in it and come all the way long to cities to get these tests done. Once the sex of the foetus is determined, if it is a female foetus, it is aborted. The increase in female foeticide has seen the proportionate decrease in female sex ratio which has hit an all time low especially in the 0-6 age group and if this decline is not checked the very delicate equilibrium of nature can be permanently destroyed.

Ultrasounds are taken to monitor the health of unborn children but sex selection is a violation of law and unethical. These unscrupulous murders of female or girls are justified on two grounds. First, it reduces the population and second is that the poor parents will be saved from the expenses which they would have to incur in the marriage of their daughter, if she had born. So the murder of a female foetus is considered to be a solution to two major problems, i.e. population problem and dowry.

But how far are these grounds justified? India was the first country to adopt family planning as an official programme to reduce the birthrate. But population of the country is still growing. One of the reasons for the growth of population in India is the desire for a son. Today, the sex-determination tests have provided an easy way out to know whether or not a woman will get a son. Each time a woman gets pregnant and she can have the sex of the foetus determined and get it aborted, if it happens to be a female child.

Abortion was punishable under Indian Penal Code but it was legalized with the passing of Medical Termination of Pregnancy Act, 1971. This Act along with its revised rules was envisaged as a milestone in the modernization of Indian society through laws. Doctors are against the ban on amniocentesis because it will lead to an underground practice in the field.

None of these arguments given in favour of the continuance of sex determination tests holds good. It is true that people should have every right to plan their families. If a man has a daughter and he wants son let him have it. But difficulty lies, if he wants son only.

The sex determination test is used to destroy the female foetus than to control the number of children or to have a child of the sex of one's choice. In India, the choice is always male child and it is the female only that is unwanted child. Though it is the individual interest that is paramount but he has a duty towards the society also as a member of it.

It is estimated that by 2020 there could be more than 35 million young "surplus males" in China and 25 million in India. Sex-selective abortion has become an issue in Southern and Eastern Asian countries, where sex-selective abortions have caused an increase in the imbalances between sex ratios of various Asian countries. Studies have estimated that sex-selective abortions have increased the ratio of males to females from the natural average of 105-106 males per 100 females to 113 males per 100 females in South Korea and China, 110 males per 100 females in Taiwan and 107 males per 100 females among Chinese populations living in Singapore and parts of Malaysia. However, a similar trend does not exist in North Korea, possibly due to limited access to prenatal sex-testing technologies.

It has been argued that by having a one-child policy, China has increased the rate of abortion of female fetuses, thereby accelerating a demographic decline. As Chinese families are allowed only one child, and would often prefer at least one son, there are fewer daughters, thus preventing the formation of a greater number of families in the next generation. Since 2005, test kits such as the Baby Gender Mentor have become available over the internet. These tests have been criticized for making it easier to perform a sex-selective abortion earlier in a pregnancy.

There are several kinds of sex-determination (SD) and sex-pre-selection (SP) techniques that have been produced by recent advances in medical science, like sonography, foetoscopy, needling, chorionic villa biopsy (CVB), and amniocentesis. The names of these techniques are becoming household words in urban India, with amniocentesis by far the most popular technique in India for determining the sex of a fetus, even thought was developed to detect genetic deformities.

Bombay and Delhi are the major centers' for SD and SP tests, and amniocentesis is used even in the clinics of small towns and cities in Gujarat, Maharashtra, Uttar Pradesh, Bihar, Madhya Pradesh, Punjab, Tamil Nadu, and Rajasthan.

Now sex-selection has become a rampant phenomenon and the technologies that are misused for this very purpose are becoming increasingly sophisticated. The use of advanced medical science and technology has made sexual discrimination and the elimination of female babies even before birth an invisible deed.

Female foeticide is one of the most nefarious crimes on this earth; perhaps what is detestable is that the people who commit crime belong to the educated class. To this menace our ancestral and biased view about male child, lack of education, ever increasing population and dowry have been good propellants. Some measures and their enforcement have to happen immediately. The ineffectiveness of the Pre-Natal Diagnostics Techniques (Regulation and Prevention of Misuse) Act is very much evident. Hence, there needs to be quick reformation in the attitude of people to look beyond the legacy and transform this world as a better place to live in.

There are several instruments dealing with the right of fetus, like—the Universal Declaration of Human Rights, the International Covenant on Civil and Political Rights, the American Convention on Human Rights, the African Charter on Human and Peoples' Rights, the European Convention.

Our constitution-makers also anticipated the social problems associated with the emancipation of women. They had seen prevailing gender inequality during their time and had visualized that the sex equality was crucial for the development of the country. In order to do away with the inequality and to provide reasonable opportunities and create awareness and the exercise of human rights and claim, it was necessary and promote with special care, educational and economics interests not only of men but women too and to provide necessary protection the social injustice and exploitation. The preamble, which incorporates chief goal enshrined in the constitution, reflects the spirit of equality.

Before the coming into force of the MTP Act, "abortion" or induced miscarriage came under the purview of the IPC, which criminalized such an act in its Sections 312-316. These provisions, drawn up over a century ago, were in consonance with the then prevalent English law on the subject. The rights of the unborn child received precedence over the reproductive rights of the mother or even her health needs.

Under this scheme of the law, not only was the person performing the abortion or 'causing the miscarriage' guilty of an offence but the woman who procured the abortion, was also guilty. The only circumstance where a person was not guilty was where the abortion was caused in good faith and in order to save the life of the woman. Thus, there was an absolute prohibition on abortion and no consideration whatsoever given to the circumstances of each case which required/compelled the woman to procure the abortion.

The MTP Act also incorporates provisions for ensuring access to safe abortion services. Hence, as the laws stand today, a woman can obtain MTP services provided that she satisfies any of the grounds contained in the Act, in a place recognized and registered under the Act and that the MTP has to be conducted by medical professional reçognized under the MTPA and the MTP Rules. Criteria for registration and qualifications/ experience of medical professionals are also provided in the MTPA, MTP Rules and MTP Regulations.

Due to excessive female infanticide in the northern and western states of India there were strong agitations and protests to curb the evil of female foeticide. The state of Maharashtra became the first in country to ban pre-natal sex determination through the enactment of Maharashtra regulation of prenatal diagnostics techniques act. Similar efforts at the national level resulted in the enactment of the Central pre-natal diagnostic techniques (Regulation and prevention of misuse) Act, 1994.

The Act has two aspects viz., regulatory and preventive, enforcement and effectiveness. It seeks to regulate the use of pre-natal diagnostic techniques for legal or medical purposes and prevent misuse for illegal purposes. The act provides for the setting up of various bodies along with their composition powers and functions. There is a central supervisory board, appropriate authorities and advisory committees.

In India, the policy environment is supportive of the reproductive choices of women and men. The medical termination of pregnancy Act is legal and it allows for induced abortions where pregnancy carries grave injury to women's health. A negative outcome of the PNDT Act was that the practice of sex determination was driven nonetheless and the availability of services proliferated correspondingly.

Ultrasound machines continued to be widely available and simple to use. In such an environment it is very difficult to enforce a law which sought to control information that travels through informal channels and can operate secretly.

Law cannot control the information that is conveyed through a mere smile or facial expression. Unsurprisingly the enforcement, if law becomes weak. There is still utmost controversy as to whom will serve as the watch dog to control the misuse of the practice of female foeticide and its implementation is difficult and considering it can only be the doctor who carries out the abortion or mother of the foetus who can be punished. This is very ambiguous as many women are indeed forced by family members to go ahead with an abortion of a female foetus.

Other reasons for limited effectiveness of the law include lack of political will to ensure enforcement. Experience has shown that in general the role of legislation is subverting a social practice is limited. The ministry of health and family welfare had proposed a series of amendments to the 1994 Act. Although there was a central Act regulating and preventing the misuse of pre-natal diagnostic techniques the menace of female foeticide continued.

So there was need for much more stringent rules to curb this evil. These were given parliamentary approval. The act was amended in 2002 and in 2003 Rules were framed by the central government under section 32 of the act. These rules may be called Pre-conception and pre-natal diagnostic techniques (Prohibition of sex selection) rules, 1996.

The Pre-Natal Diagnostic Techniques (Regulation and Prevention of Misuse) Act (the PNDT Act for short) came into being since 1996. This was as a result of a campaign in 1986 that included women's groups and health activists. The campaign resulted in the Maharashtra government appointing a committee, which followed formulation of an Act at the state level in 1988. Given the concern of the then Health Secretary of Maharashtra and other organizations this issue was taken up at the Central government level resulting in the formulation of the Pre-Natal Diagnostic Techniques (Regulation and Prevention of Misuse) Act, 1994 (PNDT Act for short) which was brought into force from Jan. 1, 1996.

The enforcement of this Act is still in this initial stage. The outcome of complaints filed under the law is still not known. What is known, however, is that discrimination against women continues unabated? In order to achieve the purpose of this Act, social change and a change in the mindset of people to regard women as equal stakeholders in society is essential. In the meantime, this law, however flawed it may be, is the only one we have to combat the phenomena of sex selection and sex determination, legally.

Public Interest Litigation was therefore, filed in the Supreme Court in the year 1998. The lawyers Collective represented the petitioners CEHAT, Masum and Dr. Sabu George in this case. The objective behind filings this petition was firstly, to obtain directions for the implementation of this Act and secondly, to seek an explicit inclusion of pre-conception techniques within the ambit of this law.

The Supreme Court took on the unique role of monitoring compliance with the law. The central government, state governments and Union Territories were directed to the file regular reports on the progress of implementation of the law. During the course of 5 years that the case proceeded, registration for clinics went up considerably, authorities were appointed in all states, districts and sub-districts, pre conception techniques were included within the ambit of the law and an evaluation format for reporting compliance was put in place. Implementing this law also revealed loopholes within the law. Hence amendments were brought into force as per the directives of the Supreme Court.

Supreme Court directed state governments to take further steps to enforce the law. Department of family welfare was directed to file an affidavit indicating the status of actions taken. Supreme Court directed 9 companies to supply the information of the machines sold to various clinics in the last 5 years. Details of about 11,200 machines from all these companies and fed into a common data base. Addresses received from the manufacturers were also sent to concerned states and to launch prosecution against those bodies using ultrasound machines that had filed to get themselves registered under the act. The court directed that the ultrasound machines/scanners be sealed and seized if they were being used without registration.

Three associations' viz., the Indian Medical Association [IMA], the Indian Radiologist Association [IRA], and the Federation of Obstetricians and Gynecologists Societies of India [FOGSI] were asked to furnish details of members using these machines. Since the Supreme Court directive 99 cases were registered and in 232 cases ultrasound machines, other equipment and records were seized. Today there is an estimated 25,000 ultrasound machines in the country, of these 15,000 have been registered. State governments have communicated to the central government in writing according to official reports received, they are satisfied that sex determination services are no longer being provided in their respective states.

However, it is widely believed that while these services are no longer openly available their clandestine availability and utilization continues all over the country. The observations of the National inspection and Monitoring Commission confirm this situation and endorse the need for stricter enforcement of laws.

Time has perhaps come for us to get rid of male chauvinism and treat children as gifts of nature regardless of their gender. We cannot imagine a society in the future where there will be only males and no females. The society will be full of crimes and evils. Only if legislations enacted in this behalf are not sufficient. Orthodox views regarding women need to be changed. The PNDT Act should penalize and punish the violators of this crime strictly. The pernicious acts of female foeticide and coercive abortions have to end before women becomes endangered species.

Therefore, a need was felt to have a comprehensive study on the topic *"Impact of Scientific and Technological Development on Human Rights: A Study with Special Reference to Sex Determination Test"*.

The objective of the study is to examine the impact of the development of Science and Technology on Human Rights with special reference to Sex Determination Test in modern perspectives. I have not only examined national issues but also evaluated them critically. An exhaustive study of Laws related to Sex Determination Test, the interrelationship among Science, Technology and Human Rights, role of judiciary have become part of this work.

The whole work has been encompassed in nine chapters. The first chapter is of introductory nature. The general aspects of science and technology have been discussed in national and international perspectives. The developments of science and technology has both positive and negative impact on ethical values, therefore, I have critically evaluated the role of science and technology in society and also highlighted the legal and ethical issues that have led me to undertake this work.

The second chapter is devoted only to discuss at length the concept of human rights. The origin of human right has been traced from primitive era and chronological developments have been explained. I have also made sincere efforts to discuss the notion of human rights in Indian perspective. The meaning, nature and kinds of human rights also form part of this chapter.

The third chapter is meant to discuss the meaning, significance and impact of science and technology in society, especially on human rights. Undoubtedly the developments of science and technology has yield a number of benefits in human life and made our life more comfortable and convenient but we can not ignore its negative aspects. Every coin has two sides. The negative side of science and technology is also depicted in this chapter. The challenges posed by the development of science and technology and judicial response to it have been discussed in this chapter.

Since I have undertaken the study with special reference to sex determination test, therefore, the meaning, nature and methods of sex determination test have been explained in fourth chapter. Initially the sex determination test was invented for a pious cause of unborn child but later on it was started to be misused. The consequences of such misuse of this technology have been fully discussed in this chapter.

The sex determination test has motivated the people to go for abortion to avoid the birth of unwanted girl child. Therefore, it was necessary to have a comprehensive discussion about the meaning, kinds and bad consequences of abortion on human life. Law is an instrument to regulate human behavior and control forced abortion, thus law has played tremendous role in controlling such illegal abortion. I have made my efforts to analyze the provisions of law pertaining to abortion with the help of decided cases in fifth chapter.

The Sixth chapter is spared to discuss the international efforts to combat the vice of sex determination test. There are a number of international instruments that directly or indirectly deals with the rights of unborn child, especially female foetus. I have tried to explain relevant part of such international instruments. The vices of sex determination test also drew the attention of some other countries and such countries have made legislative and executive efforts to deal with the vices of SDT. All such efforts have been discussed in this chapter.

The chapter seven is fully devoted to discuss the laws pertaining to sex determination test and abortion in India. All the provisions of the Constitution of India relevant to this study have been high lighted and discussed. Special laws like the Medical Termination of Pregnancy Act, 1971 and the Pre-Natal Diagnostic Techniques Act, 1994 have been analyzed critically. There are some other laws like Indian Penal Code, the Code of Criminal Procedure, the Medical Council Act, 1956, etc. that deals with the vices of sex determination test. Besides these, there are some policies of government and some NGOs are also working in this field. In this chapter there is discussion about the relevant provisions of such laws, policies and the role of NGOs.

The vices of SDT has raised many legal and ethical issues and posed several challenges, therefore, the chapter eight is devoted to discuss all such legal, ethical issues and judicial response towards sex determination test. The Indian Medical Council (Professional Conduct, Etiquette and Ethics) Regulations, 2002 lays down ethical norms for a medical practitioner, the analysis of medical ethics has also become part of this chapter.

The whole discussion was concluded in last chapter nine and I made my sincere efforts to make some viable suggestions, wherever required in the discussion.

Human Rights

(A) ORIGIN AND DEVELOPMENT OF HUMAN RIGHTS

1. Western Tradition

The general belief is that the concept of human right is western. The origin of the concept of human right in the world history found its first expression in 'Magna Carta of 1215'. It was only a deed of compromise upon the allotment of powers between king John and his subjects. It is also known as 'the great Charter of Liberty'. After it 'the Petition of Rights of 1628' came and then this 'Habeas Corpus Act, 1679' titled as "an act for the better securing the liberty of the subject and for prevention of imprisonment beyond the seas". After this 'the Bill of rights 1688' came into existence and it was officially titled as "an act for declaring the rights and liberties of the subject and for settling the succession of the crown. Then in 1789 'the French Declaration of the Right of Man and citizen' became the milestone in which the individual acquired protection against the capricious acts of kings. In 1791 'the American Bill of Rights' came into existence.

(a) Ancient Greeks

The fact that the human rights were recognized as natural rights of man is illustrated by a Greek play Antigone. In this play, Sophocles describes the Antigone's brother, while he was rebelling against the king, was killed and his burial was prohibited by the King Creon. In defense of the order Antigone buried her brother. When she was arrested for violating the order, she pleaded that she had acted in accordance with the *"immutable, unwritten laws of heaven" which even the king could not override.* The notion of natural rights of man was contributed by the Stoic philosopher in the philosophy.

Initially the natural law theory was developed by them and virtue of it they explained the nature of human rights, i.e. rights which every human being possess by virtue of being human. However, it may be noted that the citizens of the Greek City states enjoyed some basic rights even before the formulation of natural law theory by the Stoic philosophers. These were in particular:

- the right of freedom and speech (*Isogoria*)
- the right to equality before law (*Isonomia*)
- the right to equal respect for all (*Istimia*)

The Stoic philosophers formulated the theory of natural law after the break down of the Greek City States. The main notion of the Stoic philosophy was that the principles of natural law were universal in their nature. Their application was not limited to any class or persons of certain States; rather it applied to everybody everywhere in the world. It discovered by human reason and as such was superior to positive law.

The natural rights of man being its embodiment were not the particular privileges of citizens of certain State, but something to which every human being, everywhere, were entitled in virtue of the simple fact of being human and rational. They set forth further that men could comprehend and obey this law of nature because of their common possession of reason and capacity to develop and attain virtue.

In this way, the Stoic philosophers were able to preach the idea of universal brotherhood of mankind and laid stress upon the equality and freedom for all. The Stoic formulation of natural law was best suited to the Roman temperament, for they, in principle, believed that man should improve himself both rationally and morally.

(b) Roman Period

Writing about natural law, Cicero (105-43) B.C., like Stoic philosophers, laid emphasis upon the universal nature of it and said that natural law is of universal application, unchanging and everlasting. It is not permissible to alter this law, nor is it allowable to attempt to repeal any part of it, and it is impossible to abolish it entirely. We cannot be freed from its obligation by Senate or People . . . and there will not be different law at Rome and at Athens or different laws now and in the future, but one eternal and unchangeable law will be valid for all nations and for all times.[1]

Roman applied the Stoic conception of natural law in the formation of body of legal rules for the administration of justice. It was the most exceptional intellectual contribution of the Romans in the field of law. The above body of rules was developed by them on the basis of the custom as well as application of reason. Acting in this manner, they not only modernized their old law, but also laid stress upon the incorporation of high ethical standards in legal procedure.

Roman Law was divided into two categories of rules : *'jus civile'*, or Roman Civil Law dealing with citizens, things and actions; and *'jus gentium'*, or the law of non-citizens, which describe the rights of those who were not the citizens of Rome and they referred to those rights to which men were entitled in general. It also referred to the rules of international law at the same time. Many principles of *'jus gentium'*, were adopted from *'jus naturale'* (natural law) which enabled them to humanize these rules in such a way that a man of common sense and good faith could approve them as just.[2]

---

1. De Republic, III xxii, 33, quoted in d' Entreves, Natural Law, 1960, pp. 20-21
2. Swain, J.E., A History of World Civilization, 1947, pp. 172-73; It may be noted 'here with concern that in the Greco-roman system of thoughts, particularly in the teachings of Aristotle the slavery was recognized as valid practice—Aristotle; Politics, Book one.

(c) Middle Age

In the Middle Ages, the most original thinkers of their times like the scholastic philosopher—Abelard (1079-1142) and Thomas Aquinas (1224-74), laid stress upon the concept of natural law as the higher principles of law to be derived from reasons. But they did not go in quest of making the human personality as the main concern of law and social life.

Thomas Aquinas, like Aristotle, justified the existence of the practice of slavery. Thus, the "man" was dispensed with a central notion of mediaeval philosophy of law. Much attention was focused on the development of the principle of the sovereignty of State rather than on the development of respects for human qualities. This principle of "Natural Rights" later on became one of the greatest obstacles to the international protection of human rights.

Again, a set-back was also caused during 16th century to the development of the concept of natural rights by Machiavelli's teachings. He opposed the concept of natural law and supported absolute monarchy. His philosophy was not based on any mystical thought such as that of natural law, rather, it was "here-and-now-philosophy" for him the human nature was bad and selfish which necessitated the establishment of State to curb and crush the anti-social elements existing in human mind.

The concept of natural rights was again revitalized for two reasons; firstly, the rise of reformation which challenged the sole authority commanded by the Church, one of the most powerful agencies of the medieval period. It brought about revolutionary changes in the religious outlook of the people which resulted into widespread demand for the natural rights of freedom of conscience and religious belief.

Secondly, the other reason was the influence of the social contract doctrine. This influence was more profound in scope as well as in its impact. Further, the concept of natural rights was closely linked with the doctrine of social contract theory because the basis upon which the natural law theories were formulated was the same for the social contract doctrine also. This doctrine popularized during 16th and 17th century through the political philosopher's writing such as of Thomas Hobbes (1558-1778), John Locke (1632-1704) and Jean Jacques (1719-78).

In general, they took the help of the notion of social contract to explain the relationship between individual and society. Initially, the social contract writers claimed that a superior pope, either manual or legal was established in pursuance of the social contract under which the people collectively undertook to obey the commands of such superior power so long it governed them in their common interest and kept itself within the terms of contract.

However, in 17th century one of the protagonists of social contract theory, Rousseau emphasized that the State was an artifact, and artificial creation of the individuals or the result of the social contract. Rousseau began with the state of nature, in which man was free and independent in all respect. From this state of nature according to him, there emerged a political society by the separate acts of individuals, whereby they undertook with one another to set-up government which would be responsible to promote their common interests the political society, so created would, by majority will, proceed to appoint governors who would govern in accordance with the terms of contract, or the instrument of trust or an act of delegation by which he was so empowered. The governor was to act on the behalf of the people thus protecting their general interests and respecting their natural rights. The violation of the terms of social contract on the part of the governor would justify not only its disobedience but also rebellion against it.

(d) Revolution Era

(i) American Revolution

In 1663, the American Revolution began in the form of the colonial revolt. There were many factors which dominated towards the rise of this revolution, for example, the growing importance of the notion of natural rights, teaching of the writers of social contract theory, the British bill of right of 1689,[3] and the coercive actions of George III (1760-1820) and his predecessors. The British Government was of the view that the colonies should also share in the expenses incurred in their

3. British Bills of Rights of 1689 established the idea of representative government formally and became a charter of liberty for England.

administration. With this view, the British Government in the last half of the 18th Century started to take various regulatory measures under which it introduced certain new taxes. This resulted into militant opposition by the American people. They argued that since they did not have their representatives in the British parliament, it had no right to impose taxes upon them.

The Declaration of Independence on July, 4, 1776 was the result of the American notion of independence and their determination to overthrow the authority of the imperial tyrannical government. This historical document was drafted and framed by Thomas Jefferson. It attacked not only against the divine right of the king to rule, but also against a government which did not reflect the will of the people. The document describes:

> "We hold these truths to be self-evident, that all men are created equal, that they are endowed by their Creator with certain inalienable rights, that among these are life, liberty and pursuit of happiness. That to secure these rights Governments are instituted among men deriving their just powers from the consent of the governed; that whenever and form the Government becomes destructive these ends, it is that right of the people to alter or abolish it and institute new Government".[4] Thus, Americans made their claim for independence on the basis of inalienable rights of man, popular sovereignty, and the right of revolution, but at the time of drafting the Constitution in 1787 they did not include a bill of rights for them. They did in 1791 by adopting ten amendments to the Constitution.

These amendments are known as Bill of Rights and form part of their Constitution. Again, Amendments from 13 to 15 known as Civil War Amendments were adopted at the end of the Civil War. Since, the Bill of Rights was not applicable to the newly freed Negroes these amendments extended the civil right liberties to them and imposed obligation upon the State to respect these rights.

4. Friedrich and Closkey Mc, From the Declaration of Independence to the Constitution, 1954, p. 3.

The 13th Amendments prohibits slavery and involuntary servitude, the 14th Amendments widens the base of American citizenship by conferring citizenship on all persons born or naturalized in the United States. They became entitled to the citizenship of United State as well as of the State in which they reside. It is further provided that States shall neither make nor enforce any law which shall abridge the privileges and immunities of citizens of the United States, nor deprive any person of life, liberty or property without due process of law nor deny to any person within its jurisdiction the legal protection of the laws-; the 15th Amendment lays down that the citizen's right to vote shall not be denied or abridged by the United States or any state on the grounds of race, colour or previous condition of servitude; the 19th Amendment was added in 1920 providing that this right shall not be abridged or denied on the ground of sex.

(ii) French Revolution

The French Revolution was based upon those principles which were set in motion by the English and American Revolution. It differed mainly in that it was basically the result of economic and social inequalities and injustices of the French ancient regime. These inequalities were conspicuous not only among the third Estate (lower classes) but also in the First Estate (clergy) and in the second Estate (nobility).

It had caused the greatest amount of concern among the writers[5] who were apparently influenced by the teachings of Rousseau. They enthusiastically claimed that it marked the dawn of new age for the mankind in general and believed in the prospect of right reason and natural and imprescriptibly right to life, liberty and the pursuit of happiness. The government, in their option, must preserve and safeguard these rights and if it fails to do so it has no right to remain in existence.

(iii) Russian Revolution

During 1905, the social and economical inequality was at

5. Ferguson and Brun : A Survey of European Civilization, pp. 565-612; Martin, French Liberal thought in the 18th Century.

peak in Russia. The rule of czars was spreading over all corruption in the state. The society was divided into two classes, i.e. rightful and rightless class. Rightful class had all the powers whereas rightless class had no powers. Hence there was great dissatisfaction in the society, which dominated to the Russian revolution and the revolution resulted in the socio-economical equality in the society based on natural right theory.

(e) Modern Era

At the cession of World War I, although a few attempts on modest level were made through the 'Treaty of Versailles' to promote and universalize human rights but it met with not success. A proclamation of the right of man was issued by the 'Institute of International Law' in 1929. In all, the six articles were adopted which prescribed the duties of every state which were to recognize right to life, liberty and property, right of religion, right to use his own language and to recognize economic activities. Then there was human rights movement against Nazism.

It was believed that no permanent peace could be established without securing international safeguards for human rights and fundamental freedoms. President Roosevelt took the lead in the matter and in his message to Congress on January 6, 1941; he referred to the four essential human freedoms to which he looked forward as the foundation of a future world. These are:

- Freedom of speech and expression,
- Freedom of every person to worship God in his own way,
- Freedom from want, and
- Freedom from fear.

Although, the list of rights as here described is not very exhaustive but still it had exercised immense influence on the movement of human rights. Then the British Prime Minister, Mr. Churchill was equally concerned with the violation of human rights and racial persecution. He proclaimed that racial persecution would come to an end with the end of Second World War and human rights would be promoted.

The Prime Minister of Great Britain Mr. Winston, S. Churchill and the President of the United States Mr. Franklin, D. Roosevelt had met at the sea and issued a Joint Declaration on August 1941. It is known as the 'Atlantic Charter'. Through this Declaration the two leaders deemed it "right to make known certain common principles in the national policies of their respective countries on which they base their hopes for a better future for the world."

It was agreed among other things that "they respect the right of all people to choose the form of government under which they will live: and they wish to see sovereign rights and self-government restored to those who have been forcibly deprived of them. After the final destruction of the Nazi Tyranny, "They hope to see established a peace which will afford to all nations the means of dwelling in safety within their own boundaries, and which will afford assurance that all the men in all the lands may live out their lives in freedom from fear and want.

The above declaration of the United Nations was affirmed by the three powerful nations (United States, Soviet Union and Great Britain) in their conference of March 3, 1943. In the pursuit of internationalization of human rights the International Labor Organization and other private organizations have played crucial and creative role in the development of consensus of world community in this respect. The Philadelphia Declaration of the International Labour Organization at its 26th Session adopted, *inter alia*, the following resolution—

> "All human beings, irrespective of race, creed or sex, have the right to pursue both their material well-being and their spiritual development in conditions of freedom and dignity of economic security and equal opportunity".

Professor Lauterpacht prepared a draft of 'International Bill of Rights of Man' and suggested for its acceptance by the United Nations as a part of the fundamental Constitution of the world community. Internationalization of human rights received adequate attention of world powers at 'Dumbarton Oaks Conference' on 1994. At the Dumbarton Oaks Conference first tentative draft of the United Nations Organizations was prepared. Finally, it was the 'San Francisco Conference' held from 25th April to 26th June 1945 at which the 'Charter of the United Nations' had emerged incorporating human rights and fundamental freedom for all without distinction as to race, sex, language or religion.

The General Assembly has been assigned with the duty of initiating studies and making recommendations for the purpose of assisting in the realization of human rights and fundamental freedoms. 'The Economic and social Council' is authorized to make recommendations to the General Assembly, to the members of the United Nations and to the concerned specialized agencies for the purpose of promoting respect for and observance of, human rights and fundamental freedoms for all. The Economic and social council is further empowered to prepare a draft conventions for submission to the General Assembly, and to set-up commission for promotion of human rights. The Economic and social council constituted the Human Rights' Commission in its first session with the responsibility, *inter alia*, to formulate an International Bill of right.

Working in union, with the Economic and Social Council the 'Universal Declaration of Human Rights' was adopted by the General Assembly on December 10, 1948, which formed the basis for the preparation of other documents on human rights. The most prominent among them are the International Covenant on economic, social and Cultural rights, and the international Covenant on civil and Political rights.

These three documents, the 'Universal Declaration of Human Rights', the 'International Covenant on Civil and Political Rights', aiming at the Abolition of the Death Penalty and the International Covenant on Economic, Social and Cultural Rights, Constitute the 'International Bill of Human Rights'. They are followed by over ninety other global human rights and humanitarian treaties. Hence the concept of human rights reached in its present form after passing through the above described phases and movement which had dominated up to a great extent in development of the human rights.

2. Indian Tradition

The Indian culture is one of the most developed and rich among the others. The concept of the term "Human Rights" is not new in the perspective of Indian culture and civilization. The human rights are the minimal rights which the every individual must had against the State or other public authorities by virtue of his being a member of the human family irrespective of any other consideration. We can take the example of any period in Indian Civilization regarding existence of the concept of Human Rights; we shall find that these were in existence in one or in other form. It is a matter of necessity of the society, that the concept and meaning of the Human Rights had been modified according to the requirement of the people.

The phase-wise development of the Human Rights in India is discussed below in the next paragraphs. The Human Rights in India had been reached to the present position after developing through the following phases:

- First Phase of Human Rights (Ancient/Vedic Era).
- Second Phase of Human Rights (Medieval/Islamic Era).
- Third Phase of Human Rights (Modern Era/British and Afterwards Period).

(a) First Phase—Ancient/Vedic Era

The quest for truth, equality, harmony and knowledge inspired the ancient Indian minds more than their counterparts the Greeks and the Romans. About 5000 years ago, ancient Indian philosophers and thinker expounded a theory of higher moral law over and above positive law embodying certain values of universal validity like *Dharma, Artha, Kama and Moksha,* i.e. Righteousness, wealth, desires and salvation, with a view to develop and establish a harmonious social order by striking a balance between inner and outer, spiritual and material aspect of life.[6]

---

6. Dhyani, S.N., Fundamental of Jurisprudence—The Indian Approach, Central Law Agency, Allahabad, p. 79 (1992).

The ancient Indian legal philosopher were universalisms, humanists rationalists and above all moralists who evolved a system of legal theory which was based on higher values and ideals, i.e. on their conception of Dharma, which governed in an integrative manner all civil, religious and other actions of men in society be it king or his subjects.[7] Every aspect of life was regulated by Dharma the supreme Law in ancient India. The kings in India unlike the Tudor kings or French Louis XIV were subjected to the supremacy of the law of Dharma,[8] Law of Rita or Dharma in ancient India made a bold attempt of building an organized social life wherein each individual realized his goals within the parameters of social norms of morality. It is this Supreme Law which sustained individuals together in the society.

It is Dharma which has impelled men since Vedic ages to strive for "righteousness". The Natural law so revealed in *Vedas, Purans, Mahabharata, Bhagwad Gita,* etc. was extolled by the mystics, saints, poets and philosophers during the Vedic age. The philosophy expounded by the saints of Vedic time is nothing but a reinstatement of Natural law with religious fervor to enthuse people towards the path of Dharma, enlightenment and unity. It is this higher law of morality, justice and righteousness which has been continuously guiding and directing Hindu thought, spirit and action from times immemorial and would continue to mould for the realization of Dharma in a timeless fashion.

What is apparent is that the ancient Indians were not indifferent or unaware of human rights jurisprudence was Dharma—the ideal of ancient Indian legal theory was the establishment of socio-legal order free from traces of conflicts, exploitations and miseries. Indeed, such a law of Dharma was a model for the universal legal order.

It is a matter of fact, that the root of the concern for human rights in Vedic age may be traced in religion, humanitarian traditions and the unceasing struggle for freedom and equality. Theology presents the basis of a human rights

---

7. *Ibid.*
8. *Id.* at page 86.

philosophy stemming from a law higher than the state and whose source is the Supreme Being. Since the rights flow from a divine source, they are inalienable by moral authority.[9] The Natural Law thinkers believed that natural law was a body of higher law in subordination to which all human laws must be made.

It is a concept of merely value helping mankind to control its political destiny, liberties, human rights and fundamental freedoms and all omnipotent police states, legislatures and dictators.[10] They were highly of the view that the concept of human-beings created in the image of God certainly endows men and women with a worth and dignity from which there can logically flow the components of comprehensive human Rights jurisprudence.

The Rights of man were embedded in highly developed ancient Indian civilization. The study of *Rigveda* reveals that there was a rich jurisprudence in ancient India which provided an adequate frame-work for the regulation of the behaviour of the ordinary persons as well as the Sovereign, the king. Two norms, viz., Dharma and Danda, which were necessarily influence by the theological tenets of the Vedic Aryans, contained several features of a regulatory mechanism for religious practices.

Referring to the social responsibility of the king, Manu stated that to end lawlessness was crested the institution of the king whose supreme duty was to protect his subjects against disorder and anarchy. Detailed rules were laid down for the guidance of the king. It was his duty to uphold the law, and he was as much subject to law as any other person. It was obligatory upon him to enforce not only the sacred law of the texts but also the customary laws (rights and claims) of the subjects. This was possibly the human rights enforcement system in its embryonic stage.[11]

9. Jaswal, Paramjit S., Human Rights and the Law, APH Publishing Corporation, New Delhi, pp. 3-4 (1995).
10. Dhyani, S.N., Fundamental of Jurisprudence—The Indian Approach, Central Law Agency, Allahabad, p. 79 (1992).
11. Jaswal, Paramjit S., Human Rights and the Law, APH Publishing Corporation, New Delhi, p. 97 (1995).

The concept of Human Rights in India may be seen to have existed in crystallization of values that are the common heritage of mankind. References occur as early as in the Rig Veda to the three Civil Rights, that of Tan (body), Skridhi (dwelling place) and Jibhasi (life). Long before Hobbes, the Indian scriptures tell us about the importance of the freedoms of the individual (Civil Liberties) in state.

The concept of Dharma, the Supreme law which governed the sovereign and the Subjects alike covering the basic principles involved in the theory of rights, duties and freedoms. Long before second century B.C., we boast of elective kingship and the law of nature which even kings had to obey on pain of disposition. The early Samrities inculcate upon the king principles and policies of government involving the conception of a welfare state and that of ruler's complete identification with his subjects. In the early times, the original state of nature was imagined to be one of total anarchy where might alone was right.

When people were oppressed by the law of fished (Matsyanyana, according to which the bigger fish swallow the smaller ones), they made Manu, the son Vivaswat, the king. They fixed one-sixth part of the grains and one-tenth of their goods and money as his share. Kings who received this were bound to ensure the well being of their subject. In fact, Yogaksema implies the idea of welfare, well being, including the idea of prosperity, happiness and so on. That is why the Kautilya's Arthshastra asserts"? In the happiness of the subjects lies the happiness of the king, and what is beneficial to the subjects to his own benefit. The king's function was not conceived in terms of legislation but of protection and this involved the protection not only of his subjects from invasion, but also of the order of society, the right way of life for all classes and ages as laid down in the sacred texts.

The Mahabharata explicitly sanctions revolt against a King who is oppressive or fails in his function of protection, saying that such a ruler is no king at all, and should be killed like a mad dog. Kautilya also disapproved the theory of absolutism of king and subordinated him to the law of duties. Similarly, Shantiparva prescribes that king may be punished if he does not follow the path of Dharma.

Kautilya, the author of the celebrated Political treatise, Arthshastra, not only affirmed and elaborated the civil and legal rights first formulate by Manu but also added a number of Economic rights. He categorically ordained that "the king shall provide the orphan, the aged, the infirm, the afflicted and helpless with maintenance; he shall also to the children they give birth to". It revealed that society in Vedic India was well structured and highly organized. The Matsyanyana, the big fish swallowing the small was never allowed by the state, classes and individuals. It was believed that the economic development ought to be the concern of the State and an equitable division of the available wealth was a duty of the ruler.

Indeed, the state control and regulation of economy and community sharing of privileges has been a true Indian tradition even in ancient India. The traces of State socialism can be found in Arthshastra in which a positive role is envisaged for the state. On positive duties of the king (interchangeably used for state) Manu says: "It is duty of the state to support education and honour and make gifts to learned people.

The state should do many things for the welfare of the people. P.V. Kane said that in ancient India though there were bi-acts of Parliament guaranteeing services to the people, the public opinion, the views of the eminent writers and the practice of the best kings created an atmosphere in which it was thought that it was imperative for the king representing the State to encourage learning, to give employment to those who were unemployed.

The Maurya Empire of ancient India established unprecedented principles of civil rights in the 3rd century BC under Ashoka the Great. After his brutal conquest of Kalinga in circa 265 BC, he felt remorse for what he had done, and as a result, adopted Buddhism. From then, Ashoka, who had been described as "the cruel Ashoka" eventually came to be known as "the pious Ashoka". During his reign, he pursued an official policy of nonviolence (ahimsa) and the protection of human rights, as his chief concern was the happiness of his subjects. The unnecessary slaughter or mutilation of animals was immediately abolished, such as sport hunting and branding. Ashoka also showed mercy to those imprisoned, allowing them outside one day each year, and offered common citizens free education at universities. He treated his subjects as equals regardless of their religion, politics or caste, and constructed free hospitals for both humans and animals.

Ashoka defined the main principles of nonviolence, *tolerance* of all *sects* and opinions, *obedience* to parents, *respect* for teachers and *priests*, being *liberal* towards friends, humane treatment of *servants*, and *generosity* towards all. These reforms are described in the *Edicts of Ashoka*. In the Maurya Empire, citizens of all religions and ethnic groups also had rights to *freedom, tolerance*, and *equality*. The need for tolerance on an *egalitarian* basis can be found in the Edicts of Ashoka, which emphasize the importance of tolerance in public policy by the government. The slaughter or capture of *prisoners of war* was also condemned by Ashoka. Slavery was also non-existent in ancient India.

The philosophers of Vedic age endeavored to define human rights as those rights which were inherent in our nature and without which we could not live as human beings. They supported vehemently the view point that human rights and fundamental freedoms allow us to fully develop and use our human qualities, our intelligence, our talents and our conscience and to satisfy our spiritual and other needs. They considered human rights as based on mankind's increasing demand for a life in which the inherent dignity and worth of each human-being will receive respect and protection. They had a strong conviction that human rights are universal and apply to all persons without discrimination.

They felt that respect for individual rights needs to be upheld at all times irrespective of circumstances or political systems. There are many references in Vedas which focus light on the existence of human rights. The Vedas proclaim Liberty of Body (Tan), dwelling house (Skridhi) and Life (jibase). In 1367 B.C., Bahmani and Vijaynagar kings are stated to have entered into an agreement for the humane treatment of prisoners of war and the sparing of lives of the enemy's unarmed subjects. It is also apparent that protection of the rights and the individual was the main object for which the stated existed.

The philosophy of Vedic age enlightens us of the fact that the human right enveloped within its fold the "constant perpetual desire of giving to every man what is due to him". It is established beyond doubt that Vedic India had a strong tradition of respect for Human Rights. We find many references in Ancient scriptures and epics to the effect that—let every one be happy, let everyone be free from all ills. The ideal human unit and of a world free from traces of conflicts and misery has always stirred the Indian hearts since times immemorial.

Human Rights have always occupied a place of prime importance in India's rich legacy and believed in the 'Welfare of all' i.e. "Vashudhaiva-kutumbakam".[12] Panini, the great Sanskrit grammarian of the 5th century B.C., interprets Dharma as an act of religious merit, custom and usage. Mahabharata describes it as being ordained for the advancement and growth of all creatures for restricting creatures from injuring one another and to uphold all creatures. Thus in India, the Dharma of the Vedic period provided for the protection of the rights of man.

Hindus no less than Greeks and Romans excelled in propounding philosophical ideals and constructing scientific concept and methods which deeply influence the law and life of people. In the words of Max Muller (six systems of Indian philosophy):

> "It is surely astounding that such a system as the Vedanta should have been slowly elaborated by the indefatigable and intrepid thinkers of India thousands of years ago, a system even now makes us feel giddy, as in mounting the last steps of swaying spire of an ancient Gothic cathedra. . ."[13]

There is however witnessed a downfall of Human rights jurisprudence in Post-Vedic age. In the post-Vedic period, the rise of Buddhism and Jainism were certainly a reacting against the deterioration of the moral order as against the rights of

12. Dhyani, S.N., Fundamental of Jurisprudence—Indian Approach, Central Law Agency, Allahabad, p. 41 (1992).
13. *Id.*, pp. 79-80.

privileged class. A close scrutiny of Buddhist period reveals that people were equal in all fields of their life. Life was more human and liberal and repudiated caste distinction. After Buddha, Ashoka protected and secured the most precious of human rights particularly right to equality, fraternity, liberty and happiness.

It was an age of glory and greatness in every branch of national life. Hieuen Tsang says that administration in Chandragupta period was founded on benign principles, there was no forced labour, crimes were rare, and king personally supervised the whole administration.

Harsh Vardhan was the last emperor of Hindu India. His reign marks the culmination of Hindu culture. He never forgot that the object of the government was the welfare of the governed. He provided food and drinks, and stationed physicians with medicines for the poor persons without any cost. He devoted his whole time to promote the welfare of his people. Men of merit and ability were patronized irrespective of their castes, colour and creed. It is for his commitment towards his people that he is often compared with Akbar and Ashoka.

After the break up of his empire the whole India was split up. The society, too, in general had degenerated. The philosophy of human right lost sight. The downfall of Rajput gave rise to the advent of Muslim rule in India. It was under Muizz-ud-Din that Muslim empire was founded in India.

Therefore, there is no doubt that in Ancient India the Human Rights jurisprudence was rich. The State (King) was fully protecting the various rights of his people and Welfare of the citizen was the main objective of the State.

(b) Second Phase—Medieval/Islamic Era

The concept of human rights got lost on its way in the dark and narrow alley of the second phase. In the Islamic period the philosophical and ideal speculation were replaced by new ideal of chivalry, war and other heroic traditions which led to confusion and uncertainty. With the invasion of India by Muslims created new situation wherein the Muslim rulers or Sultans followed a policy of discrimination against the Hindus.

So the significance of Muslim rule in India was counterproductive to harmony, justice and equality.

The advent of Muslim rule led to systems and ideals totally different from Hindu view of society and life. Muslim conquerors—especially Mahmud Ghaznavi and others made frontal attacks on Ancient way of life and religion. The destruction of temples, idols and large scale conversion to Islam alienated the masses. It was however, at a later stage the Muslim state in India became considerably modified in its form. The Mughal rulers especially with Akbar a new era began in Mughal history of India in the field of Human rights, with his policy of universal reconciliation and tolerance. He was earnestly concerned with the welfare of his subjects like the ancient Indian rulers.

At one place, Akbar went to the extent of saying that if he was guilty of an unjust act; he would rise in judgment against himself. Various European travellers, who visited Akbar's empire, highly appreciated his zealous regard for rights and justices. His justice loving tradition was followed by his son Jehangir, too.

There was a popular legend that Jehangir arranged a chain with bells to be hung outside the palace in order to enable petitioners to approach him for the redresses of their grievances. Strictly speaking, it was an easily accessible individual petition system in comparison to our modern lengthy and expensive writ petition system.

It revived and regenerated the old Indian value of truth, righteousness, justice and morality. Great Saints like Shankara, Ramanuja, Madhava, Tulsidas, Kabir, Guru Nanak Dev and other reinterpreted the Vedic Dharma to re-establish the supremacy of Indian Vedic values over alien ideals and philosophy.

The philosophy of these social reformers and leaders was nothing but a reinstatement of natural law with religious fervor to enthuse people towards the path of 'Dharma', enlightenment and unity at a time when Hindu society was dominated and divided by the foreigners. The cult of Avatara (divine descent) as expounded by Lord Krishna in Bhagwad Gita was revived by these saints and seers (devotees) who saw God in the form of Ram and Krishna to protect the righteous persons (paritra naya Sadhunam) and punish the evil does (vinashaya duskritam).

(c) Third Phase—Modern Era/British and Afterwards Period

British Period in India was rightly depicted as 'Kaliyuga' or 'dark period' in Indian history. British Indian rulers discriminated against Indians in political and civil liberties rights. There was demand for civil, political rights and fundamental freedom. Then Raja Ram Mohan Rai led to the strong voice against discriminative policies. At that time, East India Company deprived of their political, social and economic rights. Then there was demand of human rights through 'Satyagrah' and 'Ahinsa' of Gandhiji. After this 'Charter Act of 1813' was enacted to promote the interest and happiness of the native inhabitants in India. Similarly, 'Government of India Act 1833' was passed to allow the Indian to enjoy some political rights. Next to it, the proclamation of 'Queen Victoria' on the 1st Nov., 1858 contained 'secular nature of the state'. Then there was birth of 'Indian National Congress 1885' and 'The Constitution of India Bill, 1895' was prepared by it. After it 'The Government of India Act, 1915' guaranteed equality of opportunity in the Public services regardless of race or religion. 'Indian National Congress in 1925' finalized the draft of 'The Common Wealth of India Bill' embodying a declaration of right. Then the 'Madras Congress of the Indian National Congress, 1927' came into existence. A committee under Motilal Nehru was appointed which was known as 'Motilal Nehru Committee'. Then 'The Simon Commission' appointed by the British Government in 1927. In 1930, Congress Working Committee gave a call for the attainment of 'Purana Swaraj'. In 1931, 'Karachi Session of Congress' adopted a detailed programme of fundamental rights and duties and economic and social change. Thus, the 'Government of India Act, 1935' was passed without any bill of rights. 'Sapru Committee' in 1945 stressed on the need for written code of fundamental rights. In 1946, the British Cabinet Mission was founded. After this the Constituent Assembly raised a forceful demand for the inclusion of human rights in the Constitution.

(i) Constitution of India

With the commencement of the new Constitution on January 26th, 1950, the Natural law rights have been incorporated in the Preamble, in Chapters III and IV concerning Fundamental Rights and Directive Principles of State Policy. Under Part III, Fundamental Rights are included which are right of equality, right to six freedoms, right to life and personal liberty, right to freedom of religion, right to property, cultural and educational right, right against exploitation and right to Constitutional remedies. Under Part IV Directive Principles of State Policy are included which are right to adequate means of livelihood, right against exploitation, right to both sexes to equal pay for equal work, right to work, to education and public assistance in cases of unemployment, old age, sickness, right to equal justice and free legal aid, right to living wage, right to worker's participation in management of Industries, etc.

Hence, the promulgation of the Constitution by the people of India in January 1950 is watershed in the History of India. The Preamble, Fundamental Rights and the Directive Principles of State Policy together provide the basic human Rights for the people of India. Democratic socialism spelt out in the Preamble and the Directive Principles is meant to provide rich contents in which the fulfilment of Human Rights are hoped to be achieved. Hence, the background and the philosophical history of the Constitution of India proved as the milestone in installation of the concept of human rights in modern Indian judicial process and legal system.

(B) MEANING OF HUMAN RIGHTS

Broadly speaking human rights are those fundamental and inalienable rights, which are essential for life as human being. Human Rights are the rights which are possessed by every human being, irrespective of his or her sex, colour, nationality, race, religion, etc. simply because he or she is a human being.[14] "Human Rights" mean the rights relating to life, liberty, equality and dignity of the individual guaranteed

14. As per J.E.S. Fawcett.

by the Constitution or embodied in the International Covenants and enforceable by Courts.[15] Human Rights are the rights which are attached to the individual in the Womb and remain with him till the Tomb.[16] Human Rights are those rights which are inherent in our nature, and without which we cannot live as a human being. These are those fundamental rights, which allow us to develop fully and use our human capabilities, our intelligence, our conscience, our talent and satisfy our physical, spiritual, intellectual, social and other needs. Human Rights sometimes called fundamental rights, the rights that cannot, rather must not, be taken away by the legislation or any other act of government and which are often set out in constitution. As natural rights they can be seen as belonging to men and women by their nature. They are also described as "Common rights" for the very reason, they are being shared by all human being of the world as—Common Law shared by people in England.[17]

They are based on mankind's increasing demand for a life in which the inherent dignity and worth of each human being will receive respect and protection. Human rights are sometimes called fundamental rights or basic rights or natural rights. The principal object of securing human rights is the creation of the conditions for all individuals to have the opportunity to lead a minimally good life.

(C) INTERRELATIONSHIP AMONG SCIENCE, TECHNOLOGY AND HUMAN RIGHTS

Science and technology are growing at a very fast rate in the modern world. Science influences technology and in turn, gets influenced by technology. Both are changing and both contribute to changes in other fields. Science and technology are considered two important means for socio-economic progress.

There is a close interrelationship among Science and Technology and the Human Rights. The science and

15. Protection of Human Rights Act, 1993, Section 2(d).
16. Justice Krishna Iyer.
17. United Nation.

technological advancement affected every aspect of human life. The positive and creative utilization of science and technology for human welfare prove a mile stone for human rights movement, whereas the negative utilization of scientific and technological development for destructive purpose proved a grave for human rights.

When we speak of science and technology, we speak in terms of their practical utility and convenience, and neglect their impact on human satisfaction for it cannot be demonstrated. It is true that once a new technology is accepted, its hidden consequences may be unavoidable. For example, automobiles pollute environment, mass production promotes monotony and alienation, sophisticated technology produces technological unemployment, birth control techniques augment instances of sexual immorality, pesticides cost human health, war weapons make international peace casualty and so on. These undesirable consequences of science and technology were never anticipated previously and make us believe that we are becoming helpless victims of technology.

The General Assembly of the United Nations adopted a resolution of 'Tehran International Conference on Human Rights, 1968' in which specific attention was to be paid to developments in science and technology in relation to:

- respect for the privacy and the integrity of the individual and sovereignty of nations in the light of advances in recording and other techniques;
- protection of the human dignity, physical and intellectual integrity in the light of advances in medical science, medicine and biochemistry;
- control on uses of electronics that may affect the rights of the person and the limits that should be placed on such uses in a democratic society;
- the balance which should be established between scientific and technological progress and the intellectual, spiritual, cultural, and moral advancement of humanity; and
- This resolution accentuates the dangers that technological developments harbor with respect to human rights and fundamental freedoms. It should

be clear, however, that in many cases technological developments offer opportunities for individual and collective choices and for the enhancement of human rights.[18]

These are the positive and negative impact of Science and technology on human rights.

I. Positive Impact of Science and Technology on Human Rights

The development in the field of science and technology has brought a tremendous revolution and transformation in the life pattern of man, as well as in the field of Human Rights Jurisprudence. The progress of the science and technology not only upgraded the quality of life of human society but also made it comfortable up to a maximum extent. All the spheres of human activities like business, education, communication, medical, legal, research, technological, industrial, etc. have been benefited from the advancement of science and technology. Hence, the various intellectuals related to the field of Human Rights opined that the progress of science and technology strengthen the human rights progress and helped in its advancement.

The use of science and technology as an instrument of state power is not new. The rise of the nation-state, the colonial enterprise, and the consolidation of empire went along with the patronage of selected sciences and the exploitation of local knowledge and techniques on the "periphery" to the benefit of the "metropolis". World War II did not simply consolidate the links between science and the state to achieve specific practical objectives; it irreversibly embedded science at the heart of political processes.

The theater of war displayed the immense contribution that science-based technologies, such as the atom bomb, proximity fuses, guided missiles, and radar, could make to national defense and that new drugs, such as penicillin, could make to national health. The notion of advanced technologies

18. Resolution of 'Tehran International Conference on Human Rights', 1968.

refers here both to technical appliances and to methods of their usage, leading to the replacement not only of manual work but also of the mental work of man. In this sense, an example of advanced technology is electronic communication techniques.

Today the development of science and technology has changed the whole world; let it be in any thing in transportation, communication, agriculture, and machines. Today with the help of science we can do our work easily and obtain our requirements easily. The invention of fire was a great discovery and later on the wheel, tools and so on. Today our world is fully developed world. Today by science we can talk to each other by an easy way and one can reach to any part of the world. Today with the help of electricity we can do hardest works in a few minutes. Through the electric media, we can get the news from each corner of the world at our home.

The advanced technology in electronic communication changed the whole world scenario in this field. Advanced technologies put a positive influence on productivity, the improvement of quality, and other modern features of production. They remove a whole range of adverse side-effects of mechanization and automation, such as noise, air pollution with chemical substances, dust, etc. The countries which are suffering from a shortage of trained labour, advanced technologies make it possible to overcome this problem.

Computer is the fastest means of communication. We can talk to each other in a few minutes; by Internet, we can send our messages and can receive the messages. We can get all information of the world by sitting in a small corner through Internet.

The science has brought a great revolution in the field of industry. The industrialization all over the world has uplifted the economies status universally. Today the common man, even in developing countries like India came over the poverty line. Advanced technologies exert a positive influence on labour productivity, the improvement of quality, and other modern features of production. They eliminate a whole range of adverse side-effects of mechanization and automation, such as noise, air pollution with chemical substances, dust, etc. In countries suffering from a shortage of trained labour, advanced technologies make it possible to overcome this barrier

Similarly, the science has also dominated in the field of medicine and medical science. The invention of new medical tolls and technology has made complicated operations/surgery easy. Today due to new medicines, the normal life—span of man has been increased and death ratio had been decreased. Therefore, science had contributed in human life up to a great extent. The scientific development not only uplifts the human life, but made it so comfortable and easier that was beyond the human imagination. Hence, science has contributed vitally for us.

The positive impact of science and technology is also in development of Medical Science, especially in Vaccinations, C.T. Scanning and Reproductive Technology. Scientific technology facilitates a series of pre-natal diagnostic tools to identify and cure any potential birth defects but it has also been misused especially for sex-selective abortion.

There is a positive impact of Science and Technology on Human Rights in upgradation of the quality of Human Life, especially in following fields—Medicines, machines and techniques, Agriculture (Hybrid seeds, Chemical fertilizers, etc.), Transportation, Communication, Education, Research, Business, Industries, Law, etc. not only this, but there is also development of new Human Rights due to science and technology and following are some examples—Concept of Right of Information, Education, Development, Healthy Environment, Right of Development, Right of Privacy, etc.

The development of science and technology has made the electronic media an effective tool in Promotion and Protection of Human Rights. The development of the Science and Technology accelerated the Human Rights jurisprudence by connecting particular nations to the external world. The improved information technology brought the whole world closer and generated the concept of glob.

The development of the Science and Technology encourage the awareness and education of the human rights. For instance—through TV program today we see that the ratio of the Female is going down as the result of female feticide which may cause the gender misbalance in future. Further, through public aware program of mass media we get information about the human rights. . .

The development of Science and Technology also contributed in the development of the Social and Compensational jurisprudence. The inter-cultural transformation and regional law has strengthened the concept of social justice and compensational jurisprudence.

The Development of the Science and Technology also encouraged the human being for future development and development is a consistent process which helps the man to search better ways to make the human life more comfortable. For instance, the research for serious diseases like HIV/AID and Cancer are the result of Science and Technology in the field of Medical Science.

These, like traditional technologies, have a double impact on human rights. On the one hand, they may contribute to the fulfilment of certain rights, and on the other they may simultaneously hamper the fulfilment of other rights.

2. Negative Impact of Science and Technology on Human Rights

Science and technology are racing ahead law and human rights are looking on helpless from the sidelines because there is very little that they can do to match the speed of technology. Law moves very slowly, while technology moves with lightning rapidity. The result is that technology is racing out of legal control. In consequence, there can be grave damage to human rights as well. Hon. Mr. Justice C.W. Weeramantry in his book 'The Slumbering Sentinels' and 'H.R.'s and Scientific and Technological Developments' warned that serious threats are being posed to H.R.'s by scientific and technological developments. There is a need to open the eyes of a general so dazzled by technological innovations that it is blinded to the social and human dangers that need to be seen.

The blind race of advancement of science and technology also affected the human life adversely. It has become a major destructive tool for the humanity. The excess exploitation of natural resources and industrial revolution brought damage to environment, health and mental state of the Human Life, the information technology is being used for international crimes, the man has become a machine in the era of modernization.

Hence, in this way the advancement of science and technology has become a destructive tool of the Human Dignity.

Modern science has the capacity with in it to sustain a culture of science which is incompatible with democratic governance as well as the democratic rights of those who are turned into the subjects of modern science and technology. It is in this context that the human rights community needs to further develop the ideas that emerged as the initial response to the Technology Missions. The first is the idea of an ombudsman for each mission. The various missions, especially those on SDT immunization, water, housing and family planning may generate a host of everyday complaints which the bureaucracy may not be sensitive to. In this context the ombudsman can play his role with sensitivity and, at the same time, also respond to the specific problems of technological innovation in various forms.

Today there is a blind race of chemical, biological and nuclear weapons between the different nations and danger in the modern world is comparatively more because sale of these weapons is already in process. Due to Scientific and Technological development, in the past few decades the world has accumulated Nuclear, biological and Chemical weapons, many-folds larger than the times of bombardment on Hiroshima and Nagasaki and all the States are on the neck of 'explosive bowel'.

Experimentation on human body, Female Feticide, Gene Testing, Cloning, Reproductive technique, organ transplantation, etc. have become a business which leads towards the destruction of Human value and human dignity. Sale and purchase of the human organ, the kidney trade scandal, blood sale, etc. has taken place in the form of international racket. This is the result of Science and Technology.

(i) Developed Country's Monopoly over Right of Development

The country like USA, Australia, England, France, Germany, China, Japan, etc. have developed the advance scientific techniques in every field. And these countries adopted the monopolies trends by adopting the patent law or restricting the other countries from taking the benefit of the Science and Technological development.

Preserving the future generation is the cultural right of the human being, but the advancement of Science and Technology is putting a negative effect on the future generation. For example, violation of right to privacy, Right to healthy Environment, Right of life, Adequate Standard of living, Right to livelihood, etc. Today, the misuse of scientific instruments created a great danger for the future generation. Further, the result of bombardment of Hiroshima and Nagasaki, as well as the use of Chemical and biological weapons by USA during Vietnam War are the eye opening effect on human generation.

The advancement of Science and Technology again re-generated the concept of "might is right". The country, the community who had advanced their Science and Technological field is might and the action taken by them is right. The above concept is totally violation of the natural right. It has encouraged in-human acts and crimes like abortion, female feticide, cloning, etc. It has threatens rights enumerated in Universal Declaration of Human Rights also like right to life, right to privacy, right to work, etc.

(D) JUDICIAL BEHAVIOUR

In *Subhash Kumar* v. *State of Bihar*[19] in this case Supreme Court held that right to live is a fundamental right under Article 21 of the constitution and it includes the right of enjoyment of Pollution free water and air for full enjoyment of life.

The purpose of Human Rights is to ensure the Human dignity and Science and Technology has to strengthen the Human rights.

In *Ratlam Municipality* v. *Vardhi Chand,*[20] the court observed the right to life and personal liberty includes the right to live with decency and dignity. In this context the court pointed out that the grievous failure of local authorities to provide the basic

19. AIR 1991 SC 420.
20. AIR 1980 SC 1622.

amenity of public slum dwellers to case in the streets on the for a time.

So science and technology if provides better instruments for cleanliness the drains and streets then it helps to strengthens the human right.

In *F.K. Hussain* v. *Union of India,*[21] the Kerala High Court pointed out that the right to sweet water and the right to free air is attributes of the right to life.

(E) CHALLENGES OF SCIENCE AND TECHNOLOGY ON HUMAN RIGHTS

The spectacular advances in science and technology have also created numerous problems. Moreover, as the power of science and technology keeps growing, the problems we are addressing tend to worsen. For example, right to food and a pure environment is a recognized human right, the problems facing us today are far more acute than they were earlier[22] Environment has been the first casualty as far as scientific and technological innovations are concerned. A relatively unsystematic and uncontrolled scientific and technological advance may have many unforeseen social effects particularly on the quality of the environment. Examples:

- Due to excessive use of chemicals and artificial fertilizers soil impoverishment has taken place.
- There have been fears that food additives may contribute .to human cancers, blood pressure, diabetes, nervous weakness and such other diseases.
- Atmospheric pollution caused by man may lead to climatic changes that could cause a new ice age.
- Gases sprayed through airplanes may interfere with the planer's ozone layer and allow dangerous radiation to reach the surface of the earth. Many more examples of this kind could be cited.

21. O.P. 2741/1988.
22. Bellagio Declaration on Overcoming Hunger in the 1990.

Environmental concerns also loom large in Latin America, with regard not only to the devastation of forests and contamination of air, water, and soil but also to the immense development projects, such as those in the Brazilian Amazon Basin. All of these have become important political issues and highlight the importance of the decision-making process. They also show the power of international environmental groups acting by themselves and in concert with domestic groups.

In Thailand, there has been a very active environmentalist movement, which has often been sufficiently assertive to prevent the construction of large-scale dams that would have adversely affected environment. The conflict between the demands of industry and environmental concerns has been brought out quite strongly in Thailand, for example in the matter of logging.

The preference for the most advanced medical technology without an adequate study on its utility or efficiency is a major problem, shared by all contemporary societies. In the medical field in Venezuela, it observes that the privileged status of high-technology medicine leads to an incapacity to respond at other levels of the health system.

Biomedical advances are without a doubt one of the most far-reaching areas of modern technological achievement. Their potential to affect human society in all its aspects, from macro-social organization to the micro-facets of their impact upon the human body, exceeds the power wielded by many other branches of technology. Moreover, these advances, still in their infancy, open up large vistas hitherto contemplated only in the area of science fiction. These possibilities necessitate the timely consideration of the potential for good or ill of this branch of science.

The scientific advancements in medical science made things convenient for the human kind, by unfolding the secret portal of the quality and status of the foetus, growing with in the womb of the pregnant woman and allowed scope to exercise considered choice in the matters of welcoming the new member into the life form.[23] In contra, the same science has

23. Jain, Ashok Kumar, The Saga of Female Foeticide In India, Socio-Legal Offshoots, Ascent Publications, Delhi (2006).

paved the way by providing opportunity to discriminately eliminate the female foetus after identification while exercising option for male child. Progress in technology is inexorable. As the international medical journal *Lancet* had said, new technologies have the potential to create new problems for society.

Technology is not neutral in value. It can be used to serve society and it can also be used to perpetuate biases, exploit society and even help in its extermination. The misuse of medical technology for sex determination and female foeticide is one such example. In a social context, where there are deep-rooted biases against a girl child, gender discrimination becomes a deeper 'male fixation'. Any technology that prevents the birth of girl child finds a big market. Similarly, technology that claims to promote the birth of a boy child would find an even greater market.[24] The modern technology has proved to be counter productive and has become an importa State of Punjab. The medical technology has in fact made it much simpler to get rid of the female foetus in the womb itself. Earlier it was infanticide but now the technology has transformed it into foeticide. Undoubtly the issue is very complex and cannot be addressed on a linear path. Technology alone cannot be blamed. A part from technology there are many more other factors which need to be addressed at several levels to explain the phenomenon in a more comprehensive way.[25]

It is necessary to control the application of biomedical science by various actions of society, including legislation, not only because application often, if not always, involves profit for someone but also because application without adequate planning may cause considerable harm.

Science and technology have become today tow formidable forces. Both are changing fast and are making other institutions to undergo fast changes. Interaction of other social institutions with science and technology is a great challenge of our time.

---

24. *"Darkness at Noon: Female Foeticide in India", Voluntary Health Association of India, available at* http://indiafemalefoeticide.org
25. Singh, D.P., "Female Foeticide in Punjab—Causes and Consequences", Paragon International Publishers, New Delhi (2007).

Science and technology are advancing so fast that they have irresistible effects on other institutions. Commercial establishments, business firms, industries, etc., stand to lose heavily unless they use the latest technology. Technical changes often alter the problems of the government. Religion is forced to adopt its teachings to meet new scientific interpretations. Education seeks to prepare students for scientific and technical developments.

As it is made clear, science and technology have been undergoing relatively fast changes. These changes do not always guarantee beneficial results to the society and people. These changes may often give rise to some special problems also. At the same time, we have not been able to develop a system to exercise control over scientific and technological innovations.

Sex Determination Test

(A) INTRODUCTION

The origin of the Indian idea of appropriate female behavior can be traced to the rules laid down by Manu in 200 B.C. : "by a young girl, by a young woman, or even by an aged one, nothing must be done independently, even in her own house". Manu, the arch law-giver of the Hindu religion stipulated: "In childhood a female must be subject to her father, in youth to her husband, when her lord is dead to her sons; a woman must never be independent".[1] Women's lives are shaped by customs that are centuries old. "May you be the mother of a hundred sons" is a common Hindu traditional wedding blessing. The country has a long-standing tradition of son preference. In Kautilya's Arthshastra it is said, the sole purpose of a wife is to bring forth a son 'Putra hi striyaha'. In one of the sutras it is said that the aim of existence of women

1. Agnes, F., Law and Gender Inequality—The Politics of Women's Rights in India, OUP, New Delhi, p. 11 (1999).

is to be the mother of sons, daughters are not desired, and a wife who bears only daughters should be abandoned.[2]

Upon conception, mantras from the Atharva Veda, one of the four most sacred books of Hinduism, are chanted so that if the foetus if female it will be transformed into a male.[3] The Yajur Veda speaks of girls being exposed when born. This despite the fact that "No progeny can be born without a woman. . ." (as recognized by Matsya Purana).[4]

The 'Pristine' Hindu law has been generally believed to be harsh towards women and denied than sexual and economic freedom.[5] Statistics reveal that in India males significantly outnumber females and this imbalance has increased over time. The sex ratio according to 2001 census report stands at 933 per 1000 males. Out of the total population, 120 million are women who live in abject poverty. The maternal mortality rate in rural areas is among the worlds highest. From a global perspective India accounts for 19% of all live births and 27% of all maternal deaths.

The deaths of young girls in India exceed those of young boys by over 300,000 each year and every 6th infant death is specifically due to gender discrimination. Women face discrimination right from the childhood. Gender disparities in nutrition are evident from infancy to adulthood. In fact, gender has been the most statistically significant determinant of

---

2. Ahmad, S., "Pre-Natal Diagnostic Techniques: A Source of Gender Bias", *Kashmir University Law Review-X*, p. 204 (2003).
3. Such practices and rituals are numerous in India. For example, there is a popular ritual in U.P. called jiutia in which a woman fasts the whole day without eve a sip of water in order to have a son. There is another practice in which a woman is not allowed to wash her hair in warm water until she begets a son.
4. Misra, P., "Female Infanticide : A Threat to Posterity", *NISD Journal*, pp. 23-25 (2002). While some writers maintain that there are no proofs that the exposures of female children were regularly practice among Vedic Hindus (Pinkham). Others maintain that many girl babies were exposed or put to death in every race practicing ancestor-workship. In the creative period of the Vedas, like most primitive people, they practiced the exposure of girl children (Farquhar).
5. Jain, Ashok Kumar, The Saga of Female Foeticide in India, Socio-Legal Offshoots, Ascent Publications, Delhi (2006).

malnutrition among young children and malnutrition is a frequent, direct or underlying, cause of death among girls below age 5.

Girls are breast-fed less frequently and for a shorter duration in infancy. In childhood and adulthood, males are fed first and better. Adult women consume approximately 1,000 fewer calories per day than men according to one estimate. Nutritional deprivation has two major consequences for women: they never reach their full growth potential, and suffer from anemia, which are risk factors in pregnancy. This condition complicates childbearing and results in women and infant deaths, and low birth weight infants. The tradition also requires that women eat last and least throughout their lives even when pregnant and lactating. Malnourished women give birth to malnourished children, perpetuating the cycle. Women receive less healthcare facilities than men.

A primary way that parents discriminate against their girl children is through neglect during illness. As an adult they tend to be less likely to admit that they are sick and may wait until their sickness has progressed far before they seek help or help is sought for them. Many women in rural areas die in childbirth due to easily preventable complications. Women's social training to tolerate suffering and their reluctance to be examined by male personnel are additional constraints in their getting adequate health care.

Girl children are particularly vulnerable to human rights violations, simply because they are girls, and therefore require additional protections. They may face the different protection issues listed in the above sections from being subjected to abuse and violence to being involved in armed-forces or being discriminated in reason of disability, caste or social origin as at the same time they are at risk of discrimination and violence on the basis of their gender. According to Human Development in South Asia 2000, in India, 18% more girls than boys die before their fifth birthday. In Bombay, 84% gynaecologists admitted that they performed sex-determination tests.

There are 57 million more men than women globally, a UN report said on 21st October. In China, the ratio is 108 men per 100 women. Every year, 12 million girls are born—three million of whom do not survive to see their 15th birthday.

About one-third of these deaths occur in the first year of life and it is estimated that every sixth female death is directly due to gender discrimination.[6] Son preference is one of the most evident manifestations of gender discrimination in our society.

The girl child may also be less accessible than boy children. Both protection and development services have to strive to reach girl children. Out-patient data from hospitals in northern Indian cities shows lower admissions of girl-children, and girls who are in a more serious condition than boys when brought for treatment. An August 2004 spot-check at one hospital showed 25,538 boy-children and 12,645 girl-children in the OPD records, 3,822 boy-babies as against 3,160 girl-babies born in hospital, and 1,954 boy-children admitted to a pediatric ward as compared to 1,091 girls.[7]

Though India was not the only country with a strong preference for sons, it was the only country using pre-natal diagnosis for this purpose. The doctors who said they would perform pre-natal diagnosis for sex selection argue that by aborting female foetuses they help in bringing down the rate of female infanticide. The 2001 Census highlighted the drastic disparity between the sex ratios in several states in north and west India and continued decline in major southern states.

Many of the challenges girls face will start from the moment they are born; in fact in some parts of the world girls are the target of social preference before they are even born. This is the first in a series of reports to be published in 2015, which will follow a cohort of 135 girls born in 2006 inlook at how their gender impacts on their lives.[8] Declining sex ratio in various parts of the country, specifically the ratio of the girl child, compared to the boys in the age group of 0-6 years has been a cause of deep concern to Government of India.[9] During the last ten years, this ratio has declined significantly in almost

6. Government of India's first periodic report to the UN Committee on the Rights of the Child, 2001.
7. Women Watch: available at www.un.org/womenwatch.
8. Because I am a girl, the state of the world's girls, Plan International, 2007.
9. Female Foeticide, in Haryana and Punjab: A Situational Analysis, Shakti Vahini, 2003.

all parts of the country, barring Kerala, and notably in—Delhi, Haryana, Uttar Pradesh, Punjab (one of the worst sex ratios in the country), Andhra Pradesh and Karnataka.[10] Datamation Foundation's extensive research in this regard concluded that selective sex tests and abortions are the main reasons for the abandonment of the female foetus.[11]

TABLE 1
Indicators of Sex Preference in India[12]

Indicator		*Number/ Percentage*
1.	Mean ideal number of:	
	Sons	1.4
	Daughters	1.0
2.	Percentage who want more sons than daughters	33.2
3.	Percentage who want more daughters than sons	2.2
4.	Percentage who want at least one son	85.1
5.	Percentage who want at least one daughter	80.1

TABLE 2
The Trend of Sex Ratios in the Age Group of 0-6 Years all over India[13]

Year	*Sex Ratio*
1961	976
1971	964
1981	962
1991	945

10. Census, 2001.
11. Gender Equity Policy, Save the Children, 1999.
12. *Source* : National Family Household Survey (NFHS), 1998-99.
13. *Source* : Census, 1991.

TABLE 3
Distribution of District by Ranges of Child Sex Ratio in the 0-6 Age Group in Maharashtra[14]

Sex Ratio	Number of Districts
Less than 800	16
800- 849	33
850- 899	72
900- 949	213
950- 999	245
1000- 1049	21
Total	591

TABLE 4
District-wise Sex Ratio for Population Aged 0-6 Years (No. of males per thousand females), Maharashtra, 1991 and 2001[15]

District	2001	1991
(1)	(2)	(3)
Ahmednagar	890	949
Akola	936	934
Amravati	947	950
Aurangabad	884	933
Bhandara	958	97
Bid	898	939
Buldana	915	945
Chandarpur	944	965
Dhule	907	960
Gadchiroli	974	980

(Contd.)

14. Provisional Census Tables, 2001.
15. Computed from Provisional Population Totals, Paper-I of 2001 and RGI (1991) C series 2.

TABLE 4 (*Contd.*)

(1)	*(2)*	*(3)*
Gondiya	964	
Hingoli	935	
Jalgoan	867	925
Jalna	914	951
Kolhapur	859	931
Latur	923	947
Mumbai	898	920*
Mumbai (suburb)	919	
Nagpur	949	951
Nanded	944	960
Nandurbar	966	
Nashik	936	954
Osmanabad	927	947
Parbhani	926	955
Pune	906	943
Raigarh	943	961
Ratnagiri	954	961
Sangli	850	924
Satara	884	941
Sindhudurg	946	963
Solapur	897	935
Thane	933	952
Wardha	934	952
Washim	921	
Yavatm	942	961
Maharashtra	917	945

The child sex ratio is calculated as number of girls, per 1000 boys in the 0-6 year age group. The 2001 census reported a child sex ratio of 927 girls per 1000 boys. Therefore, there are 73 'missing girls' for every 1 000 boys in our country, and soon it may become very difficult to make up for them. The practice of eliminating female foetuses is believed to be one of the main reasons for the adverse child sex ratio. Millions of female foetuses were and are still, being, terminated creating a serious imbalance in child sex ratio in the country. Sex Determination Test seems to be more prevalent in urban areas than in the rural areas, but the gap is fast decreasing because of the easy availability of sex-determination tests in rural areas.[16]

Though the PNDT Act has been in place since the past six years the latest sex ratio figures of the 2001 Census (Tables 3 and 4) reveal alarming trends. The Census figures of the 0-6 age group show a steep decline in the number females especially in states like Haryana, Punjab, Himachal Pradesh, Maharashtra, Gujarat and Tamil Nadu. Within Maharashtra economically better-off districts such as Aurangabad, Sangli and those on the 'sugar belt' show the most adverse sex ratios.

Depressing socio-economic, cultural and demographic practices also have led to reduction in enrolment and retention of girls in schools, extracting excessive work from them, and providing them least recreational and rest facilities.

The four major causes for this problem were women were considered as an economic liability to the family; women were neglected in the process of decision-making in the family and in the community as a whole; very low female literacy rate and lack of job knowledge and earning capacity; and prevalence of dowry and other customary practices that are specifically related to women.

The Indian girl child is part of the society, which idolizes sons. Right from childhood, girls are made to accept the norms of patriarchal and male dominated society and they thus grow up accepting themselves to be inferior to boys. It is unfortunate that our society consider 'male' as the breadwinner for the family, and therefore a more valuable asset than a girl child, who is looked upon as a liability in the family. In the pursuit of sons, women have become, with some pressure from the families, consumers of the new ultrasound technology which allows them to choose and bear sons.

A 1997 UNFPA report "India towards Population and

16. "Pre-Birth Elimination of Females—A Handbook of Guidelines", by National Commission for Women, 2008.

Development Goals", estimates that 48 million women are missing from India's population. The report states that, "if the sex ratio of 1036 females per 1000 males observed in the State of Kerala in 1991 had prevailed in the whole country, the number of females would be 455 million instead of the 407 million (in the 1991 census). Thus, there is a case of between 32 to 48 million missing females in the Indian society as of 1991 that needs to be explained.

Commitment to human dignity is a widely shared value and the foundation for our understanding of human rights. The preamble to the Universal Declaration of Human Rights, adopted by the United Nations General Assembly in 1948, states that "recognition of the inherent dignity and of the equal and inalienable rights of all members of the human family is the foundation of freedom, justice, and peace in the world".[17]

Development of technology in the field of medical science had played a significant role in controlling of death and birth rate, to treat serious disease to save the life by organ transplantation, to adopt new surgery technique, to invent new machines, etc. But, on other hand, these inventions of medical science is being misused by the man that had resulted into gross violation of the "Human Rights". The female foeticide in India is a current example of the misuse of medical science.

The concept of the sex determination is even existed in the primitive societies. The sex of the unborn child, who is developing in the womb of the mother, was being determined by the "Dai" by the behaviour of the mother (in whose womb the child is developing, i.e. appetite, tastes, dreams and walk of the expectant mother.

Now, due to advanced scientific technology, the same is being determined by new technology like—ultrasound, sonography, amniocentesis, chorion villi biopsy, foetus copy, maternal serum analysis, etc. Ultrasound applications has evolved and over-whelming and spontaneous demand for its use in obstetrics and gynecology. In the world's most populous nation it is being, used to determine the sex of unborn. The non-invasive technique ultrasound scanning helps to screen

---

17. United Nations General Assembly, General Assembly Resolution, 217A (III), UN Doc A/810.

mother and foetus in complete safety, convenience and lack of trauma. It is pertinent to mention here that sex organs develop after 16 weeks of pregnancy in the mother's womb and it is possible to detect only after attaining definite twentieth week of gestation. The ultrasonography shows genitalia at and after four months of intrauterine life.

Innovative techniques, like biopsy, ultrasound, scan tests and amniocentesis, devised to detect genetic abnormalities, are highly misused by number of families to detect gender of the unborn child. Technology for foetal sex determination came to India in the mid-70s in the form of amniocentesis. Other sex-selection techniques: both 'pre-conception and post-conception'—became available in the country as medical science advanced in later years.

Amniocentesis tests were introduced in India in 1974 to detect any genetic abnormalities. They were used to detect gender for the first time in 1979 in Amritsar, Punjab, and then became a tool for sex determination and for female foeticide. The practice of this test was stopped by the Indian Council of Medical Research, but it was too late, people started using it as an instrument for selecting foetus.[18]

In 1975, amniocentesis techniques for detecting mention foetal abnormalities began to be developed in India, at the All India Institute of Medical Sciences (AIIMS), New Delhi. It was soon known that these tests could detect the sex of the foetus also, and doctors at the Institute noted that most of the 11,000 couples who volunteered for the test wanted to know the sex of the child and were not interested in the possibility of genetic abnormalities. Most women who already had two or more daughters and who learnt that their expected child was female went for an abortion. Both the availability and affordability of such techniques after penetrating in the urban communities are also making inroads in the rural areas shown by the proliferating ultrasound scan machines in several hundred small towns across the country aiding in sex determination.

In fact, parents can find out the sex of their baby at just six weeks by using a home test available on the internet, it emerged. The $ 189 mail order kit works by testing a single

18. CRIN: available at http://www.crin.org.

drop of a pregnant woman's blood. It produces the same information usually first given at 20 weeks by an ultrasound scan. Some parents will use the test to help them plan ahead but pro-life campaigners warned that a result at six weeks could lead to a sharp rise in the number of abortions. It could lead to babies being aborted simply for being the "Wrong sex."

There is a real risk that some people will choose to abort babies of a certain gender. The 20 week scan-most mothers have their first at 12 weeks—comes a month before the legal limit for an abortion. Some health authorities have already stopped revealing the information at twenty weeks for fear of "wrong sex" terminations.[19]

Unfortunately, even male geneticists seem to have no qualms about abetting sex selection. Wertz and Fletcher (1995) surveyed the attitudes of 71 medical geneticists in four developing countries (Brazil, Greece, India and Turkey) and 611 geneticists in the 15 developed countries. They found that 52 per cent of the geneticists in India (the highest percentage amongst the developing countries) would perform pre-natal diagnosis to select a male foetus for a couple with four daughters and no son.

Information furnished by the Office of the Registrar General of India indicates that the Sex Ratio (SR) (number of females per thousand males) has increased from 927 to 933 from 1991 to 2001. However, the Child Sex Ratio (CSR) has declined from 945 to 927 during the same period. The figures further reveal that the CSR is comparatively lower in the affluent regions, i.e. Punjab (798), Haryana (819), Chandigarh (845), Delhi (868), Gujarat (883) and Himachal Pradesh (896). State/UT-wise SR and CSR as per 1991 and 2001 Census can be seen at Table 5. Medical professionals and sex determination clinics are mostly present in the urban areas. The decline in urban areas is more than twice that seen in rural areas (935:903 and 948:934, respectively) over the inter-Censal period 1991-2001. In fact of all the 35 states and union territories of India,

19. Edward, Richards P. and Katharine Rathbun, C., Medical Care Law, ,edition, An Aspen Publications, 1999.

it is only in the small states of Kerala and Manipur that urban child sex ratios have not declined.

TABLE 5
State/UT-wise Sex-ratio and Child Sex Ratio during 1991 and 2001

India and State/ Union Territory/District*	*Sex Ratio*		*Child Sex Ratio*	
	1991	*2001*	*1991*	*2001*
(1)	*(2)*	*(3)*	*(4)*	*(5)*
India	927	933	945	927
Jammu & Kashmir	896	892	NA	941
Himachal Pradesh	976	968	951	896
Punjab	882	876	875	798
Chandigarh*	790	777	899	845
Uttaranchal	936	962	948	908
Haryana	865	861	879	819
Delhi	827	821	915	868
Rajasthan	910	921	916	909
Uttar Pradesh	876	898	927	916
Bihar	907	919	953	942
Sikkim	878	875	965	963
Arunachal Pradesh	859	893	982	964
Nagaland	886	900	993	964
Manipur	958	978	974	957
Mizoram	921	935	969	964
Tripura	945	948	967	966
Meghalaya	955	972	986	973
Assam	923	935	975	965
West Bengal	917	934	967	960
Jharkhand	922	941	979	965
Orissa	971	972	967	953
Chhattisgarh	985	989	974	975

(Contd.)

TABLE 5 (Contd.)

(1)	(2)	(3)	(4)	(5)
Madhya Pradesh	912	919	941	932
Gujarat	934	920	928	883
Daman & Diu*	969	710	958	926
Dadra & Nagar Haveli*	952	812	1013	979
Maharashtra	934	922	946	913
Andhra Pradesh	972	978	975	961
Karnataka	960	965	960	946
Goa	967	961	964	938
Lakshadweep*	943	948	941	959
Kerala	1036	1058	958	960
Tamil Nadu	974	987	948	942
Pondicherry*	979	1001	963	967
Andaman and Nicobar Islands*	818	846	973	957

Some of the reasons commonly put forward to explain the consistently low levels of CSR are son preference, neglect of the girl child resulting in higher mortality at younger age, female infanticide, female foeticide, higher maternal mortality and male bias in enumeration of population. Easy availability of the sex determination tests may also be proving to be catalyst in the process, which may be further stimulated by pre-conception sex selection facilities.

With the latest report on sex ratio at birth in 2010, the Maharashtra's Health Management Information System (HMIS) also corroborates the grim scenario. According to the HMIS' circle-wise child sex ratio at birth 2010 data, the state has an average of 904 girl child per 1,000 boys. "As per global trends, the child sex ratio should be more than 960 girls per 1000 boys", said Prakash Doke, Executive Director, SHSRC.

After winning prizes for improving sex ratio in 2009, the best districts in Haryana have lost the battle this year. Figures of first nine months in 2010, in a state in famous for skewed male-female ratio, show a sharp decline in Jhajjar, Gurgaon and

Faridabad districts—which had secured first, second and third place and won a cash prize of Rs. 5 lakh, 3 lakh and 2 lakh respectively in 2009. Jhajjar had secured first place, registering improvement by adding 22 girls for each 1000 boys in the district, while Gurgaon had added 20 girls for the same number of boys. The sex ratio in Jhajjar was recorded 825:1000 while it was 859:1000 in Gurgaon. But as per the figures up to September 2010, the sex ratio was 792 in Jhajjar and 840 in Gurgaon. There were 903 girls for 1000 boys in the 0-6 year age group in Faridabad in 2009, but latest figures suggest that it was just 877 till September this year. The situation has become worse in Rohtak, the home district of CM Bhupinder Singh Hooda, where ratio has dipped to 810 in the first nine months of this year—from 822 in 2009. Not only this, districts like Sonipat, Palwal, Kurukshetra and Ambala have also registered a decline. While economically developed districts have shown a downtrend, the most backward district of Haryana, Mewat, has registered an improvement in the sex ratio from 888 of last year to 902 till this September. Yamunanagar and Panipat are two other districts, which have shown a marked change in comparison to last year, while Panchkula has succeeded registering a slight improvement.

Table 6
Falling Trend in Sex Ratio

District	*Upto Sept. 2009*	*In 2009*	*Up to Sept. 2010*
(1)	*(2)*	*(3)*	*(4)*
Jhajjar	825	825	792
Gurgaon	843	859	840
Faridabad	902	903	877
Ambala	825	829	782
Bhiwani	858	863	830
Fatahabad	882	885	856
Hisar	874	874	857
Jind	859	861	857

(Contd.)

TABLE 6 (Contd.)

(1)	(2)	(3)	(4)
Kaithal	844	847	831
Kurukshetra	809	810	783
Karnal	832	836	810
Mahendragarh	791	789	787
Panipat	825	836	853
Panchkula	868	867	868
Rewari	779	781	756
Rohtak	820	822	810
Sonipat	813	821	810
Sirsa	895	884	868
Yamunanagar	824	824	834
Mewat	889	888	902
Palwal	902	919	890
State	849	853	837

TOI had recently reported how the sex ratio in Haryana had dipped to a five-year low with just 837 girls for 1000 boys in the age group of 0-6 years. Sociologists say while 'kuan pujan' has been performed even after the birth of a girl in isolated places, it is for the first time that such a large number of women took part in the ritual, calling it the 'beti bachao abhiyan' (save the girl child campaign). These women went to the well situated in Shree Dera Baba Shyoran Dass Mandir of Sirsa in a procession with dhols and nagadas (drums) playing.

On the occasion, other family members of the newborn girls also took the pledge to oppose the practice of female foeticide. The success of Haryanvi girls in the Commonwealth Games too seems to have made a difference. "We are excited about the performance of girls in CWG. I hope one day my daughter would win gold medals and make the country proud," said Kritika, mother of a new born girl. Another first time mother, Sharda Sharma, a resident of Ratta Khera, said such functions would motivate the common man about the importance of girl child in the family.

The facility of an ultrasound is easily available. Since the people have the power to pay the doctors (not all) have started pre natal sex-determination as a profit earning venture. These doctors see entrepreneurial opportunities in fulfilling the demand of a male child. Now there are private clinics providing the sex determination tests even at place which don't have the basic civic amenities like water and electricity. One finds several advertisements in the newspapers that encourage people to abort their female fetus to save the future cost of dowry. This nexus between technology and the parents aspiring for a son has become an industry where there are eager consumers and equally efficient "service providers". Though there is a ban on these ultrasound test but the cases have only multiplied rapidly and widely.

The emergence and spread of prenatal sex determination clinics are the early warning signals on the imbalance of sex ratios at birth in the coming decade following selective abortion of female foetuses. The recently available urban-rural figures for 2001 on child sex ratio provide further confirmation that these declines are caused by the relative availability of sex determination facilities.

In a society dominated by gender bias, the sex determination test is widely used to kill female foetuses, and continues to be available despite a ban. Such technologies either deprive women of their right to life or affect the quality of their lives.

(B) THE MEANING AND CONCEPT OF SEX DETERMINATION TEST

Before knowing about the meaning and concept of sex determination test firstly, it will be better to know some thing about foetal growth and development in pregnancy. Following are the different stages of foetal development in womb:

1. Foetal Growth and Development in Pregnancy

In the very early weeks, the developing baby is called an embryo. Then, from about eight weeks onward, it is called a foetus, meaning 'young one'.

(a) First Month

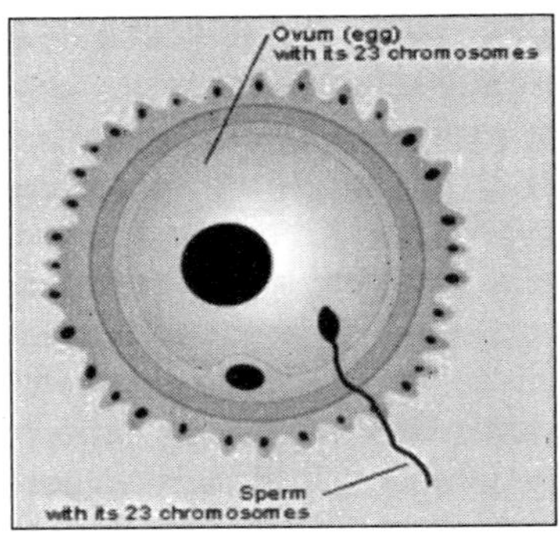

Three weeks from the first day of last menstrual period the fertilised egg moves slowly along the fallopian tube towards the womb. The egg begins as one single cell. After the egg has been fertilised by the sperm, it starts to divide into more cells. This cell divides again and again. By the time the egg reaches the womb it has become a mass of over 100 cells, called an embryo, ant is still growing. Once in the womb, the embryo burrows into the womb lining. This is called implantation.

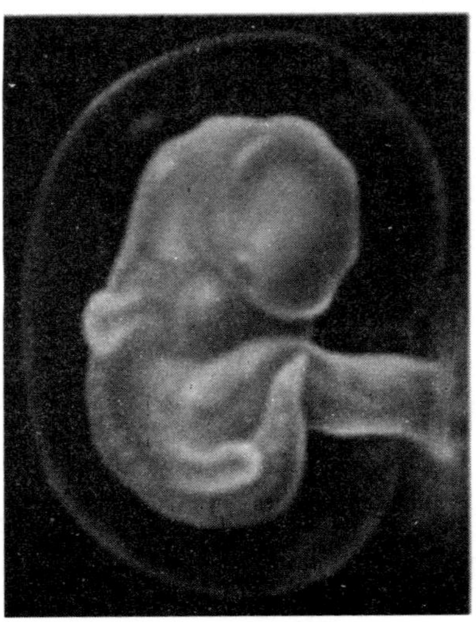

Three Weeks

The embryo now settles into the womb lining. The outer cells reach out like roots to link with the mothers blood supply. The inner cells form into two and then later into three layers. Each of these layers will grow to be different parts of the baby's body. One layer becomes the brain and nervous system, the skin, eyes and ears. Another layer becomes the lungs, stomach and gut. The third layer becomes the heart, blood, muscles and bones.

(b) Second Months

At **five weeks** the embryo is the size of a grain of rice (about 2 mm long) and would be visible to the naked eye. The fifth week is the time of the first missed period when most women are only just beginning to think they may be pregnant. Yet already the baby's nervous system is starting to develop. A groove forms in the top layer of cells. The cells fold up and round to make a hollow tube called the neural tube. This will become the baby's brain and spinal cord, so the tube has a 'head end' and a 'tail end'. Defects in this tube are the cause of spina bifida.

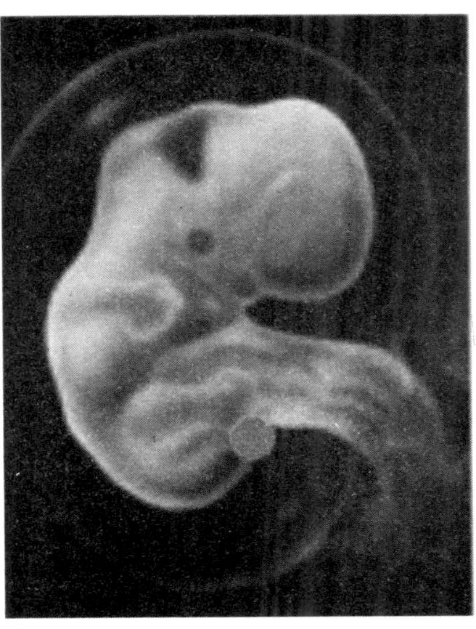

Second Months

At the same time the heart is forming and the baby already has some of its own blood vessels. A string of these blood vessels connects baby and mother and will become the umbilical cord.

There is now a large bulge where the heart is and a bump for the head because the brain is developing. The heart begins to beat and can be seen beating on an **ultrasound scan**. Dimples on the side of the head will become the ears and there are thickenings where the eyes will be. On the body, bumps are forming which will become muscles and bones. And small swellings (called 'limb buds') show where the arms and legs are growing.

At **seven weeks** the embryo has grown to about 10 mm long from head to bottom. This measurement is called the 'crown-rump length'.

A face is slowly forming. The eyes are more obvious and have some colour in them. There is a mouth, with a tongue. There are now the beginnings of hands and feet, with ridges where the fingers and toes will be. The major internal organs are all developing; the heart, brain, lungs, kidneys, liver and gut.

(c) Third Months

At **nine weeks**, the baby has grown to about 22 mm long from head to bottom. The umbilical cord is the baby's lifeline, the link between baby and mother. Blood circulates through the cord, carrying oxygen and food to the baby and carrying waste away again. The placenta is rooted to the lining of the womb and separates the baby's circulation from the mother's. In the placenta, oxygen and food from the mother's bloodstream pass across into the baby's bloodstream and are carried to the baby along the umbilical cord. Antibodies, giving resistance to infection, pass to the baby in the same way, but so too can alcohol, nicotine and other drugs. Inside the womb the baby floats in a bag of fluid called the **amniotic sac**. Before or during labour the sac, or 'membranes', break and the fluid drain out. This is called the 'waters breaking'.

Just **12 weeks** after conception the foetus is fully formed and its **sex organs are well developed**. The external genitals appeared in week 9, and now, by week 12, have **fully**

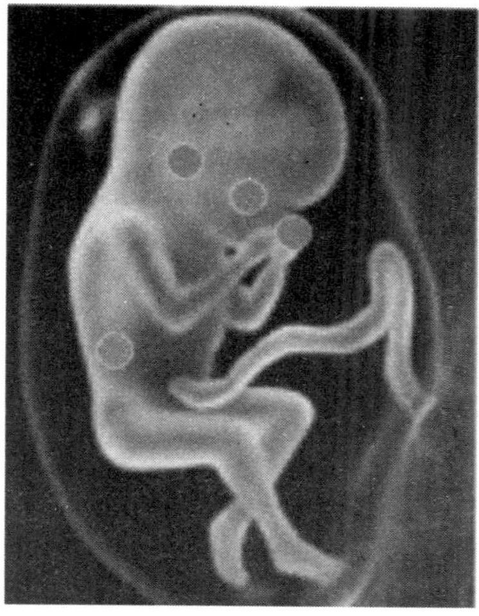

Third Months

differentiated into male or female genitals. It has all its organs, muscles, limbs and bones. From now on it has to grow and mature. The baby is already moving about, but the movements cannot yet be felt.

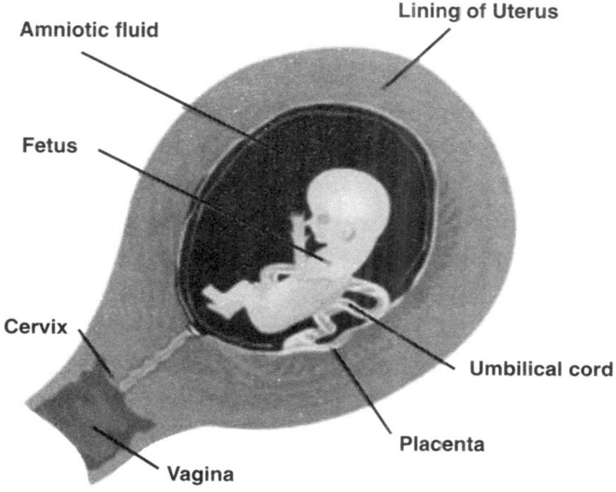

Twelve Weeks

(d) *Fourth Months*

By about **14 weeks**, the heartbeat is strong and can be heard using an ultrasound detector. The heartbeat is very fast, about twice as fast as a normal adult's heartbeat. At 14 weeks the baby is about 85 mm long (about 9-10cm long) from head to bottom. The pregnancy may be just beginning to show, but this varies a lot from woman to woman. The baby is now growing quickly. The body grows bigger so that the head and body are more in proportion and the baby doesn't look so top heavy. The face begins to look much more human and the hair is beginning to grow as well as eyebrows and eyelashes. The eyelids stay closed over the eyes. The lines on the skin of the fingers are now formed, so the baby already has its own individual fingerprint. Finger and toenails are growing and the baby has a firm handgrip. Your baby may suck its thumb now.

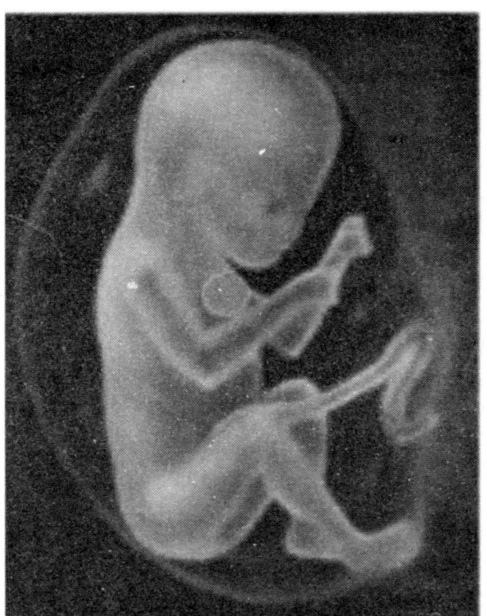

Fourth Months

(e) *Fifth Months*

By **week 20** your baby measures about 18 cm from crown to rump and is half as long as it will be when born. At about **22 weeks**, the baby becomes covered in a very fine, soft hair called 'lanugo'. The purpose of this isn't known, but it is

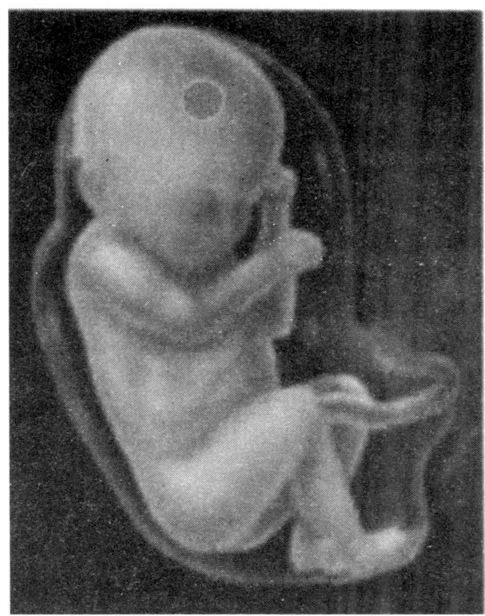

Fifth Months

thought that it may be to keep the baby at the right temperature. The lanugo disappears before birth, though sometimes just a little is left and disappears later.

At about **16 to 22 weeks** you will feel your baby move for the first time. If this is your second baby, you may feel it earlier, at about 16 to 18 weeks after conception. At first you feel a fluttering or bubbling, or a very slight shifting movement, may be a bit like indigestion. Later you can't mistake the movements and you can even see the baby kicking about. Often you can guess which bump is a hand or a foot and so on. The baby is now moving about vigorously and responds to touch and to sound. A very loud noise close by may make it jump and kick. It is also swallowing small amounts of the amniotic fluid in which it is floating and passing tiny amounts of urine back into the fluid. Sometimes the baby may get hiccups and you can feel the jerk of each hiccup. The baby may also begin to follow a pattern for waking and sleeping. Very often this is a different pattern from yours so, when you go to bed at night, the baby wakes up and starts kicking.

FETUS AT 20 WEEKS

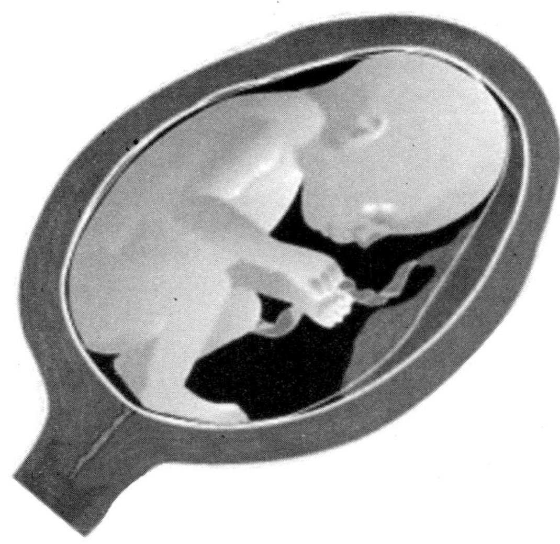

16 to 22 Weeks

The baby's heartbeat can now be heard through a stethoscope. Your partner may even be able to hear it by putting an ear to your abdomen, but it can be difficult to find the right place. The baby is now covered in a white, greasy substance called 'vernix'. It is thought that this may be to protect the baby's skin as it floats in the amniotic fluid. The vernix mostly disappears before the birth.

(f) Sixth Months

At **24 weeks** the baby is called 'viable'. This means that the baby is now thought to have a chance of survival if born. Most babies born before this time cannot live because their lungs and other vital organs are not well enough developed. The care that can now be given in neonatal units means that more and more babies born early do survive. At around **26 weeks** the baby's eyelids open for the first time. The eyes are almost always blue or dark blue. It is not until some weeks after birth that the eyes become the colour they will stay, although some babies do have brown eyes at birth. The head to bottom length at 30 weeks is about 33 cm.

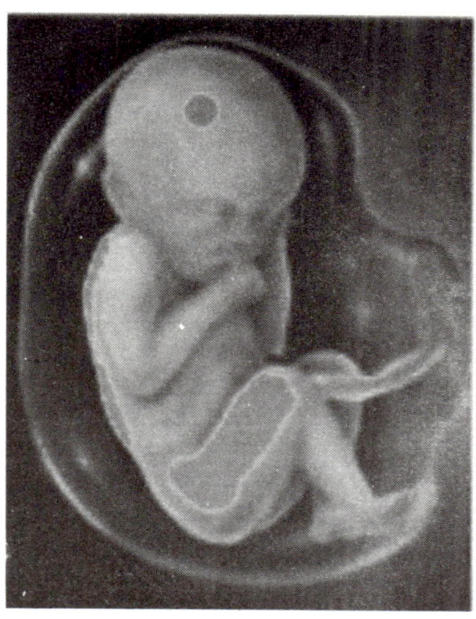

Six Months

(g) Seventh Months

By **28 weeks** lanugo hair has almost gone and hair is present on the head. Fat is being deposited under the skin. The

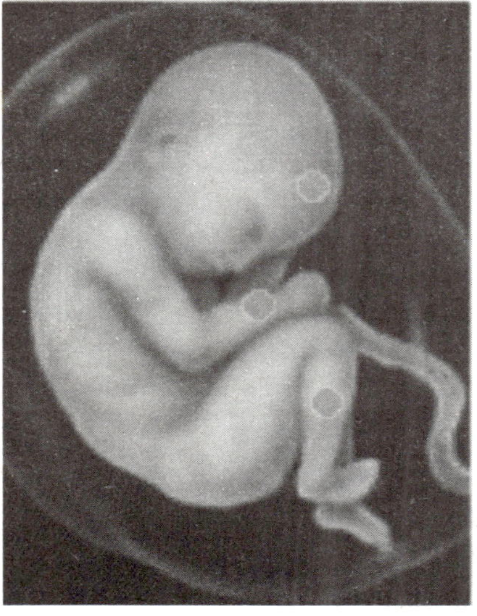

Seventh Months

baby is growing plumper so the skin, which was quite wrinkled before, is now smoother. Both the vernix and the lanugo begin to disappear.

(h) Eighth Months

Your baby is becoming plumper. By **30 weeks** the toenails are present and by **32 weeks** the fingernails have reached the ends of the fingers. The baby's eyes will be open when the baby's awake. By about 32 weeks the baby will have settled into a downward position as there is no longer enough room left in the womb for it to move about freely. You will feel occasional vigorous jabs of the baby's arms and legs. If your baby is a boy, his testes will migrate down into the scrotum in the eighth month. By about 32 weeks the baby is usually laying head downwards and is ready for birth.

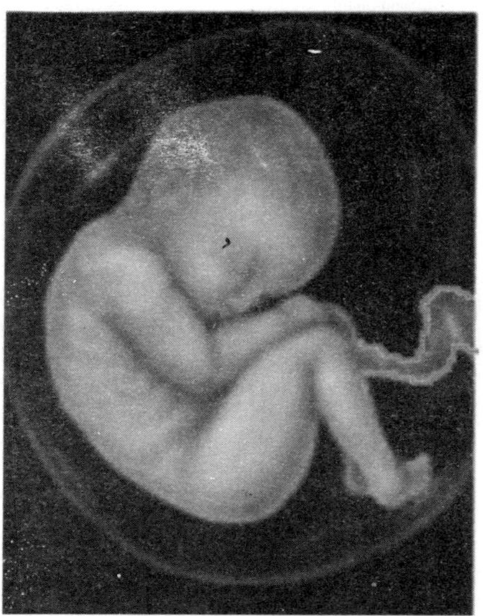

Eight Months

(i) Ninth Months

Some time before birth, the head may move down into the pelvis and is said to be 'engaged', but sometimes the baby's head does not engage until labour has started. Sometime

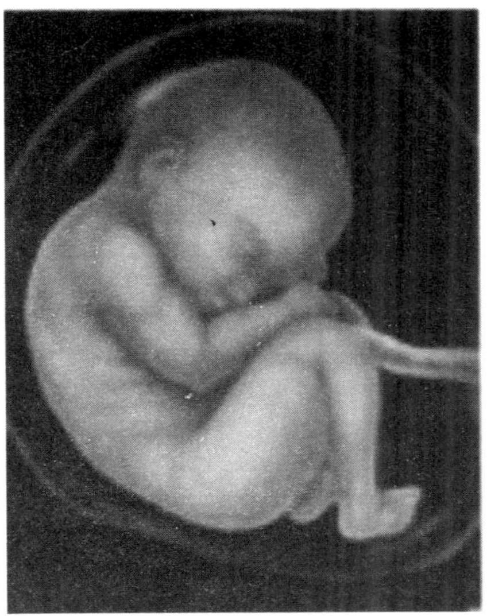

Ninth Months

between 36 and 40 weeks, the baby's head will engage—that is, the head will be lying just on top of your cervix. By 40 weeks, your baby should be plump and healthy. The lanugo hair that had covered your baby has now mostly disappeared, although some hair may remain low on the forehead, in front of the ears and down the centre of the back. The toenails should have reached the tips of the toes.

(j) *Full Term*

By full-term, your baby should weigh about 2.7-3.5 kg, although full-term babies can weigh anything from 2.5-5 kg, and measure 35-38 cm from crown to rump and 44-55 cm from the baby's head to its toes. These are just average figures, though, and there can be wide variation in the measurements. So now, 38 weeks after conception, your baby has all its organs and body systems ready for the big moment when it is born into the world.[20] The development of baby in the womb is a wonderful process. We have compiled a month-by-month

20. Dr. Copyright CMP Medica (NZ) 2002.

FETUS AT 40 WEEKS (FULL TERM)

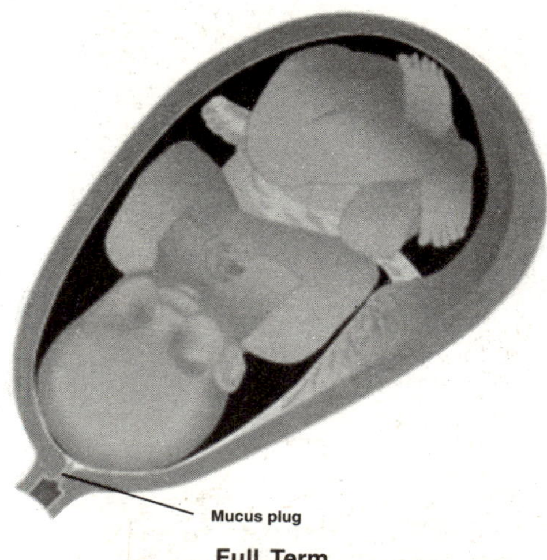

Full Term

timescale of what happens in the womb. But keep in mind that different pregnancies do develop at different rates.

2. Meaning and Definition of Sex Determination Test (SDT)

In general sense SDT means to know the sex of the fetus. Hence, in simple words—Sex Determination Test means to know the sex of the fetus—i.e. whether male or female in prenatal stage. In its generic sense, "Sex Selection" means the procedure which helps in known the probability whether or not an embryo will be of a male or female sex. For this purpose the Act specifically defines the term "Sex selection" in Section 2(0) thereof, which runs as follows: "Sex selection" includes any procedure, technique, test or administration or prescription or provision of anything for the purpose of ensuring or increasing the probability that an embryo will be of a particular sex".

On no account sex determination test shall be undertaken with the intent to terminate the life of a female foetus developing in her mother's womb, unless there are other absolute indications for termination of pregnancy as specified in the Medical Termination of Pregnancy Act, 1971. Any act of termination of pregnancy of normal female foetus, amounting to female foeticide, shall be regarded as professional misconduct on the part of the physician leading to penal erasure besides rendering him liable to criminal proceedings as per the provisions of this Act (Clause 7.6). It is here important to note that the penalty for unindicated sex determination and female foeticide is striking off the name from the register apart from criminal action.

A perusal of the above definition goes to show that the said term is not defined precisely providing for any full-fledged meaning but is in ambiguity and inclusive nature. However, this situation permits to interpret the term multifariously.

(i) Medico-Legal Definition of SDT

The determination of the sex of an individual, with regard to both the primary sex—i.e., whether the ovaries or the testes develop—and the various secondary sexual characteristics may be rigorously controlled from the start of development or may be subject to later influences of a hormonal or environmental nature.

However, this may be, in order to appreciate the action of the control systems, the point of departure is that animals were primitively hermaphrodite, that during early stages of evolution every individual probably possessed both male and female gonads. Differentiation into separate sexes, each possessing male or female gonads but not both at the same time, is a device to ensure cross-fertilization of eggs, whether this is accomplished by having the two types of sexual gland mature at different stages of the growth of the individual, as in some shrimp and others, or whether by the production of two distinct types of individuals, as in most species of animals.[21] This point of view is important because the question ceases to be how testes are caused to develop in the male organism and ovaries in the female but how, in a potentially double-sexed organism, the development of one or the other sex are suppressed.

21. Derek Morgan, Issues in Medical Law and Ethics, Edition, Cavendish Publishing Limited 2001.

That such is the case is seen as clearly as anywhere in the human condition itself. Neither sex is completely male or female. Females have functional, well-developed mammary glands. Males also have mammary glands, undeveloped and nonfunctional although equipped with nipples. Males have a penis for delivering sperm, but females have a small, nonfunctional equivalent—the clitoris. These are secondary sexual features, to be sure, but the difference between the sexes is in the degree of their development, not a matter of absolute presence or absence.

The basis for this is seen in the very beginnings of the development of the reproductive system, in frog, mouse, and man alike. In the young embryo a pair of gonads develop that are in different or neutral, showing no indication whether they are destined to develop into testes or ovaries. There are also two different duct systems, one of which can develop into the female system of oviducts and related apparatus and the other into the male sperm duct system. As development of the embryo proceeds, either the male or the female reproductive tissue differentiates in the originally neutral gonad of the mammal.

(ii) In the Frog and Other Lower Vertebrate Animals

The picture is even clearer. The original gonad consists of an outer layer of cells and an inner core of cells. If the individual is to be a male, the central tissue grows at the expense of the outer layer. If it is to be female, the outer tissue grows at the expense of the central core tissue. If both should grow, which is a possibility although a rare occurrence; the individual will be a hermaphrodite. Anything that influences the direction taken therefore may be said to determine sex.[22]

One of the modern scientific technological developments in the field of medicine is the use of pre-conception and pre-natal diagnostic techniques. These techniques are used not only of the diagnosis and treatment of certain physical problems connected with pregnancies, but also for knowing in advance

22. Cox, H.W.V., Medical Jurisprudence and Toxicology, 6th edition, 1998, The Law Book Co. (Pvt.) Ltd.

whether or not the embryo or the foetus is that of a male or female. It has become a usual practice among some fractions of the society to get rid of the growing pregnancy if it is found that the sex of the embryo or foetus living in the womb is of female character, for a variety of reasons. One such reason is that of the hatred and the anticipated socio-economic contingencies connected with the birth of female child in the family. This situation is not only depriving the right of birth of a female unborn child, but also a social evil in immoralising the human society. In this immoral activity the role of the parents/doctors/hospitals/clinics play pivotal role. The evil of gender discrimination with the accelerated pace of modernization of medical technology, the chances of abuse of liberal abortion rule by members of medical profession are increasing.

(C) OBJECTIVES OF THE DEVELOPMENT OF SEX DETERMINATION TEST

The primary objective of developing the technique to check the conditions of the fetus in womb was purely humanity oriented.[23] But, due to his own intention, the man begins to misuse the technique and violated the human rights. The basic objectives of the above techniques were:

- To know about the health of fetus in womb of mother.
- To treat the fetus, if suffering from any deformity.
- To help the mother in case of negative effect on her health due to development of the fetus.
- To detect and treat other pregnancy related problems.
- To assess the normal development of fetus.
- To ban the use of sex selection techniques.
- Prevention of misuse of such techniques for the prenatal sex determination leading to female foeticide.

---

23. "Pre-Birth Elimination of Females—A Handbook of Guidelines", by National Commission for Women, 2008.

(D) FACTORS RESPONSIBLE FOR SDT

Factors prevailing in India and responsible for SDT are:

(i) Socio-Cultural

- Preference for a son by family and society (as lie carries forward the name of the family, is considered a source of support during old age and performs last rites at the time of cremation)
- Social and familial pressure on women to produce sons
- Lower status of women in the society
- Inheritance system where a girl child has no right to her father's property.
- Social evil of dowry prevalent in our society.
- Discrimination against the girl child.
- Socio-economic and physical insecurity of women a stigma attached to being an unmarried woman.
- Unethical medical practices

(ii) Economic

- Child rearing cost *vis-à-vis* benefits that may accrue when the child becomes an adult.
- Cost related to marriage, especially in form of dowry.
- Most women lack financial independence.
- Easily accessible and affordable procedures for sex determination during pregnancy.

(iii) Political

- The issue does not attract attention of political party.
- Weak enforcement of existing policies and laws aimed at curbing the practice.
- Little political interest in bringing innovative policies to deal with the problem.
- Two-child norm of certain state governments.

(iv) If we Practice Sex Determination Test we deny the right of

- the female child to be born,
- the woman bearing the foetus to take a decision about her health and family,
- the woman to a satisfying and healthy sex life,
- the woman to decide about pregnancy—if, when and how often,
- the woman to have access to safe, effective, affordable and acceptable methods of family planning, and
- the woman to a safe pregnancy, child birth, and a healthy infant.[24]

(E) MYTHS ABOUT SDT

(i) Myth

Sex selective abortion is an effective tool for population control/family planning.

(ii) Fact

- Son preference.
- Poverty is an important cause.
- Women mostly want a small family.
- Women's education awareness and participation in economic can effectively curb population growth.
- Eliminate the undesirable sex:
  (i) *Myth*: Sex determination Tests are safe and accurate
  (ii) *Fact*
- The risk of spontaneous abortion & infections leading to further complications.
- Side effects:
  (i) *Myth*: SDT would not alter the sex ratio of the population.

24. "Pre-Birth Elimination of Females—A Handbook of Guidelines", by National Commission for Women, 2008.

(ii) *Fact*

- Average desirable family is 2 sons and a daughter.
  (i) *Myth*: Laws cannot curb SDT.
  (ii) *Fact*
- A socio-cultural revolution is needed.
- Measures for creating awareness and suitable policy interventions.
  (i) *Myth*: Banning SDT would infringe upon women's right to choose the sex of the offspring.
  (ii) *Fact*
- Women from poor countries have never asked for a right to decide the offspring sex.
  (i) *Myth*: Sex Selective abortions are more human than dowry murders and sati.
  (ii) *Fact*: Can poverty be eradicated by bombing slums or minorities problems be solved by eliminating minorities? Women aren't the problem. The problem is society's attitude towards them. The remedy lies in making daughters wanted and welcome and riot in refusing them their existence.

(F) EFFECT/CONSEQUENCES OF SEX DETERMINATION TEST

There are several ill effects techniques, for instance, amniocentesis can lead to abortion or premature birth. The use of a needle while performing amniocentesis can lead to spreading of infection. In some cases, the foetus may suffer hemorrhage, bleeding or breathing problems. The needle can pierce the foetus causing death or permanent disability.

Though considered less painful than amniocentesis, chorionic villi biopsy is not free from risks either. It can also lead to abortion, spreading of infection, limb defects and in some cases the limb may even come out. There can be bleeding when the sample is taken leading to mental and physical defects in the baby.

The pregnant woman's health may be affected and, in some instances her life may be threatened, due to complications during abortion like septic, gangrene and tetanus, hemorrhage due to incomplete abortion or injury to internal organs, poisoning from abortifacients (drugs used to induce abortion) resulting in kidney failure and tubal infections that may lead to infertility.

Other physical risks include excessive bedding, ripping or perforation of uterus, anesthesia complications, convulsions, cervical injury enhanced risk of miscarriages in future and long term health complications.

Associated mental trauma, crying, nightmares, flashbacks to abortion, hysterical outbreaks, nervous breakdown, depression, loss of self-esteem, self-destructive behavior, sexual dysfunction, sleep disturbances and a feeling of guilt or punishment from God may become a daily reality for the woman.

Risks are increased manifold because foetus is terminated not necessarily in hospitals under proper care and supervision, but in private nursing homes, mobile ultrasound vans and also at homes. The methods used in such situations are often very crude.

A huge majority was of the opinion that female deficit would give rise to increase in number of sex-related crimes like rape, abductions and immoral trafficking in female. Over the last years, the immoral traffic has increased. There are a few instances where the brides have been brought from other states by purchasing them from the poorer families. For more than two-fifth persons, finding a suitable bride within one's own community and area has already become a huge problem in the state.

Some of the other consequences were that the female deficit would result into the revival of century old practice of polyandry. It was quoted (From Mahabharata) that Draupadi was also married to five 'Pandavas'. Another point that came out was that if there would be fewer girls, then the practice of dowry would diminish because the girls would be highly valued. At that stage, getting a girl as a ride would gain ultimate importance than the accompanying dowry. It may even happen that instead of the bride's the groom's parents might offer dowry/money to get the girl married to their son.

(G) METHODS OF SEX DETERMINATION TEST

Three major pre-natal diagnostic tests that are being used as sex determination tests are as follows:

- Amniocentesis (normally performed after 15-17 weeks of pregnancy).
- Chorionic Villus Sampling (more expensive and normally performed around the 10th week of pregnancy).
- Ultrasound (least expensive and normally performed around 10th week of pregnancy).[25]
- The two new methods for pre-conceptual sex selection, which are now becoming quite popular, are the Ericsson's method and Pre-implementation Genetic Diagnosis (PGD).[26]
- In the Ericsson's method first a semen sample is diluted and then centrifuged. X and Y bearing sperms are separated when placed in a chemical solution. The faster moving Y sperms penetrate the solution's denser bottom layers, which are collected and centrifuged. The process is repeated and the Y concentrate is collected for artificial insemination. The method is said to have a success rate of about 70 percent of producing a male child and is very expensive, but is still being tried by many families in the Metropolitan Cities.[27]
- The Pre-implementational Genetic Diagnosis is a much more complicated technique which is done in order to study the genetic blue print to determine

25. "Pre-Birth Elimination of Females—A Handbook of Guidelines", by National Commission for Women, 2008.
26. "Pre-Natal Diagnostic Techniques: A Source of Gender Bias", by *Kashmir University Law Review-X* (2003).
27. Mehta, Swati and Kothari Javna, "Pre-Natal sex selection and Law", *Lawyers Collective*, November 26, at p. 6.

> whether the embryo is male or female. The extricated cell from this technique for the sex selection purpose is douse with two fluorescent probes. Chemical stains that single out the X and Y chromosomes from the intricate genetic master plan. It is then bathed in a stainless steel water bath to wash away unwanted cellular debris that could interfere with the analysis. Freshly scrubbed X (female) shows up as a pink dot under a special fluorescent microscope, while Y (male) reveals itself as a bright green speck. The embryos that turn out to be male, which are always fewer in number, are then implanted in the woman's uterus and the remaining female embryos are simply discarded.

This procedure finally results in sex selection of embryos which for the doctor and government a like falls out of the purview of the PNDT act, as it is pre-conceptual and not 'pre-natal'.

These are the common methods of sex determination before birth as well as before conception.

I. Amniocentesis (Amnion: Membrane, Kentesis: Pricking)

This test is conducted on the amniotic fluid obtained from the womb of a pregnant woman to predict whether an unborn foetus is a male or female.

In this technique, amniotic fluid is drawn from the amniotic sac surrounding the foetus in the uterus through a long needle inserted into the abdomen. Foetal cells present in the fluid help in determining the sex of the foetus. It is normally performed after 15-17 weeks of pregnancy.

Amniocentesis (Amnion; Membrane, Kentesis, Pricking) was brought in India in 1975, as a measure of detecting genetic disorders and abnormalities. It is a diagnostic procedure performed by inserting a hollow needle through the abdominal wall into the uterus and withdrawing a small amount of fluid from the sac surrounding the foetus. The test can detect chromosomal disorders, such as structural defects (open spine, where the vertebrae fail to close), (anencephaly) a conditions in which the brain is incomplete or missing), and many rate, inherited metabolic disorders.[28] The test may also be used to identify suspected problems or infections late in the pregnancy: lung maturity can also be determined. Amniocentesis was meant to be used in high-risk pregnancies, in women over 35 years.

In this technique, about 10 mls of amniotic fluid is removed. The risk of harming the foetus or causing the miscarriage is 0.5-1 percent. The test is done at between 15-18 weeks gestation. The technique developed to discover birth defects, incidentally, could also reveal the sex of the foetus. Unfortunately, this invention of medical science has resulted in 'quickening the pace of death of the female child from the born to the unborn stage'.[29] Amniocentesis in India has become synonymous with the sex determination test, which has led to sex-selective abortions.

Amniocentesis test is the clinical study of amniotic fluid only in diagnosing the actual existence of the disorder in the existing fetus. Amniocentesis test thus offers the means of discovering antenatal, unborn metabolic disorder, chromosomogenetic abnormalities, sex linked aberrations and deficiencies in neural—tube development. Moreover, this test also helps in detecting genetic disorder of the foetus and findings out whether a child born would be deformed or abnormal. The chromosome test done on the amniotic fluid taken from the womb of pregnant woman can be used to predict whether an unborn foetus is male or female.[30]

2. Chorionic Villi Biopsy

This refers to the removal of elongated cells (called villi) of the Chorion, which is the tissue surrounding the foetus, through the cervix. The tissue cells are tested to determine sex

---

28. Stranc, L.C., *et. al.*, Chorionic Villus Sampling and Amniocentesis of Pre-natal Diagnosis, p. 349 (1997), Ahmad, S., "Pre-Natal Diagnostic Techniques : A Source of Gender Bias", *Kashmir University Law Review-X*, pp. 205-06 (2003).
29. Grover, A., "Amniocentesis of Female Foeticide", *The Lawyers*, p. 3, March (1986).
30. Percival Robert, Mannual of Obstetrics (14th ed.) 1990 at p. 17.

of the foetus. This technique enables sex determination between the first 6-13 weeks of pregnancy and abortion can be carried out in the first trimester itself.

Another method similar to amniocentesis is Chorionic villi biopsy. The latter involves the removal of the elongated cell (villi) of the chorion (tissue surrounding the foetus), through the cervix. This tissue is then tested for determination of sex. This new biotechnology enables sex determination between the weeks 6 and 13. Abortion, if desired can be carried out in the first trimester itself, with greater ease. Claimed to be less painful than amniocentesis and 100% accurate, this technique carries a 3 to 5% risk of bleeding, pain and spontaneous abortion.

3. Ultra Sonography/Ultrasonic

Here inaudible (to humans) sound waves are used to get a visual image of the foetus on a screen. Normally, it is used to determine the foetal position or abnormalities, but it can also be used to find the sex if external genitalia of a male foetus is seen on the screen. It is normally performed around the 10th week of pregnancy. It is the most commonly and rampantly used method for sex determination.

The discovery of the cheaper Ultrasound technique likewise has proved to be the nemesis of the female foetus in India. It is non-invasive and can identify up to 50 per cent of abnormalities related to the central nervous system of the foetus. But sexing has become its preferred application. The technique uses inaudible sound waves to get a visual image of the foetus on a screen. Normally employed to determine the foetal position or abnormalities, the technique can be used to determine sex if external genitalia of a male foetus is seen on the screen.

The medical fraternity was quick to see entrepreneurial opportunities in catering to insatiable demands for a male child. The "portable" ultrasound machine allowed doctors to go from house to house in towns and villages.[31] Depending on the ultrasonologist's expertise, chances of a correct prediction

31. In some interior villages of Punjab and Haryana, they say the mobile scan is more easily available than water supply.

are 95-96 per cent, with greater accuracy as the pregnancy advances. If the foetus is female, a second trimester, even a third trimester abortion is carried out either by a doctor or a quack.

In recent decades, many new and sophisticated reproductive technologies have come up complicating the problem of female foeticide. One needs to spend just half an hour with infertility experts to be educated on the newest technologies. The menu is an impressive one: karyo-typing, with analyses chromosomal abnormalities and incidentally reveals the sex of the foetus, a procedure that takes 11 days and costs around Rs. 5,000; Fluorescent in situ hybridization, with has 95% accuracy, take 2 days and coast Rs. 10,000; Comparative genomic hybridization requires 2 days; Polymerase chain reaction, the results of which are available in a day with a cost of Rs. 5,000; and Pre-implantation genetic diagnosis (PGD), where the results take about a week. PGD is made available in Thailand for sex selection of Indians who are aware of the law against such tests in the country, at a cost of about Rs. 1.5 lakh.[32]

All these techniques can be used to detect the sex of the foetus within 4-6 weeks of pregnancy, making abortions a less serious business than the usual methods (like amniocentesis) that come into play only 14 weeks after pregnancy. Thereafter, abortions not only become medically dangerous for the mother but also acquire entirely different moral dimensions.[33]

Using these new techniques, sex selection of the foetus can now take place pre natal even before conception. The two new methods for pre-connectional sex selection, which are now becoming quite popular, are the Ericsson's method and PGD. Both these techniques involve the identification and discarding of the female embryo.[34]

---

32. Dani, A., "Death in the Womb", *The Times of India*, New Delhi, November 19 (2004).
33. *Ibid.*, Under the Medical Termination of Pregnancy Act, 1971, in India all abortions after 20 weeks are illegal.
34. 'Embryo' refers to the developing human organism formed after fertilization till the end of 56 days; 'Foetus' refers to the period from the 57th day ending at birth.

4. Pre-Conception Techniques to Select Sex

(i) Ericsson Method (X and Y Chromosome Sperm Separation)

A male child requires an XY combination of chromosomes. Sperms may have either X or Y chromosome, but eggs have only X chromosome. In this method, sperms are separated into those bearing X chromosome and those bearing Y chromosome—by filtration when put in a chemical solution. The faster moving Y sperms penetrate the solution's denser bottom layers. The egg is then fertilized with a high concentration of Y sperms to produce a male.

In the Ericsson's method only XY sperms, which can produce boys, are used for artificial insemination. In this method, first a semen sample is diluted and then centrifuged. X and Y bearing sperms are separated when placed in a chemical solution. The faster moving Y-sperms penetrate the solution's denser bottom layers, which are collected and centrifuged. The process is repeated and the Y concentrate is collected for artificial insemination. The method is said to have a success rate of about 70 per cent of producing a male child and is very expensive, but is still being tried by many families in the metropolitan cities.[35]

(ii) Pre-Implantation Genetic Diagnosis (PGD)

One of the latest technologies to be used for sex selection, it involves chromosomal analysis of a few cells taken from a test tube embryo (fertilization is done outside the uterus) to determine the sex.

The Pre-Implantation Genetic Diagnosis (PGD) is a much more complicated technique (which was developed in the West to sort out embryos with inherited diseases like hemophilia). While ultrasonography and amniocentesis determine the sex of the foetus during pregnancy, and the foetus is aborted if found to be female, in the PGD mechanism sex selection takes place much before.

---

35. Mehta, S. and Kothari, J., "Pre-natal Sex Selection and Law", *Lawyers Collective*, p. 6, November (2001).

Under it, the first step is "pickup" which involves the collection of unfertilized eggs from the female ovaries. They are fertilized, outside the woman's body, in a Petridis with active perms. The resulting embryos are then carefully nurtured in an incubator. After 72 hours, each eight-cell embryo is biopsied by a micromanipulator, which includes glass pipettes and powerful microscope. While one of the pipettes holds the embryo in place, the second delicately extricates a single cell from the little clump. The extricated cell is taken to a tiny FISH (fluorescent *in-situ* hybridization) laboratory and transferred to a slide under a Stereo Zoom Microscope, specially designed for single-cell analysis.[36] The genetic blueprint of the cell is studied in order to determine the sex of the embryo. Chemical stains are used to single out the S and Y chromosomes from the intricate genetic master plan. It is then 'bathed' to wash away unwanted cellu!ar debris, which could interfere with the analysis. The freshly scrubbed X chromosome (female) shows up as a pink dot while the Y chromosome (male) appears as a bright green speck. The male embryos which are always fewer in number are then implanted in the woman's uterus,[37] and the female embryos are simply discarded.[38]

36. Rajalakshmi, T.K, "Sex Selection and Questions of Law", *Frontline*, p. 103, October 27 (2000).
37. *Ibid*.
38. The entry of an American company promoting a gadget which helps gender selection is both pathetic and hilarious. Priyanka Kakodkar in her article on 'XY Terror' (Outlook, December 10, 2001) says: "A first glance, it seems like an innocuous spiel for baby-food. The advertisement, tucked away on page 19 of The Times of India, shows a mop-haired and diapered toddler, gleefully clutching its hands. Then, you notice the disquieting catch phrase: 'gender Selection now a Reality'. It goes on to offer Gene-Select-a pill-and-douche kit from a US firm which claims to help couples choose the sex of their child that too before conception. The product, which has been on offer for more than two weeks on son-craving Indian shores, has sparked a wave of protest from women's rights groups and health activists. "Gen-Select"—its claims have been dismissed by doctors in Mumbai—is clear product of Orangeburg, a South Carolina, firm. That it has specifically targeted the Indian market, which reveres sons and despises daughters, is clear from its website. The only overseas toll-free number listed is for India. The product

Thus, gender discrimination can be in the form of infanticide, foeticide, embryocide or before conception as 'future sperm separation'. Since female infanticide requires at least nine months, female foeticide up to three months, female embryocide, potentially just a few weeks, and sperm separation, a few days, it is becoming easier to produce only boys. So, the earlier the stage at which sexing is done, the graver the social consequences.

A writer has summed up the complexities of the issues in pre-natal sex-determination in the following words.[39] "Feminists are loath to confer the right to life on the foetus, and the women's movement the world over has fought for a woman's right to control her own body. Unconditional access to safe, legal abortion is a non-negotiable demand to ensure some measure of reproductive autonomy in a situation where women are not in a position of refuse sex, especially in the marital context, where men do not shoulder the responsibility of contraception, where sexual abuse is rampant and safe contraceptives are neither freely accessible nor fool-proof. Yet, feminists also fight against patriarchal notions, which lay down that a female has no place in the society, and the campaign against sex-determination and sex pre-selection is but one aspect of this battle. Pre-selection is even more complicated—a sanitized and less messy way of eliminating the female. There is no 'life' to contend with, no 'murder', no blood and gore. Yet, the violence is in no way diminished. If anything, this is extreme form of misogyny unimagined until a couple of decades ago."

---

costs $ 119.95 (roughly Rs. 6,000) and can be ordered online. When contacted by Outlook, the firm's managing director Scott M. Sweazy said he had received a "tremendous response" in India both from the public and distributors. For more on Gen-Select one can visit their website www.genselectKIT.com. See http://www.indiafemale foeticide.org

39. Murthy, L., Sex Selection: Getting Down to Business, available at http://www.infochangeindia.org, in V. Kumari, 'Fertility Revolution and Changing Concept of Family and Identity", *Delhi Law Review*, Vol. XXV, p. 120 (2003).

According to the non-official jargon for telling couples that they have a baby boy, doctors in Delhi would use "congratulation", "touch the right ear", give a "thumbs up sign" and even tell the parents "not to worry". These gestures effectively convey and let the couple know of the sex of the baby.[40] Similarly, in Gujarat, erring doctors and radiologist are employing code language to inform expectant parents about the sex of the foetus. Religious greetings are the most popular-while a male foetus is announced with a "Jai Shri Krishna", "Jai Ganesh", "Jai Shri Ram" or "Har Har Mahadev", indicators of a female foetus include "Jai Mataji", "Jai Ambe" and so on. Other popular code words include, Report barabar chhe (The report is alright) for a male foetus, and, report barabar nathi (with doctors grimly looking at the parents) for a female. Another way of sending out signals is by distributing sweets—pedas for a boy and jalebis for a girl.[41]

In a study conducted on the women in Gujarat and Haryana, it is found that the awareness about a ban on sex determination tests is fairly widespread among them. Many women also felt that the ban should be removed and couples should have the choice to decide the sex composition of their children. They desire and want fewer children while ensuring that at least one if not two of them are sons. This has also led to increased acceptance and use of sex selection tests to achieve parental preference to, have sons while not exceeding the desired number of children.[42]

A senior Delhi government official explained: "Sex determination tests are conducted when families and the pregnant woman demand it. Therefore, we cannot expect a situation wherein people will file complaint against such clinics. The only way we can nab errant clinics and doctors' is by sending decoy customers".[43] 'Pay Rs. 500 now and save Rs. 5,00,000 later' is how these technologies are advertised.

40. Anonymous, *The Hindu*, New Delhi, December 20 (2004).
41. Anonymous, *The Times of India*, New Delhi, November 26 (2004).
42. *Ibid.*, at p. 29.
43. *Ibid.*, August 20(2001).

(H) SEX DETERMINATION TEST AND ABORTION

God made the world
Then He made a creator
I was created to create mankind
To me He gave motherhood

You are a mother
Mother to only sons
You are the creator
You'll create to order
You'll love
Love only the sons of man

May I never see myself?
Can I never guide her?
Can I never adorn a bride?
May I never mother a daughter?
Where have all the baby girls gone?
Sent to heaven by sex sensitive death

My daughter
They call you Devi
Yet you are a curse
You are Annapoorna
Yet denied food
You are Saraswati
Yet unlettered
You have a temple
Only my womb is denied
You have divinity
But denied life

My daughter, a mother bears the burden of your death
Guilty condemned again...again...and again till I bear a son

Is the gift of creation?
To be tarnished by destruction
The gift of life sullied by death

Am I a creator?
Or just a procreator
Am I an identity?
Or just a womb
Am I a woman?
Or just a channel for man
Am I a mother?
Or just a son bearer

—*By UNFPA on Motherhood*

'World wide fully 42% of all unborn girls are aborted, compared to 25% of boys.' over 3 thousand female fetuses are aborted every day in India one million per year. As per Ms Conly most families still appreciate the worth of daughters "most families do want a daughter a daughter to help the mother with child care and other household chores. Also woman often wants an emotional bond with their daughter" describes. "But if you are talking about more than one daughter then it becomes a huge problem. A second daughter is going to bring financial ruin or at a minimum, significant financial stress. So I think both female infanticide and sex selective abortion are driven to some extent by the dowry system."

Whereas, In New Delhi Rashmi name changed got a 12 week old foetus aborted when she discovered it was a girl. This was following ultrasound screening which determined the sex of the foetus. Acc to R.P. Ravindra 'Choosing the sex of one's child is the most sexist sin.'

Selective abortion affected the overall male and female ratio. 'Sex selective abortions are on the rise'. As per Dr. Pater "Daughter is a manes a liability and son means an asset. Sons are called blank checks" Acc to Delhi Health and Education Minister Harsh Vardhan acknowledges the problem but says: We cannot do anything unless someone registers a complaint against such practices." Nobody does is seems amniotic and fetal cells are called primary cell and have value really only in sex determination which is possible after completion of 15th week and up to 20th week of pregnancy. If done earlier, it is difficult to detect sex of unborn and if done latter than 20th

week it would be too late for considering termination. Incidentally 12th week to 20th week of pregnancy is period during which therapeutic abortion is medically feasible and legally permissible.

With the modernization of medical technology the chance of abuse of the liberal abortion law by members of medical practitioner have increased considerably. It is well known that in India a male infant is more welcome on birth than a female one. A study reveals that out of 15 million abortions carried out in the world in 1997, India alone accounted for 4 million, 90 per cent of which were intended to eliminate the girl child (Law against Practice of Female Foeticide and Infanticide, Shalu Nigam, Indian social Institute).

A female baby is considered a burden to the family. This after knowing the sex of foetus the parents do not tell the gynecologist that they do no want the child because it is a female child. The doctor who ultimately does the MTP may not even be aware that he or she is doing it on the ground that the female child was not need by the parents. The parent may only say to the doctor that they do not just want the child at this particular moment which as per the MTP Act they have right to do so.[44]

This abuse of medical sciences, deprive a female foetus to be born alive. Law does not confer a right on unborn person to be born. However, the increasing incidence of female foeticide seems to an encroachment on right of a child and a worst form of discrimination. The practice hurt not only social morality but is counter—productive. If allowed to continue unchecked it may de-establish the natural proportion of male and female population.

The studies suggest that doctors in government hospitals and other private medical practitioners have been conducting this test to determine the sex of the foetus and have been aborting it if it happens to be female. A survey conducted in 1992 even in cosmopolitan Bombay revealed that 7,999 out of 8,000 aborted fetuses were femakle.[45] It has been reported in a national daily that as many as 50,000 female fetuses are aborted

---

44. *The Hindustan Time,* Aug. 9, 1994 at p. 18.
45. *Ibid.,* Aug. 9, 1994 at p. 18.

every year after such test. In Delhi alone, there are 2000 clinics conducting sex determination tests and 70 percent of all abortion in capital is female foeticide.[46] It is pity that this life saving technique of ultrasonography and amniocentesis is sometime used for denial of life to an unborn person only on the basis of gender. As many as 50,000 female fetuses are aborted every year after such test.[47]

One of the latest developments in reproductive technology has been the use of IVF and which will in time refine the sex pre-selection technique by removing genetic material from the fertilized pre-embryo eight cell stages and testing them for X-bearing spermatozoa which showed signs of female formation. Some doctors have been reported to prefer sex pre-selection to sex-determination that involves amniocentesis or Chorionic Villus sampling, as this would avoid the need later on for abortion and risky or intrusive surgical operations (such as caesarean and cervical surgery, etc.)[48]

So a reproductive technology which was developed to detect chromosomal abnormalities in the foetus has now been appropriated for sex determination primarily. If the finding of such tests reveals that a female child has been conceived the foetus is being invariably terminated. According to the Indian Medical Association, for instance, five million female fetuses are aborted every year. Keeping in view the seriousness of the problem, the National Human Rights Commission (NHRC, India) has asked the Medical Council of India to examine the ethical aspects of sex determination tests which it too acknowledges are causing a high rate of female foeticide.[49] Many activist groups are agreed that female selective abortion is a serious problem that deserves high priority from international and national policy-makers.

Sex determination has become a lucrative business for many doctors and clinics for over a decade now. It was in 1977

46. *Ibid.*, Sep. 28, 1994 at p. 13.
47. *The Hindustan Times*, Sept. 1994 at p. 13.
48. Bilimoria Purushottama and Sharma Renuka: Issues in Health Ethics in Modern India, in the Other Revolution, edited by Sharma, Renuka, Sri Sat Guru Publications, Delhi, 1999, p. 263.
49. *Ibid.*, p. 264.

that a leading hospital in Bombay, the Harkisondas Hospital inaugurated its pre-natal sex determination clinic and advertised it through a circular which referred to the "humane and beneficial test". This circular, however, added that "abortion, if necessary, will not be performed in this hospital". This in any case was no problem as there were several other clinics to do the job. The problem caught media attention when a doctor in Amritsar advertised his ante-natal sex determination clinic in 1979. It was in 1982 that a wrong diagnosis leading to the abortion of a male child created a lot of hue and cry.

There were angry protests and agitations by women's organizations and activists, and surveys were conducted which revealed that sex determination tests have become a lucrative business in several parts of the country. There are many clinics in Bombay and in smaller towns of Maharashtra. There are clinics with sex determination services in various other states also. It is believed that in some states there are courier services to carry samples of the amniotic fluid of pregnant women from rural health centers to big towns and cities. In Haryana there are said to be mobile vans which conduct sonography as the latest sex determination technique in villages.

Sex determination test has been an important issue for the women's movement, especially in the 80s. The feminist response has been to end the practice. The campaign at the time resulted in state and national legislation.

Maharashtra was the first state in India that has passed a law in 1988, outlawing the use of pre-natal diagnosis for sex selection and also made it illegal to reveal the sex of the foetus even when the procedure is done for legitimate medical reason, for example—to detect the chromosomal abnormalities. Several other states like New Delhi, Karnataka, Haryana and Rajasthan have also passed a similar legislation. At the national level, the Pre-Natal Diagnostic techniques (Regulation and Prevention of Misuse) Act, 1994 was passed, which made sex test, a cognizable, non-bailable and non-compoundable offence.

Now it is an offence to have recourse to pre-natal diagnostic techniques under the pretext of detecting chromosomal abnormalities. It is also an offence on the part of the pregnant woman who undergoes the test. The national law requires that all institution providing prenatal resting be registered with purpose of gaining greater oversight and monitoring.

Miller comments that, while this provision might have some effect on large institutions, it is completely useless for regulating the use of the new portable ultrasound machine. According to Miller, a new GE model offers most of the conventional functions in a 20 pound unit that can fit in the back seat of car, allowing physicians to provide ultrasound scanning for foetal sex selection anywhere that a car can go. The national law also says nothing about sex selection through sperm separation which is legally permissible in Bombay.[50] As reported by Nivedita Menon,[51] women's groups are dissatisfied with the national Act, and in August 1994 urged the President to send it back for consideration to parliament. Some of the points that their memorandum raised are as follows.[52] All ultrasound machines and other equipments which can be used for sex determination test should be registered. The Joint Committee had earlier considered this suggestion and rejected it as unfeasible because such equipment is used for various purposes other than pre-natal testing.[53] Future techniques for sex determination as well as for sex pre-selection should be brought within the ambit of the central law.

The Act Punishes the woman if it can be proved that she was not coerced and that she went in for the test and the abortion of her own will. The memorandum says that punishing, the woman is misguided, even on the presumption that she was coerced unless proved otherwise. This is unjust in a context where women rarely take autonomous decisions. The

---

50. Miller, Barbara, The Endangered Sex: Neglect of Female Children in Rural North India, Oxford University Press, New Delhi, 1997, pp. 197, 208, 212.
51. Menon, Nivedita, Rights Bodies and the law: Rethinking Feminist Politics of Justice, in Gender and Politics in India, edited by Menon Nivedita, Oxford University Press, New Delhi,. 2001 p. 279.
52. *Saheli Newsletter*, 1995, Vol. 5, No. 2.
53. *Report of Joint Committee*, 1992, pp. 20-21.

act in this respect is anti-women, and would create conditions that would limit its effectiveness.

Here this is to make it clear that the national Act has come into force with many loopholes, as perceived by women's groups. It is true that women may take decision of pre-natal sex determination on their own in certain cases but it is not always true. In fact, women in our society are the oppressed victims of tradition and patriarchy, and are often forced to undergo abortion of a female foetus by their families. Sons are a major obsession throughout India. The rising levels of education, economic opportunities and the constitutional guarantees of equality have not helped to raise the status of women significantly. Son preference ha penetrated in all sections of society. It is the woman who is blamed and ridiculed for delivering a baby girl. Often parents insist that their sons remarry if the daughter in law is unable to bear a son. Sometimes women are abused and battered if they fail to deliver a boy, and if they refuse to abort a female foetus. It appears that women are rarely in a position to make self-decision and therefore, should not be criminally responsible for sex selection.

I. Implications of Declining Sex Ratio

Historically, the imbalance in sex ratio led to the competition for bridegrooms (and not brides who were scarce) and payment of exorbitant dowry. The son was actually given to the highest bidder. Among the Jats in particular the scarcity of girls led to a widespread system of polyandry.[54]

A further consequence of the requirement that women marry was that the lowest caste males had great difficulty in obtaining wives. Daughters were often sold to higher castes, and even poor males often paid a bride-price to obtain a wife. The intensity of competition for wives was so great that child betrothal and early marriage was practiced in an attempt to

54. Panigrahi, L., British Social Policy and Female Infanticide in India, Munshiram Manoharlal, New Delhi (1972), in Snehi, Y.U., "Female Infanticide and Gender in Punjab: Imperial Claims and Contemporary Discourse", *Economic and Political Weekly*, October 11 (2003), available at www.epw.org.in

cope with the problem.[55] Thus, there are various socio-economic and health implications of declining sex ratio.

2. Distorted Sex Ratio in the Society

An increase in sexual and social crimes against women, such as rape, abduction of women for marriage, child marriage, bride selling, forced polyandry, etc., sexual violence is likely to become more of a problem as the number of unmarried men increases. The various factors responsible for such criminal activities of unmarred youth would be to fulfil their desires; no social bond; and lack of responsibility.[56] Shortfalls in the 'supply' of women will lead to their being subject to greater restrictions, control and violence, as in China, where shortage of marriageable women from other regions.[57] Social imbalance with a decline in moral values; purchasing brides from other States would affect the State's culture. An increase in prostitution, sexual exploitation, cases of SDT, HIV/AIDS and psychological disorders, particularly amount women. The health of the women is affected because of repeated

55. Guttentag, M., *et. al.* Too Many Women? The Sex Ratio question, Sage, Beverly Hills (1983), in Snehi, Y.U., "Female Infanticide and Gender in Punjab: Imperial Claims and Contemporary Discourse", *Economic and Political Weekly*, October 11 (2003), available at www.epw.org.in
56. Things have come to such a pass that in some villages of Madhya Pradesh, no marriages have taken place for years because there are no girls and the boys are married by buying girls from far away villages of Bihar for paltry sums. In one district in west Rajasthan, in 1997, the first "baraat" was received after 110 years and in another clan, there are only two female surviving children compared to 400 male children.

    A recent newspaper article says that in Hathin (Haryana), two decades of female foeticide have caught up with the people. Men are resorting to the tactic of buying brides from other States like Assam and West Bengal. The price put on such a girl is much less than what people pay for cattle! After marriage, they are condemned to a life of slavery. See the *Hindustan Times*, New Delhi, July 12 (2003).
57. Sudha, S. and Rajan, S.I., "Persistent Daughter Disadvantage: What Do Estimated Sex Ratios at Birth and Sex Ratio of Child Mortality Risk Reveal?" *Economic and Political Weekly*, p. 4361, October 11 (2003), available at www.epw.org.in

pregnancies and forced abortions. Women are a vital part of India's labour force, especially in rural areas and now in urban areas also. Further, women's unseen work is often not valued in economic terms.

An argument frequently used by the supporters of sex selective abortion is that the decline in sex ratio will result in an elevation of the status of women and reform of the dowry system. However, there are no indications that the declining sex ratio over the past century has elevated the position of women or eliminated dowries. In fact, ostentatious weddings and dowry has become the order of the day.[58]

By the early 1980s new reproductive technologies like announcements is had appeared on the scene. The scientific sounding justification for using sex determination to produce only sons were first given in 1975 by 'eminent' scientist from the All-India Institute of Medical Science (AIIMS), New Delhi. A doctor at the Institute involved in genetic research into sex-specific diseases had obtained access to this technology, and was offering clinical services to certain patients. To her horror she discovered that in many of the cases the diagnosis that the foetus was a female (even without any evidence of genetic disorder) was being followed by abortions. The Indian Council of Medical Research (ICMR) directed the AIIMS to stop offering clinical services, leaving the tests only for research purpose.[59]

However, the AIIMS scientists asserted in the journal Indian Pediatrics that destruction of a few female fetuses will not affect child sex rations. They advocated sex determination as a way to liberate Indian women from undergoing endless pregnancies to have sons.[60] They however, did not realize at that time the serious repercussions of such a technology. In 1982, Prof. Lotika Sarkar picked up a handbill being distributed

58. Chandra, S., "Female Foeticide : Causes, Laws and Preventive Strategies", Paper presented at a Symposium held at New Delhi, July (2005).
59. *Ibid.*, Amniocentesis as a technology was first used outside India in 1937 and for sex determination in 1951.
60. George, S.M., "Baby Boys on order", *The Times of India*, New Delhi, January 4 (2003).

in railway compartments by a clinic in Amritsar offering amniocentesis tests to expectant parents (no mention of genetic disorders).[61] The arguments offered in the handbill in support of the test included: "the birth of a daughter in these days is a threat to the family economy, and to the nation". National women's organizations condemned the use of these tests for making money and recommended that they be only permitted at teaching and research institutions for the limited purpose of preventing genetic diseases. The resolutions were carried to the Health Ministry by the Joint Secretary in charge of the Women's Bureau, and brought forth loud condemnations of the practice from the Union Health Minister.

Meanwhile, studies in Bombay brought out the unsavory fact that 98% of abortions following sex determination tests were of females. About 41% gynecologists performing the abortion felt that the pregnant women were under pressure from their families. Joint campaigns mounted by some ethically committed doctors, scientists and women's groups have finally forced the Maharashtra Government to legislate a ban on such tests.[62] Similar legislations followed in States of Gujarat and Goa and finally at the national level.[63]

The Central Act came into force in 1996. The practice of female foeticide, however, continues with impunity. Abortions being legal, the nexus between sex detection (permissible in various situations under the Central PNDT Act) and the subsequent abortion is difficult to establish. The various escape routes in the existing legislations coupled with weak enforcement have helped commercialization of medical

---

61. The first private clinic in India was established in Amritsar in 1979 and the practice spread rapidly over Haryana and Punjab. Even now facilities for sex determination are not easily available in rural areas, especially in Bihar and Uttar Pradesh, where the female ratio has declined substantially. However, what matters presumably is the access to such facilities in towns nearby. See Krishnaji, N., "Trends in Sex Ratio", *Economic and Political Weekly*, September 9-15 (2000), available at www.epw.org.in
62. The Maharashtra Regulation of Use of Pre-natal Diagnostic Techniques Act, 1988.
63. The Pre-natal Diagnostic Techniques (Prevention of Misuse) Act, 1994.

procedures for the satisfaction of personal prejudices and choices.[64]

The new policy of liberalization of imports accelerated the spread of new Reproductive Technologies for sex determination and mobile vans providing these tests followed by abortion are reported to be carrying the practice even into rural areas.

3. Response of the Civil Society and the State to such Technologies

The drive against female foeticide and sex determination techniques gained strength in 1980s. The 1976 partial ban on sex determination tests in government hospitals had only led to the proliferation of private clinics/hospitals offering the facility. The ban was imposed because amniocentesis advent in 1975 caused a dramatic increase in female foeticide cases. Since then, different parts of the country have witnessed several campaigns against the misuse of science and technology to continue discrimination against women. In 1982, the Centre for Women's Development Studies (CWDS) launched the first campaign. It was initiated by Dr. Veena Mazumdar and Dr. Lotika Sarkar in Delhi as a protest against an advertisement for Bhandari antenatal sex determination clinic; Amritsar, Punjab. The clinic was openly advertising its services through press, in railway compartments and other pubic places. The advertisement referred to daughters as liabilities to the family and a threat to the nation, and exhorted expectant parents to avail the services of the clinics to get rid themselves of this danger'.

More campaigns like the Forum against Sex Determination and Sex Pre-Selection (FASDSP) in 1985 in Maharashtra and the Campaign Against Sex Selective Abortion (CASSA), Tamil Nadu came up. FASDSP lobbied to regulate

64. Kusum, "Mother of All Crimes", *The Hindustan Times*, New Delhi, June 26 (2001), Though facilities for sex determination are not easily available in rural areas, especially in Bihar and Uttar Pradesh, where the female ratios has declined substantially. However, what matters presumably is the access to such facilities in towns nearby. See Krishnaji, N., "Trends in Sex Ratio", *Economic and Political Weekly*, September 9-15 (2000), available at www.epw.org.in

the practice of sex determination in Maharashtra by formulating a separate legislation, instead of modifying the Medical Termination of Pregnancy (MTP) Act, 1971, that had the danger of curtailing women's right to abort. As a result, the Maharashtra Regulation of Use of Prenatal Diagnostic Techniques Act, 1988, came into being.

Serious drawbacks in the state legislation and poor implementation caused the awakening of interest in the issue across the entire country. A move for an all-India ban on sex determination tests gained momentum, and the Pre-Natal Diagnostic Tests (Regulation and Prohibition of Misuse) Act, 1994, (called the PNDT Act) came into existence. Though the PNDT Act entered into force in January 1996, no evidence of decline in the practice of female foeticide came forth even after four years. Lack of concern and political will to implement the legislation by the Centre and states led to Public interest litigation (PIL) in the Supreme Court (SC). The PIL was filed by three petitioners. Dr. Sabu George—a social activist, Mahila Sarvangeen Utkarsh Mandal (MASUM), Pune, and Centre for the Enquiry of Health and Allied Themes (CEHAT), Mumbai, in February 2000. In May 2001, the SC directed the Centre to implement the PNDT Act in all its aspects and called upon all state governments to take necessary steps to implement the Act. However, a further dip in 2001 sex ratio suggests that a lot more needs to be done in this regard.

In the light of new techniques available to determine sex before conception, it was felt necessary to amend the Act. From February 14, 2003 the Pre-natal Diagnostic Techniques (Regulation and Prevention of Misuse) Amendment Act, 2002 came into force. The PNDT Act 1994 was renamed as 'the Pre-conception and Pre-natal Diagnostic Techniques (Prohibition of Sex Selection) Act, 1994.[65]

4. Various Views on Girl Child

Manjeet Rathee (2005) expresses concern that in this modern age of development new technologies like ultrasound diagnostic methods are being used to identify the gender of the

65. "Pre-Birth Elimination of Females—A Handbook of Guidelines" by National Commission for Women, 2008.

foetus in women leading to large scale female foeticide. This kind of 'civilized' extermination of particular sex and that too in the name of democratic 'choice' speaks volumes of the kind of values and human essence that is being created today in the global world of liberalization. Both these practices of female foeticide and infanticide are the result of the deep rooted son preference prevalent in most sections of our society. This son preference is actually acquiring new dimensions and is being strengthened by certain economic and social processes underway today.

Sharad Vyas (2005) in his article bring forth the point that the Delhiites have begun to speak up against pre-natal sex determination. And now lodging a complaint has become easier no visits to the police station no fear of disclosing identity. The solution is available on the internet www.indian-femalefoeticide.org. Here people can lodge anonymous complaints against practitioners and institutions that use reproductive technologies to inform families about the sex of the foetus. The website has recently won the Ministry of Information Technology's e-governance award.

Yashphal Kaur (2005) while outlining the rights of a Sikh woman stresses that she is equal to man. She has religious rights. She has independence. But sadly, these basic rights are denied to many Sikh women today. In some cases even before a girl is born she is killed by abortion because of a desire for a male child. Upon, birth, many relatives are not even informed for day s that a daughter has taken birth. Yet in the same family if a son is born, everyone will know by the end of that day. The following year Lohri is celebrated and ladoos and sweets are distributed in the village if a son is born. Nothing is done in celebration for many daughters who are born in Sikh families.

Rob Stein (2004) highlights that growing number of Americans who are selecting the sex of their children using techniques developed to help couples who are infertile or at risk for having babies with genetic diseases. In addition to the standard in vitro fertilization procedure, some clinics have another testing approach that can sort sperm by sex an easier and far less expensive method, albeit not quite as reliable. The doctors offering the services as well as some medical ethicists who defend them argue that the procedures make it possible for parents to fulfil a natural desire, harm no one, and enhance the joys of parenthood and family life.

Madhu Gurung (2004) opines that the two child norm only leads to female foeticide. The phenomenon of declining sex ratio that showed up in Census 2001 in Punjab, Haryana, Chandigarh, Delhi, Western Uttar Pradesh, Gujarat and Maharashtra. This defies all demographic theories as these are prosperous states. One expects that when people live better, have better education and economic security, there will be less traditional bias against the girl child. But the situation is different. The two child norm has only worsened the situation. In India, there is an unholy alliance between tradition and technology. Today ultrasound is the sex selective technology that is widespread in most prosperous states. The reasons are easy to define prosperity ensured better infrastructure, more machines and more doctors to perform the tests. People had money power to pay for the technology and, of course, as infrastructure improved the people could access the clinics easily. All this made foeticide rampant.

Puneet Kaur (2002) expresses concern that the sudden fall in the number of girls in the youngest age group is believed to be the proof of the increased incidence of sex selective abortions or female foeticide. Most of these abortions are the result of the misuse of sex determination technologies such as ultrasound scanning and amniocentesis. These medical technologies otherwise very useful to check the health and other status for the foetus are proving to be hazardous. The sex selective abortions are also highly profitable for much of the medical community and they are able to get legal or punitive action hindered through political pressure or by bribing the local police authorities.

T.K. Rajalakshmi (2002) in the article female foeticide in Punjab presents some cases who have got the sex determination done and were charged under section 312 to 120 of the Indian Penal Code 1860. The provisions of the pre-natal Diagnostic Techniques (Regulation and Prevention of Misuse) Act, 1994 were not invoked. However, a staff nurse who allegedly performed the abortion was booked under the

Medical Termination of Pregnancy (MTP) Act 1971. The author argues that female foeticide would not stop as long as other manifestations of fender violence in the form of domestic violence stemming from dowry demands, son preference and so on continued in the society.

Datt Ruddar (2001) reiterates that sex ratio is an important indicator to measure the extent of prevailing equity between males and females at a given point of time. The author underlines that some of the important reasons put forward to explain sex ratio are female abortions and female infanticide. The Indian States indicate wide variations in the sex ratio. Those responsible for the poor sex ratio are Delhi, Haryana, Punjab, Uttar Pradesh, Jammu and Kashmir, Madhya Pradesh, Bihar, Gujarat, Rajasthan and Maharashtra. The states which have shown significant improvement in sex ratio are Goa, Karnataka, Uttaranchal, Himachal Pradesh, Orissa, Andhra Pradesh, Tamil Nadu, Chhattisgarh and Kerala. The only state that has consistently shown a sex ratio of more than unity is Kerala. The author argues that unless there is an improvement in Uttar Pradesh, Madhya Pradesh, Rajasthan, Gujarat, Bihar, and Maharashtra, the chances of improvement in the country's sex ratio remain bleak.

Dagar Rainuka (2001) stresses that the predominance of male child preference and the simultaneous rejection of the girl child are reflected in the adoption methods to beget a male child and subsequent resort to female foeticide. In her study, 45 percent respondents mentioned conscious use of methods to beget a male child. In numerable places pilgrimage, extensive customs and rituals reveal the preoccupation with begetting a male child.

Aruti Nayar (2001) highlights the fact that sex selective abortions have acquired the shape of an industry in which you have eager consumers and equally efficient service providers. It is not easy to break the nexus between the patient's family, the doctors and the radiologist. According to Aruti, it is the human traits such as the need for social approval, longing for the continuity of the lineage and the ever present lure of son that lie behind such a disturbing demographic trend. One cannot help wondering how all rhetoric about empowerment of women and improving their status is just hogwash, something that often keeps feminists and the elite urban women busy. The ground reality is a different story altogether. Mothers themselves don't want to bring daughters into the world.

According to *Mallik Rupsa (2000)* establishment of permanent and an autonomous commission on reproductive and genetic technology, including representation from government, medical associations, research institutes, and civil society organizations is required. The government must act to ensure adequate and effective implementation of the PNDT Act as well as a wide range of laws and regulations that address gender inequity at different should include enforcement of the Child Marriage Restraint Act, 1976, the Dowry Prevention Act, 1961 and various provisions in the family laws guaranteeing equal rights to property and inheritance to daughters.

Mishra Vinod K. and Retherford, Robert D. (2000) estimate levels of child malnutrition and examines the effects of mothers' education and other demographic and socio-economic factors on the nutritional status of children. Findings suggest that women's education and literacy programmes could play an important role in improving children's nutritional status.

T.K. Rajalakshmi (2000) presents a public interest petition filed in the Supreme Court which asserts that the Pre-natal Diagnostic Techniques (Regulation and Prevention of Misuse) Act, 1994 has failed to achieve its goals. The petitioners Sabu George, Centre for Enquiry into Health and Allied Themes (CEHAT) and the Mahila Sarvangeen Utkarsh Mandal (MASUM) say that female foeticide continues to exist in various garbs and they huge sought the intervention of the court to interpret the act in such a way that it takes into account new techniques such as Pre-implantation Genetic Diagnosis (PGD). The petition draws attention to the gross misuse of reproductive technology in a society characterized by a strong bias against the female child. Even as female infanticide is yet to be eradicated technique like PGD have widened the gap in the already skewed sex ratio. They argue that there exists a link between female foeticide and infanticide and the widening sex ratio. The sophisticated technique of PGD helps couples but this does not out weigh the damage caused by its misuse by unscrupulous practitioners.[66]

The studies give a clear signal that all is not well with the girl child in our society. The social and religious traditions, values and norms with economic discrimination against women and girls ensure that the boys have preferential treatment in all aspects relating to education, health, food, and clothing. The roots of the son preference are deeply entrenched in our social, cultural and economic environment. In extreme cases the neglect and discrimination of the females take the form of female foeticide and infanticide. The use of modern medical technology has added another dimension to the problem. The sex of the child in the womb is determined for subsequent abortion in case the foetus is found female. So there is an urgent need to develop multi-sectoral strategies to address the issue of gender bias. Given what is at stake, there is no time to wait.

The phenomenon of anti-female bias and pre-natal sex selection is widespread in our society. The discriminatory practices against the girl child pervade in all groups—the rich and the poor, the higher and lower castes and in all religions. The incidence of poverty, the prevailing misconceptions, negative attitudes and adverse socio-cultural factors accentuate the problems of the girl child all the more.

There is an utter lack of sensitivity and hundreds of gender selective deaths keep taking place each passing day. Despite all claims of development, we have miserably failed n achieving the goals of gender parity in all walks of life. Girls remain vulnerable in the vicious circle of gender stereo-types. They continue to be marginalized and discriminated against. The discrimination is spread all over in the sectors of education, employment and health, etc.

And of late, the easy availability of sex determination technology has added another dimension to this discrimination in the form of pre-natal sex selections. The modern technology has provide counter productive and is responsible for sex ratio imbalance particularly in the 0-6 age group. Despite legislations

66. Singh, D.P., "Female foeticide in Punjab—Causes and Consequences", Paragon Publishers, New Delhi, pp. 18-21, (2007).

anti-female biases coupled with commercial interests and availability of technology has posed a great threat to the survival of girls.

(I) SEX DETERMINATION TEST AND HUMAN RIGHTS

I. Positive Impact

Genetic Tweak helps Avert Miscarriage

In Mumbai, two years ago, Priya was diagnosed with a rare genetic disorder called the Robertsonian Translocation. An arm of one of her chromosomes was attached to another chromosome; it caused no obvious abnormality in the 28-year old woman but was possibly the cause for her repeated miscarriages. But thanks to the use of a low profile technique called the Pre-implantation Genetic Diagnosis (PGD), Priya, who lives in Central Mumbai, left Jaslok Hospital with her new-born daughter. "We now have Laxmi in our house, at last," said the proud mother. PGD is not a new technique, but given the fast pace of growth in the field of genetics, it is now possible for doctors and geneticists to locate more genetic abnormalities in embryos. A recent study by the European Society of Human Reproduction and Embryology showed that only 94 of the 235 women with the disorder got pregnant using PGD. The law permits PGD only in cases where there is a basis for genetic intervention. This is possibly the first time it was used for Robertsonian Translocation. Thus, there are many positive impacts of this technique which are as follows:

- Prevent from suffering of Human being
- Service of Humanity
- Protecting Right of life—both Mother and Unborn child
- Protecting Human dignity
- Widening the Concept of Human Rights
- Broad interpretation of "Right to Life"
- Upgradation of Human Life
- Treatment of fetus at initial stage
- Timely treatment to mother
- Advancement of Human Rights Jurisprudence

- New Direction to Human Rights jurisprudence
- Concept of noble cause for service of mankind
- Right to Family and Children
- Positive use of scientific development
- Most Advanced Technology
- Emancipate women from the burden of repeated pregnancies in their quest for producing a son
- Eliminate the undesirable sex
- To prevent the misuse of sciences of the technology to determine the sex leading to female infanticide
- To ameliorate the status of women
- Answer to population control and keeping the family size small
- Allow families to balance their desire for a daughter
- Helps women overcome some of their insecurities and burdens
- Detection of 5 types of abnormalities, i.e. chromosomal abnormalities genetic metabolic diseases, hoemoglobinopathies, sex linked genetic diseases congenital anomalies
- Helping families to cope with intransigent problems especially dowry

2. Negative Impact

- Violation of Natural rights
- Violation of individual rights
- Violation of right to life of fetus
- Encouragement to female feticide (an in human act)
- Experimentation on Human being
- Against human valued
- Degradation of Human dignity
- Gross violation of Human rights
- Misuse of medical science against human ethics
- Effect on future generation
- Violation of right to health
- Gender in-equality
- Principle 10 the International conference on Population and Development, 1994 at Cairo: Practice like female infanticide and misuse of technologies to

determine foetal sex and selectively abort female fetuses, and realities such as higher mortality rate among small girls . . . violate the basic human rights of female children

- Exposes women to additional health risks
- Scarcity of women would increase crimes against women like rape, abduction and forced polyandry
- Worse effects on the sex ratio in the country
- It is the violation of women's the right to survive
- Discrimination against women in the womb
- Negates the Fundamental right to equality
- Girls are denied the right to be born
- Imbalance sex ratio.

Sex Determination Test and Abortions

(A) SEX SELECTIVE ABORTIONS

Discrimination against girl children and threatens on their life remain a global phenomenon that may occur before birth and continue beyond childhood into adulthood. Girl children are exposed to discrimination and violence in all settings, often in places where they should be protected, in their home, school, and immediate community. They are also often among the most vulnerable when familial, social or community structures collapse, such as when they are deprived of parental care or familial support, during humanitarian emergencies or armed conflicts. The low value placed on girl's subjects them to exclusion, exploitation and violence.

In many parts of India, the girl child is not valued and is even in danger of being unwelcome before birth. At every stage of her life she may be discriminated and neglected for basic nutrition, education and living standard. Much of what should be considered maltreatment is socially regarded as the 'normal/accepted' way to treat a girl child in the home or community.

Girl Children discrimination may damage them mentally, behaviorally and physically, the impact can result in both short and long-term consequences on the individual, on their family and on the community. The impact of discrimination is largely determined by the nature, duration, extent of the discrimination that affects them as well as by the relationship of the perpetrators to the victim and the behaviour of the adults. It can affect their mental and physical health and development, impair their ability to learn and socialize.

Low weight at birth, insufficient feeding, inadequate care and nutrition depletions caused by repeated illness may impair growth in the critical first years and reduce their learning abilities. It destroys their self-confidence, undermines their development as functional adults and mothers later in life as they are denied access to education, medical care, and sanitary basic knowledge. Gender discrimination replicates itself from generation to generation. If girls remain illiterate, they are likely to be less capable to raise healthy and educated families, to think and judge independently as well as to develop civic sense. There is discrimination even in the field of higher education. At least a 40% of girls are not allowed to pursue higher studies, due to the conservative familial ideologies.

Women are the main victims of malnutrition, poverty, high illiteracy and infant mortality; they have often no power themselves even though they have legal recourse. It is rather impossible for a woman to stand up against her husband, in-laws or parents if she wants to save her daughter.[1] The cultural beliefs in India mandate marriage for women as a necessity, which, is possibly the root cause of all forms of discrimination against them. There is often subtle perpetuation of inequalities between girls and boys. The religious and cultural beliefs uphold women's roles as self-sacrificing duty bound and relegated to the domestic spheres, whereas the sons are charged to carry on the family name. They have to support their parents in old age as they live with them when old. They are also

1. Save Girl Child Organization available at http://www.savegirlchild.org

responsible for funeral rites of their parents as it is believed that parents achieve moksha only if their sons lit their pyre.

Likewise there are several other reasons which contribute to put the girl child at the second place. For instance, the custom of dowry, which has been escalating considerably over a period of time and has been viewed as status symbol, has been responsible for various forms of gender inequalities at all levels.

Due to these reasons we have witnessed an increase in the sex selective abortions and consequent imbalance in the sex ratio of the country. This means that the phenomenon of sex selective abortions continues to go unabated in spite of all affirmative actions of the state. If such a trend continues then, it has many potentially serious consequences. One fairly obvious social consequence is that there would not be enough women for men to marry. The paucity of potential brides might result into various problems such as increase in immoral trafficking of women adultery sex crimes and increase morbidity. There is thus a need for a more balanced sex ratio. Only a breakdown of patriarchy and change in the perception of woman's role in society can achieve this balance.

Women are commonly denied their fundamental rights to education, to access to medical care, services and information, to involve in their communities or to express freely but there as also denied their most basic rights such as their right to name and nationality and even their right to be born (female foeticide) and to live (girl infanticide). Sex selective abortions are one of the recent forms of discrimination against the girl children.

Sex selective abortions or female foeticide involve two steps. The first step is the determination of the sex of the foetus and second step in the therapeutic abortion. Female foeticide also known as sex-selective abortion is the use of medical technology to identify the sex of the foetus and to selectively abort female fetuses. But, by the passage of time, the technique of sex determination test which developed for the noble cause started being misused by man and violated the human rights of the fetus in mother's womb. Female infanticide is the deliberate killing of female infants soon after birth for the purpose of eliminating the female child. The phenomenon of female infanticide is as old as many cultures, and has likely accounted for millions of gender-selective deaths throughout history.

No one wants girls any one. Eliminate the now, instead of dealing with the problems of raising a girl goes the thinking behind the deadly actions.[2]

Female foeticide is now practiced in different parts of the world but is especially prevalent in Southern Asia. The biological norm for birth ratios is about 105 boys born for every 100 girls worldwide, but in India and China an average of respectively 120 and 117 boys are born for every 100 girls. Female foeticide is also largely practiced in Bangladesh, Indonesia, Pakistan, South Korea, Taiwan, Vietnam and the Caucasus (Armenia, Azerbaijan, Georgia).

These countries account for nearly half of the world's population (3 out of the world's 6.5 billion Inhabitants), the killing of girls causes a significant increase in the imbalance of the number of men and women in the world and consequently fewer wives and mothers for future generations.

On the contrary, there will be increased incidences of rape, abduction and forced polyandry. In certain communities in Madhya Pradesh, Haryana and Punjab, the sex ratio is extremely adverse for women. A set of brothers share wife and sometimes even by patrilineal parallel cousins. To think it is better to kill a female foetus than give birth to an unwanted female child is very fatalistic. By this logic, it is better to kill poor people or third world masses, rather than let them suffer poverty and deprivation.[3]

The practice of Female Foeticide or the selection of the sex of the foetus is a combination of personal choices, family issues, social, ethical, medical and even legal reasons. Within all these reasons, technology has also come to play an increasingly crucial role. Sex Determination Techniques, that is, Pre-Natal Diagnostic Techniques (PNDT) are used for predicting the sex of an unborn offspring after conception preferably in the first

2. Sharma, Kalpana, 'No Girls Please, we're Indian', *The Hindu*, Sunday, August 29, 2004.
3. Kameshwari, G., "Sex Selection and Sex Selective Abortion Problems and Perspectives, 413, Brindavan Apartments Red Hills, Hyderabad, 500004.

four months of pregnancy. From foetoscopy, ultrasonography, chorionic villus biopsy, to foetal blood sampling, genetic technology has evolved over the last three decades.[4]

The overall sex ratio in India has declined over the century from 972 in 1901 to 927 in 1991. The adult sex ratio has since gone up to 933 in 2001. By contrast, the child sex ratio for the age-group 0-6 years in 2001 was 927 girls per 1000 boys against 945 recorded in the 1991 census. The widespread use of sex-determination tests and rampant female infanticide are thought to be the main causes. Worldwide, in 2006, the sex ratio was 1.01 males to 1 female.[5] The practice of female foeticide has now taken over infanticide, the practice of killing children at birth. However girl infanticide is still practiced. Some of the methods used to eliminate girl babies after their birth are: poisoning, throat splitting, starvation, smothering and drowning. Many other girl children are disposed of, often in garbage dumps, where most die. These practices illustrate the insignificance accorded to the lives of the girl children.

Sex selection and abortion has become a lucrative business for some individuals. Medical technology and policy of liberalizing abortion now gives the status conscious Indian families the choice between payment of large dowry for their daughters and eliminations of daughters.

UN figures out that about 750,000 girls are aborted every year in India. Abortion rates are increasing in almost 80% of the India states, mainly Punjab and Haryana. Today, the nationwide average number of girls to every 1000 boys is 927.[6] This has been on a decline since the 1991 Census. From 945 girls for every 1000 boys in 1991, the child sex-ratio has declined to 927 in 2001. The situation is alarming in some states and cities, Himachal Pradesh 896, Punjab 793, Chandigarh 845, Haryana 819, Delhi 865 and Gujarat 879.

Unlike many other social evils attributed to poverty, the killing of female foetuses through sex-selective abortion cannot

4. Elimination of all Forms of Discrimination and Violence against the Girl Child, Expert Group Meeting, 2006.
5. NDTV, September 6, 2007.
6. The 2001 Census.

be attributed to poverty and ignorance.[7] Indeed, it is the economically affluent states of Punjab, Haryana, districts of Gujarat, and Delhi that have the distinction of having more people who can pay for expensive tests to help choose male children over females.[8] The capital city Delhi has 919 and 859 for slum and non-slum areas respectively. Clearly it is those who can "afford to choose", who use the technology to do so.

Nation-wide, the sex ratio continues to fall, and the sex ratio 0-6 years fell from 945 in 1991 to 927 females per 1000 males in 2001. Around 150 female infants were put to death each year in a cluster of 12 villages of Rajasthan. The Bhati community in Jaisalmer has the lowest sex ratio of 550 in the world. In Jaipur, Rajasthan, pre-natal sex determination tests resulted in an estimated 3,500 abortions of female foetuses annually. In Bihar, a girl child is stuffed in a clay pot.

In Bihar, holding the baby from the waist and shaking it back and forth snaps the spinal chord. In certain blocks in Katihar district, Bihar 35 dais accepted having killed three to four babies a month, making the total number of female babies who were killed approximately 560 per month.

Studies have revealed that female foeticide and infanticide are practiced specifically among certain communities.

The inefficient legislative implementation further adds to the vulnerability of the girl child in India. Non-registration of medical facilities, the use of pre-natal diagnostic techniques, communication of the sex of the foetus, determination of sex, advertisement of sex determination, and non-maintenance of records explain also the large number of abortions.[9] The study exposes the darker side of society and the profession that abets the crime.[10]

In spite of Government legalization the efforts of social organization against the obnoxious practice, illegal sex

7. "Pre-Natal Diagnostic Techniques: A Source of Gender Bias", by *Kashmir University Law Review-X* (2003).
8. NGO Working Groups on Girls available at www.girlsrights.org
9. HIV Status, Sexual Preference, Religion, Race and Ethnicity Available online:http://www.savethechildren.net
10. Ms. Phavalam, Organizer of the Campaign against Sex Selective Abortion (CASSA).

determination and female fetus MTP continue to be carried out widely in out country. The doctors have come across several instances of severe adverse psychological reactions in women following repeated MTP's of this nature. Further studies are warranted to identify the factor related to this phenomenon and its physiological impact on women and on the society at large.

(B) CONCEPT OF ABORTION IN VARIOUS RELIGIONS

In ancient India abortion was denounced as a sin of the highest order, thereby recognizing the legitimacy of protecting the unborn. The Atharva Veda compose between 1500 and 1000 B.C. is the earliest available document on Indian medicine. Ayurveda is the name given to an Upanga (sub or supplementary Veda) of Atharva Veda by Susruta, one of the founders of the Hindu system of medicine. In Atharva Veda abortion is opposed and is considered as a serious sin.

Abortion is severely condemned in Vedic, Upanishad, the later puranic (old) and Smriti literature. Paragraph 3 of the Code of Ethics of the Medical Council of India says: I will maintain the utmost respect for human life from the time of conception.

According to Manu, a woman has to be reborn as a man to attain moksha (redemption). A man cannot attain *moksha* unless he has a son to light his funeral pyre. Hindu lawgivers of later ages also treated abortion as a crime, Manu (200 B.C.), the major law giver, dismissed abortion as a cause of impurity. According to him, libations shall not be offered to women who drink alcohol, live with many men, kill their husbands or have abortions.

According to ancient Hindu philosophy any menstrual flow in the second and third months or pregnancy should be considered an abortion. The limbs of the foetus gain in firmness in the fifth and sixth months of pregnancy and its issue at this time is called garbhapata (Susruta Samhita II, 8, 9). According to Vishnu Smriti, the destruction of embryo is tantamount to killing a holy or learned person. Yagnavalkya recognized garbhapata (being guilty of abortion) as one of the valid reasons for abandoning one's wife. In Charaka Samhita and Susruta Samhita certain obligations are imposed on pregnant women so as to prevent even induced abortion.

Foeticide was prohibited and classified as murder, equal to neglect Vedas incest and drinking of spirituous liquors. Man even considered a woman as murderer of her husband or of Brahmin or as an outcaste who had undergone abortion.

Buddhists view is that the bhiku who intentionally destroys a human being by way of abortion is no samana and no follower of Sakeyaputa. Gandhi said that an abortion was more in violation of the principle of the ahimsa than the artificial birth control which was morally blamed worthy.

Holy Quran states that who stupidly kill their children without knowledge and deny to themselves of what Allah has blessed them with. According to Christianity abortion as a grievous sin and was included in the Ten Commandments, which contain the forbidden acts. Every human being including the unborn child in the womb of its mother receives the right to life directly from the almighty God but not from parents, society or any other authority.

Thus, abortion was denounced as a sin of the highest order in ancient India, it could be resorted to only on narrow grounds. Nature has ordained a primary role to women in procreation of children. It is women who bear and give birth to children. Logically they should, therefore, be able to decide whether to have a child or not and be equally responsible for aborting a foetus.[11] She has a right to self-defence and in exercise of that right she can kill her foetus if it is necessary to save her own life or health.[12]

The religious texts of Islam, Hinduism and Christianity forbid abortion.[13] Woman by nature possesses a right to have a

---

11. Jain, Ashok Kumar, The Saga of Female Foeticide in India, Socio-Legal Offshoots, Ascent Publications, Delhi (2006).
12. An unborn child's right to be born is said to be qualitatively inferior to the right of the mother to preserve her own health.
13. "No man, no indication—medical, eugenic, social, economical nor moral, could show or give a valid legal right to dispose of an innocent life directly and deliberately, that is, to dispose of it with a view to its destruction, whether this is regarded as the end, or as

child. She should not be deprived of such a natural right just by a statute. A woman having become pregnant, it is her fundamental right to have a child. She cannot be forced to abort the child.

Girl children who escape foeticide, infanticide, or neo natal denial are still in the 0-6 high risk frames for early disposal. She is less fed, less encouraged to explore the world, more likely to be handed jobs to do, given less health care and medical abortion, socialized not to ask. Most of Indian children aged below 3 years suffer from anemia no one has cared to investigate whether girls predominate among these under nourished children but chances are that they do. Outpatient data from hospitals show lower admissions of girl children, and girls in more serious condition than boys when brought for treatment.[14]

(C) MEANING AND DEFINITION OF ABORTION

Abortion has been derived out from the abort which means miscarries in giving birth. Abortion means the pre mature detachment of the fetus from mother's body. It means to detach the fetus from mother before the maturity attainment. In abortion there is a deliberate ending of a pregnancy at an early stage. By abortion there is a expulsion of the products of

---

the means to an end which may not in itself be in any way harmful: (PIUS XII).

Biologically man is a tiller and woman is a field and the foremost purpose of the inter-relationship between the two is the procreation of the human race . . . the tiller of the soil cultivates the land not in vain but for the produce. Take away this purpose and the entire pursuit become meaningless" (Sayed Abdul A'la Manududi's Birth Control). "Muslim jurists agree unanimously that after the foetus is completely formed and has been given a soul, aborting it is haram" (Dr. Yusufal Quardawi Halal and Haram). Hindu sage Manu in his dharmashastra said that a killer of a priest of destroyer of an embryo casts his tilt on the willing eater of his provisions (Ch. VIII, verse 317).

14. http://ww.crin.org/docs/resources/treaties/crc.37/India Alliance for Child Rights IACR (The site visited on 3 May 2007).

conception at any period of gestation before full term. it is an act of giving premature birth, specially the expulsion of human foetus prematurely particularly at any time before it is viable or capable of sustaining life.[15] It refers to an induced procedure at any point in the pregnancy; medically, it is defined as a miscarriage or induced termination before twenty weeks gestation, which is considered non-viable. In Medico legal term an abortion or miscarriage means the spontaneous or induced termination of pregnancy before the foetus is independently viable be to become independent extra uterine life which usually is taken as occurring after 28th week of conception.

Abortion is an expulsion of the foetus before it has reached a state of development sufficient to permit it to live outside the uterus. It is the removal or expulsion of an embryo or fetus from the uterus, resulting in, or caused by, its death. This can occur spontaneously as a miscarriage, or be artificially induced through chemical, surgical or other means.

The role played and the liberal attitude adopted by courts in interpreting the strict provisions of the law of abortion with a view to exempting doctors and others acting in good faith from criminal liability for causing miscarrying has been elaborately examined.[16] It is of interest to note that the law of miscarriage (i.e., induced abortion) contained under the Indian Penal Code (IPC) in sections 312 to 316 have been incorporated in penal laws of the countries of the Indian sub-continent, Pakistan[17] Bangladesh,[18] Shrilanka[19] and in Malaysia[20] and Singapore[21] of ASEAN region. Hence the provision relating to abortion (causing miscarriage) in India and these countries are almost similar.

---

15. Singh Gurdev, India in Population and Law: Luke, Lee T. and Larson Arthur (1971) at p. 110.
16. Rex *v.* Bourne, [1938] 3 AII E. R. pp. 615-21.
17. Pakistan Penal Code, Sections 312-16.
18. Bangladesh Penal Code, Sections 312-16.
19. Penal Code of Ceylon, Sections 303-07.
20. Penal Code of Malaysia Sections 312-16.
21. Penal Code of Singapore Sections 312-16.

(D) TYPES OF ABORTION

Abortion may be classified into various categories depending upon the nature and circumstances under which it occurs. For instance, it may be,

- natural;
- accidental;
- spontaneous; and
- induced or artificial abortion.

Abortion falling under the first three categories is not punishable, while induced abortion is criminal unless exempted under the law.

I. Natural Abortion

Natural abortion is a very common phenomenon and may occur due to many reasons, such as bad health, defect in generative organs of the mother shocks fear, joy, etc.

Natural abortion means abortion which result due to gynoecia problem or incidentally/accidentally or we can say due to problems uncontrolled by human being. Natural abortion is a very common phenomenon and may occur due to many reasons, such as bad health, defect in generative organs of the mother, shocks, fear, joy, etc.

(i) Causes of Natural Abortion

The root causes for discrimination, female foeticide and infanticide are complex and reflect diverse political, economical, social, cultural and religious practices. Factors prevailing in India that are responsible for female foeticide/ infanticide are:[22] Dowry is increasing with the rise of consumerism propagated by commercial TV advertising, and the growing greed is reflected in higher and higher demands for dowry and the increasingly high cost of marriage.

The main sources of information about the pre natal sex selection technology were friends, newspapers TV/Radio and

22. Jain, Ashok Kumar, The Saga of Female Foeticide in India, Socio-Legal Offshoots, Ascent Publications, Delhi (2006).

seminar/conference/nuked nataks. TV and radio remain the effective methods of awareness generation, in rural areas because they are easily available and remain the main source of entertainment and information.[23] Thus, there are many causes of natural abortion those can be sum-up as under:

- Patriarchal ideology
- Discrimination against the girl child
- Introduction of automation
- Socio-economic and physical insecurity of women
- Evil of dowry
- Modern technology
- Unethical medical practices
- Non-implementation of legislation relating to foeticide
- Two child norm
- Social-economic development and modernization
- Traditions and cultural values influenced by son preference
- Social silence about domestic violence, household abuse, and submission of a woman to the will of her husband and relatives
- Vulnerability relating to the social/community/ cultural identity of the girl child
- Persistence of child marriage that prevent most of the time young women from accessing to education and emancipation
- Lack of enabling education and socialization of girls and women
- Large development of innovative medical, scientific techniques allowing sex detection
- Lack of implementation of the existing legislation to effectively protect the girl child.

(ii) Causes directly referable to the Mother

- Acute infections.

23. Singh, D.P., "Female Foeticide in Punjab—Causes and Consequences" Paragon International Publishers, New Delhi (2007).

- Diseases affecting the blood.
- Through the nervous system: Psychic trauma, sudden shock, fear Joy sorrow.
- Abnormalities of reproductive organs.
- Physical trauma.

(iii) Causes affecting the Foetus

- Death of the Foetus: Genetic abnormality, hormonal imbalance.
- Diseases of decidua and fibrinoid necrosis.

2. Accidental Abortion

Accidental abortion is very often takes place because of trauma Consequent to accidents. In accidents there is always some direct or indirect forceful impact on the uterus dislodging the ovum, embryo, or placenta from tile natural attachment.

3. Spontaneous Abortion

Spontaneous abortion sometimes may take place because of pathological reasons where pregnancy cannot be completed and the uterus empties before the maturity of foetus. This may happen because of 'metabolic circumstances or accumulation of poison which interfere with the development of embryo and advancement of pregnancy.[24]

4. Induced or Artificial Abortion

Induced or artificial abortion is defined in law as an untimely delivery voluntarily procured with intent to destroy the foetus. It may be procured at any time before tile natural birth of the child.[25] However, in medical terminology abortion means untimely delivery of a child before it is viable, i.e., capable of being reared, if born at the time of the act of

---

24. Jhala, R.M. and Raju, V.B.: Medical jurisprudence 426-8 (5th ed., 1990)
25. Queen Empress *v.* Ademma (1886) I. L.R. 9 Mad 369 Glanville Williams. The Law of Abortion: Current Law Problems. Vol. 5, pp. 128, 138 (1952). In ancient and particularly classical culture and interruption of regency was viewed with all seriousness and was an offence punishable under the law.

abortion. A child is considered viable from tile twenty-eighth week of pregnancy.[26]

Induced Abortion means intentional and direct act of the termination of pregnancy due to personnel or forced factors. Induced abortions are denied in law as an untimely delivery voluntarily procured with intent to destroy the foetus. It may be procured at any time before the natural birth of the child.

Induced abortion signifies voluntary or wilful termination of pregnancy, whether permitted by law or not, before viability. Induced abortion may be illegal (mostly septic abortions) or legalized abortions usually Medical Termination of Pregnancy (MTP).

(i) Reasons of Induced Abortion

- Unmarried women to get rid of illicit intercourse.
- To avoid additions to their families.
- By widows who are prevented from remarriage by rigid social custom.
- Premature births are more common and generally the babies run a more.
- Than normal risk of mental or physical handicap.
- Want to delay their next birth.
- They are too young or too poor to raise a child.
- Uneasy terms with their sexual partner.
- They do not want a child while they are working.

(ii) Types of Induced Abortion

Induced abortion is of two types, i.e.:

- Therapeutic/Legal/Justifiable abortion.
- Criminal Abortion.

26. Paul and Schopp, "Abortion and the law in 1980", 25 Nyl. Sch. L Rev. 497, 500-2 (1982); P. Thomas, Indian women: Through Ages (1964). Mahabharata, a great epic of the time depicts the Hindu widow as letting a woman's *ritu* (fertile period) go waste was a sing tantamount to embryo murder: Kamala Manakar, Abortion: A Social Dilemma, 24 (1973).

Induction legally allowed under MTP Act :

- Therapeutic Induction
- Eugenic Induction
- Humanitarian Induction
- Social Induction
- Environmental Induction

(iii) Unsafe Methods of Induced Abortion

Unsafe abortion as a procedure for terminating an unwanted pregnancy [carried out] either by a person lacking the necessary skills or in an environment lacking minimal medical standards or both. Unfortunately the decline in illegal abortions that one might have expected when abortions were legalized has not taken place. The term "unsafe abortion" proposed by the World Health Organization (WHO) lately has been accepted by most other international health institutions. Unsafe abortion means "abortion not provided through approved facilities and/or persons. Unsafe abortion is one of the great neglected problems of health care in developing countries.

Unsafe abortions are performed 15-20 times more often than safe legal abortions in India, at present. Unsafe abortion are mostly performed by untrained village abortionists, chiefly female dais or untrained midwives, village unlicensed doctors called quacks, licensed doctors without any training in midwifery and family planning, as well as trained doctors including gynecologists who do not wish to disclose these procedures for socio-economic and legal reasons. In both these cases, the abortions were performed by doctors without any training in midwifery, and family planning.

Mortality and morbidity rates following illegal abortion are very high and make the life of many women miserable. All attempts must be made to reduce the incidence of illegal abortion by proper legislation, propaganda and increasing availability of contraceptive and abortion services. Medical Termination of Pregnancy (MTP) is a maternal health care measure, which helps to avoid the maternal mortality and morbidity resulting from illegal abortions.

The assertion that abortion is too simple a procedure to warrant formal training is not supported by facts. Complication rates are significantly higher when general physicians, without any training, perform abortions. Examination of rates of complications occurring in a teaching hospital based abortion clinic show that rates are significantly lower for resident physicians after training than before training.

The findings demonstrate that first and second trimester abortion techniques can be improved by training and that, when properly supervised trainees can accomplish these procedures safely. Many of the General practitioners or Primary Health Center (PHC) doctors are unable to provide services when first approached either because of lack of skill to perform the procedure or lack of required physical facilities. A crash training programme, specially for medical officers working at Block level Primary Health Center, in MTP and other surgical procedures is being implemented in four states with the grants-in-aid from the Government of India (Ministry of Health and Family Welfare, Government of India, 1990).

Only after the successful performance of 25 suction evacuations under supervision is the practitioner licensed to perform abortions on his own (Ministry of Health and Family Planning, Government of India, 1975). The risk of women dying from legal abortion is exceedingly rare. Mortality from legal induced abortions has declined substantially in recent years. The risk is clearly related to the type of procedure used, length of gestation and recognized/unrecognized general health problems present at the time of abortion.

In fact the provision of induced abortion in MTP Act 1971 was described for the safety of health of the mother. The services are completely free of charge/cost in government and municipal centers. It is important to understand that establishment of good abortion services on a completely free basis is a cost benefit measure.

Section 3 of the MTP Act 1971, provisioned the period of 12 weeks for termination of pregnancy by RMP on the following grounds:

- Threat to the life of the mother (risk of life)
- Grave risk of physical or mental effect on mother.

- Risk to the un-born child suffering from consistent physical or mental abnormalities.
- Rape.
- Failure of contraceptive measures.

Justifiable abortion is the induction, which is justifiable only when caused in good faith to save the life of the woman if it is materially endangered by the continuance of pregnancy. Termination of pregnancy is possible in different ways. Medically, three distinct terms, viz., abortion miscarriage and premature labour are used to denote the expulsion of foetus at different stages of gestation. The term abortion is use only when an ovum is expelled within the first three moths of pregnancy, before the placenta is formed. The term miscarriage is used when a foetus is expelled from the fourth to the seventh month of gestation, before it is viable. Premature labour is the delivery of a viable child possibly capable of being reared, before it has become fully mature.[27] It is reported that children born at or after 210 days or 7 months of uterine life are viable, i.e. are born alive and are capable of being reared.

(iv) Criminal Abortion

When the abortion is carried out without fulfilling the conditions laid down in the termination law. It is termed criminal abortion in India criminal abortion is resorted to mostly by widows who are prevented from remarriage by rigid social custom and in a few instances by unmarried women to get rid of illicit intercourse.

There can be many means of criminal abortion and the intake of drug is one of them. Such drug may act directly on the uterus or may act indirectly on the uterus. There may be mechanical violence that may be general or local. General violence is the method used during the first month like severe exercise, riding cycling jumping from heights use of alternate hot and cold baths.

Local Violence is a method, which is usually resorted to in the third or fourth month when other methods have failed. Violence may be skilled that may be by expert for specialized

27. Modi's Medical Jurisprudence, at 325.

person or it may be unskilled like penetration of pencil, knitting needle, hair pin, nail, etc. A young girl died of tetanus. She had resorted to self-abortion by a nail. At autopsy a rusted nail was found in the uterus.

Many complications may occur from criminal abortion—

- Death may occur from shock
- Haemorrhage
- Air of fat embolism
- Sepsis

(v) Punishment for Criminal Abortion

Sections 312, 313, 314, 315 and 316 of the Indian Penal Code refer to the offences of criminal miscarriage and punishments awarded for these offences.

(E) SIGNIFICANCE OF CONSENT OF THE WOMEN FOR ABORTION

Causing miscarriage without the consent of woman is illegal. Section 313 of the IPC and MTPA, 1971 provides that no pregnancy shall be terminated except with the consent of the pregnant woman.[28] In other words, consent in an act of reason accompanied with the deliberation, the mid-weighing, as in a balance, the good and evil on each side. At present the abortion is illegal and it cannot be done without the consent of mother.[29] Consent of the mother raises another issue that if a mother wants to miscarry her foetus, can she does that? Answerer according to the present legal system is no. But it could be done under the provisions of MTPA the abortion can be done after having the consent of mother and advice of medical

28. To understand the importance of these sections it is necessary to know as to what constitutes consent. Section 93 of the IPC states that consent is not such consent as is intended by any section of this code, if the consent is given by a person under fear of injury or misconception of fact or under the unsoundness of mind or in intoxicated state, or by child below twelve years of age.
29. Consent is the knowledge or consciousness of the act consented to, which means an active will in the mind of a person to permit the doing of the act complied of.

practitioners, if they advice that pregnancy is detrimental to the physical and mental health of the mother.

It may be argued that pregnant women should have personal liberty to destroy any foetus of her own if she finds it intolerable. An unwanted pregnancy may impose a kind of slavery upon her. It is more important to consider her life and health than that of an early foetus representing only a child to be which has not yet been fully formed, cannot feel pain and cannot live outside the womb.

According to the 'Transplantation of Human Organ Act 1994', one may understand that life ends with the brain-stem death, so life starts with development of Brain. Daniel Callahan explains in his book "Abortion Law, Choice and Mortality", that the brain structure is essentially complete by the twelfth week. Now, it may be observed that before that period the woman has the absolute right to decide whether or not to terminate a pregnancy. It is the woman who has to undergo the entire process and therefore, she must be prepared for it both mentally and physically. But absolute right of abortion also throws up the issue of sex determination tests and female foeticide, which are of serious nature. Incases female foeticide the net result is the strengthening of gender bias against woman.[30]

Section 3(4) (b) of the MTPA recognize the free choice of woman to decide whether and when she will terminate her pregnancy and make guardian consent irrelevant incase the woman is of the age of eighteen years or above.

The question arises whether woman can terminate her pregnancy without the consent and against the wishes of her husband and if so, whether such action on her part would entitle the aggrieved husband to obtain a decree of divorce against her. This quest came for decision in *Smt. Satya* v. *Shri Ram*,[31] in which the High Court of Punjab and Haryana held that termination of pregnancy at the instance of wife but without the consent of her husband amounts to cruelty.[32]

30. Kumar, Santosh, Abortion: The Law and the Reality, 1998, Cri L.J., pp. 171-74.
31. AIR 1983 P&H 252.
32. On the Concept of Cruelty see Lajwanti Chandhok *v.* O.N. Chandhok (1981) 2.D.M.C. 97; Atmaprakash Arora *v.* Neelam (1981) 2 D.M.C.43; King *v.* King Law Reports (1953) AC (HL) 124; Gollins

In this case the court found on record the husband himself, his sister and his parents were languishing a child in the family but the appellant always frustrated their hopes by termination of pregnancy. The husband contended that such an act on the part if the appellant amounted to mental cruelty at least (if not physical) to him who has within his right to claim a decree of divorce on that ground. The court quoted the following passage from the judgment in *Forbes* v. *Forbes*[33] with approval:

If a wife deliberately and consistently refuses to satisfy her husband's natural and legitimate craving to have children, and the deprivation reduces him to despair and affects his mental health the wife is guilty of cruelty.

Quite contrastingly the desirability of husband's consent in the matter of termination of wife's pregnancy has been viewed on woman's right's basis in the United States of America, as Mr. Blackmun, J. expressing the unanimous view of the U.S. Supreme Court in 1976 in *Danforth v. Planned Parenthood of Central Missouri,*[34] etc. It was held that states might not constitutionally require a married woman to have her husband's consent to abortion not might they impose a blanket parental consent requirement for unmarried minors. On spousal consent the court held 6-3 that a state might not delegate to a husband a veto power over abortion which the state itself did not have. Similarly, with regard to parental consent the court rules 5-4 that "the state does not have the constitutional authority to give a third party an absolute, and

---

v. Gollins (1963) 2 All E.R. 966; Dastane *v.* Dastane A.I.R. 1975 S.C 1534 at 1541. For deprivation of parenthood, see, Kusum, "Deprivation of Parenthood: Whether amounts to cruelty" (1978) II M.L.J. 28.

33. (1955) 2 All E.R 311. In this case the wife insisted on the use of contraceptive and refused the husband the chance of a child. This in the opinion of the Court, caused injury to the husband's mental health, since the conduct of the wife was intentional in that she pursued it in spite of knowing that her persistence was causing him anxiety and misery. Accordingly she was held guilty and the husband was entitled to a decree of divorce.
34. 428 U.S. 52 (1976).

possibly arbitrary, terminate the patient's pregnancy, regardless of the reason for withholding consent".

Husband's right to restrain the wife from undergoing termination of pregnancy is at stake in England as well as in 1979 in *Paton* v. *Trustees of BPAS and another* the case of first impression in England on the husband's right to prevent abortion sought by wife, Sir George Baker P. the President of the Family Division sitting as an additional Judge of the Q.B.D. denying any right to the husband to ask for an injunction restraining the wife from undergoing her termination of pregnancy, stated that within section 1(1) of the 1967 Act of England the pregnant woman had choice to decide with her doctor whether to procreate or not and this choice was circumscribed only to the extent of an almost unchallengeable medical discretion.

The 1967 Act, according to Sir George Baker P. gave no right to a father to be consulted in respect of the termination of a pregnancy. In fact the husband had no legal right enforceable at law or in equity to stop the doctors carrying out the abortion.

Likewise, it was ruled by the court that the foetus could not in English Law, have any rights of its own unless at least it was born with a physical entity, separate from that of the mother. Sir George Baker P. stressed that the abortion Act laid great responsibility to the doctors deciding on the legality of the rumination of pregnancy, and it was expected that doctors exercised their medical skill and knowledge in good faith to arrive at a conclusion, while issuing a certificate on the existence of indications calling for termination. To Sir George Baker P., it was for either too brave or foolish a court to intervene into the medical judgment passed about the woman's need of the termination of pregnancy.

Paton, aggrieved with the decision, complained to the European Commission of Human Rights, which held the application inadmissible, as it found that there was no violation of the European Convention of Human Rights. Faced with the task of deciding on the issue for the first time, the commission interpreted on Article 2(1), first sentence reading: Everyone's right to life shall be protected by law. The commission, taking into view, the ordinary meaning of the provision in the contexts both Article 2 and of the convention, observed that the undefined term everyone was mentioned such a way in Articles 1, 2(1), 5, 6, 8, to 11 and 13, that meant for its postnatal application.

The Commission emphasized that none of the Articles indicated that 'everyone' had any possible pre natal application with exception of a rare case, under Article 6(1) when it was applicable pre-natally. Life as the next important term of the Article 2(1) called for an interpretation by the commission which observed that Article 2 could not be construed to recognise an absolute right to life of foetus as the life of the foetus was intimately connected with and inseparable from the life of the pregnant woman.

The commission reasoned that giving the foetus an absolute right under the Article, abortion would be prescribed even where the continuance of the pregnancy would involve a serious risk to the life of the pregnant woman. This would be regarding the unborn life of the foetus as possessed of a higher value than the life of the pregnant woman as well as right to life of a person already born subjected to a future implied limitation added to the express limitations of Article 2. The Commission found such an interpretation contrary to the object and purpose of the convention.

Further, the commission, though not considering upon the broader issues, such as whether Article 2 does not cover the foetus at all or whether Article 2 recognizes a right to life of the foetus with certain implied limitations, found that the authorization, by the U.K. authorities, of the abortion complained of was compatible with Article 2(1), first sentence because abortion at the initial stage of the pregnancy was covered by an implied limitation of the right to life of the foetus protecting the life and health of the woman at that stage.

In context of the applicant's right to respect for this family life as provided by Article 8 of the convention *vis-à-vis* an abortion procured with the wishes of the wife in order to avert the risk of injury to her physical or mental health, the commission found the Paton decision justified under Article 8(2) in so far as it interfered with Paton right to respect for his family life for the protection of the right of the wife (another person).

Having regard to the right of the pregnant woman, the commission refused to interpret the husband's and potential father's right to respect for his private and family life, so widely as to embrace such procedural rights as claimed by the applicant, i.e. a right to be consulted, right to make applications about an abortion which his wife intended to have preformed on her.

The commission observed that any interpretation of the husband's and potential father's right under Article 8 of the convention to respect for his private and family life, wit regard to an abortion which his wife intended to have performed on her, must first of all take into account the right of the pregnant woman, being the person primarily concerned in the pregnancy and its continuation or termination to respect for her private life.

In *Scheinberg* v. *Smith,* where a U.S. District Court had declared a 1979 statue of the state of Florida requiring a married woman neither separated not estranged from her husband to give him notice of her decision to terminate a pregnancy and an opportunity to consult with her even if he was not the father of the expected child to be an unconstitutional limitation on a woman's right to an abortion. On appeal however, the U.S. Court of appeals for the fifth circuit overruled the decision, finding that the state had a compelling interest in maintaining and promoting the marital relationship and in protecting the husband's interest in the procreation potential of the marriage.

The desirability of the husband's consent for the termination of wife's pregnancy specifically and expressly finds mention in some jurisdictions. As in Kuwait, the regulations of the Ministry of Public Health providing for conditions under which abortion may be performed stated *inter alia* that the consent of the woman and her husband must be obtained for termination of wife's pregnancy. In India where the MTPA does not mention husband's consent needed for abortion of the wife, such an abortion has been the subject of controversy.

Judicially this has been held to be an act of cruelty on the part of the wife against the husband in as much as it may affect the mental health of the husband who desires a child. Desire for a child is very natural to the husband who may suffer tremendously due to the MTP, if the wife is very much bent upon exercising her legal status in matters of procreation with regard to adopting the legal resort to abortion.

Recently in 1987 in *Sushil Kumar Verma* v. *Usha*[35] such a matter came before the High Court of Delhi where the wife who became pregnant within one month of her marriage got the foetus aborted the following month in a government approved pregnancy termination centre with the help for a registered medical practitioner without consulting her husband. The husband was kept completely in dark about the fact of pregnancy as also of its abortion. The husband being aggrieved filed a petition for the grant of a decree of divorce on the ground of cruelty, which was dismissed by the district Court, but the High Court granted.

Justice Mahinder Narain of the High Court of Delhi held that aborting the foetus in the very first pregnancy by a deliberate act without the consent of the husband amounted to cruelty within the meaning of Section 13(1)(ia) of the Hindu Marriage Act, 1955. Justice Narain quoted with approval, *Deepak Kumar Arora* v. *Sampuran Arora*[36] where a division bench of the High Court of Delhi had observed: "If, however, a wife undergoes abortion with a view to spite the husband then it may in certain circumstances be contended that the act of getting herself aborted has resulted in an act of cruelty".

Whether or not an act relating to procreation would amount to cruelty would also depend upon whether one of the parties desires the child and the other does not consent to it. Such a situation had arisen in *White* v. *White*[37] in which case the husband had insisted upon the petitioning wife did not conceive. Conversely, the wife was anxious to have a child but did not conceive due "*coitus interrupts*. The court held that the practice adopted by the husband denying the wife a chance to have a child, amounted to cruelty.

Undoubtedly, aborting the foetus in the very first pregnancy by a deliberate act, without the consent of the husband, would amount of cruelty.

---

35. AIR 1987 Del 86.
36. (1983) 1 DMC 182.
37. (2001) 1 A.C. 596.

He further observed: "It is important to bear in mind that it is no more the requirement of the law that cruelty must be of such kind that it should be a cause of danger to life and limb. The old provision which existed in Section 12 of Hindu Marriage Act was taken out from that section and reenacted as a part of Section 13 by virtue of the amendment made by the marriage Laws (Amendment) Act, 1976. Since the Marriage Laws (Amendment) Act 1986, S. 13(1)(ia) only requires that the other party has treated the petitioner with cruelty".

On the facts and circumstances of the case the respondent was held guilty of cruelty towards the appellant and the appellant was entitled to a decree of divorce under S. 13(1)(ia) of the Hindu Marriage Act 1955. Weighing the decisions in *Satya* v. *Sri Ram*[38] and *Sushil Kumar Verma* v. *Usha*[39] against the provisions of the MTPA permitting free choice to the woman without husband's consent except in case when she is minor or lunatic, in matter of terminating pregnancy, the holding of the court is uncomfortable to the married users of MTP as the decisions do not care for the right to personal liberty and human dignity of women. To hold that it is cruelty on the part of the woman to refuse to give birth to a child while her husband wants it, is to undermine her free choice whether when and how her body is to become the vehicle for the procreation of another human species.

It may be further argued that to ask a woman to give birth to child against her will constitutes the starkest form of violation of an individual right to privacy. Therefore, should the question of cruelty in such cases come up before the court, the fact that abortion stands primarily for emancipating women from unwanted pregnancy deserve to be taken into consideration. After all, it is the woman who suffers the hazards of pregnancy before it culminates into the pangs of child birth. Since the ground is invoked by the respondent in such cases for seeking a decree of divorce it is likely to be abused by the male spouses.

Also equally significant is the caution that if divorce is granted as in Sushil Kumar Verma or other cases it would be

38. AIR 1983 P & H 252.
39. AIR 1987 Del 86.

in turn greater cruelty within the law towards the wife who is punished for doing a legal thing under the MTPA and practicing right to liberty or right to life or right to privacy in matters of procreation. Lord Denning's words deserve appraisal in this context. "If the door of cruelty were opened too wide, we should soon find ourselves granting divorce for incompatibility of temperament... the temptation must be resisted lest we slip into a state of affairs where the institution of marriage itself is imperiled".

It is therefore, worth submitting that the court deciding on these decree of divorce in such cases should take into notice the fact that abortion is nothing like sterilization, that the husband would lose probability of procreation in future, and any abortion on the part of the wife without husband's consent should not be considered in isolated circumstances of the Hindu Marriage Act, but the emancipative tempo of the MTPA and the governmental interest in promoting birth of wanted children only as well as the noble idea of the upliftment of womenfolk from their traditional roles should be accorded equal value and consideration.

Lest there is a separatist treatment within section 13(1) (ia) of the Hindu marriage Act 1955 and other marriage laws legislative intervention is called for a devise a comprehensive legal scheme to bridge the gulf between the MTPA and the marriage laws in matters of abortion without the consent of the husband. Otherwise the MTPA is the cruel in itself.

In order to collect popular responses to this controversial aspect of the MTPA a question was asked about the desirability of husband's consent for termination of wife's pregnancy. The question provided for positive and negative replies. The responses are presented in the following table.

On the analysis of the responses contained in the table the following conclusions can be put forward:

- Three fourth majorities of the respondents consider husband's consent essential for the MTP of wife and one fourth of the respondents consider it not essential.
- Large numbers of Hindu, Muslim and Christian respondents approve essentiality of husband's

consent. Hindus have, moreover, the largest number of approvers.

- Forward and backward castes have sizable number of approvers of essentiality of husband's consent. Schedule caste respondents have, however, the largest number of disapprovers, as compared to forward and backward caste respondents. All of the others (no caste respondents) approve essentiality of husband's consent.
- Large numbers of rural, urban and mixed environ respondents consider husband's consent essential. The rural population has, however, the largest number of approvers.
- Compared to the literate respondents educated respondents have larger number of approvers of the essentially of husband's consent. Moreover, in each educational set up, husband's consent is considered essential by large majority of respondents.
- Although in every occupation, there are large numbers of approvers, agriculturists and businessmen have the largest and the smallest numbers of approvers respectively, servicemen and students have numbers of approvers in between those of agriculturists and businessmen.
- While amongst respondents of no-income group and various income groups there is a common majority approval of the essentiality of husband's consent, the no income group has the largest number of the approvers and the highest income group has the smallest number of approvers.
- Amongst males and females there are sufficiently large numbers of approvers. Moreover, larger number of females than that of males considers husband's consent essential.
- Large majority numbers of married and unmarried respondents consider husband's consent essential; however married compared to unmarried respondents have larger number of approvers.
- Large numbers of respondents of all age groups consider husband's consent essential.

It is submitted that the court while declaring wife's resort to MTP without husband's consent as cruelty to husband should ensure that its declaration is not detrimental to the welfare of wife, children and the family unit; and the MTPA's objective of emancipation of womenfolk from burden of unwanted pregnancy is not undermined. There should be an explanatory provision should be carved into Section 3(4)(b) of the MTPA that no MTP without husband's consent after having two children irrespective of their sex, shall amount to cruelty within the meaning of this concept in any of the statutes or religious code regulating marriage in India.

Taking into view the lack of medical literacy amongst people, and delicacy of the medical operations like MTP it is desirable that woman's consent for MTP should be an informed one. Accordingly a provision should be added to Section 3(4)(b) of the MTPA making it a legal duty on part of the registered medical practitioner to inform the woman asking for MTP of the possible risks to her person during the course of MTP, as well as of the possible benefits and consequences following MTP, before the woman gives her consent for MTP after having enough time for thoughts over benefits *vis-à-vis* risks and consequences.

(F) LEGAL STATUS OF UNBORN CHILD OR FOETUS

The law recognizes legal personality to unborn children. A child in mother's womb is by fiction treated as already born and regarded as person for many purposes. The Hindu law has equated 'person in womb' to a 'person in existence' for many purposes. Similar is the position under the Transfer of Property Act, 1882. Some of the instances are:

> Hindu law of partition requires a share to be allotted to a child in womb along with the other living heirs. If pregnancy is known, the partition should be postponed till the birth of child, but if (male) coparceners do not agree to this, than a share equal to share of a son should be reserved. If a son is born, he takes it, and if a female is born, a marriage provision should be made for her. In case, no share is reserved for a son in womb, he can, after

his birth, demand re-opening of partition. However, if the child does not take birth alive, his share may be equally partitioned between the surviving heirs. A child in womb can inherit property. Under the Hindu Succession Act, 1956,[40] the property of a male Hindu dying intestate (without making a will) shall devolve firstly upon the Class I heirs, which includes Son/Daughter. 'Son' means inter alia a posthumous son (i.e. child in womb at the time of death of intestate, born alive later). The position of 'daughter' is same as that of a son. Likewise, posthumous children are included in the scheme of succession to the property of a female Hindu dying intestate[41]

The traditional Hindu law did not recognize gifts to unborn persons. The rule of pure Hindu law that a gift in favour of an unborn person is wholly void so that it cannot be made even through the medium of a trust was modified by the Hindu Disposition of Property Act 15 of 1916, by the Madras Act 1 to 1914, and by Act 8 of 1921.[42] Thus, a gift can be made to a child and could be accepted on its behalf.[43] A person capable of taking under a will must either in fact, or in contemplation of law, be in existence at the death of the testator. Thus, a bequest can be made to an unborn person.[44] A child in womb may be beneficiary of a trust. Sec. 9 of the Indian Trusts Act, 1882, says: "Every person capable of holding property may be a beneficiary". If some of the beneficiaries of a trust are unborn persons, the trust cannot be varied without obtaining court's consent on their behalf.

The recognition of the legal personality of a child in the womb of the mother is illustrated in the rule of procedure,

---

40. Sections 8-11, Hindu Succession Act, 1956.
41. *Ibid.*, Sections 15-16. The child must be in womb (justo matrimonio, i.e. moment of conception) at the time of the death of intestate and the child must be born alive (Sec. 20).
42. Mulla, The Transfer of Property Act, ninth Edition (Ed. Soli Paul), Butter worths India, New Delhi, pp. 1299-1300 (2000).
43. Sec. 122, Transfer of Property Act, 1882. The words 'accepted by or on behalf of the donee' show that the done may be a person unable to express acceptance.
44. The Indian Succession Act, 1925 governs the wills made by Hindus.

which lays-down that a pregnant woman condemned to death cannot be executed until she has delivered her child.[45]

To sum-up:

- Rights of an unborn person, whether proprietary or personal, are all contingent on his birth as a living human being. He, thus, has a contingent or a qualified kind of legal personality. His contingent rights, however, get transformed into vested rights on his birth as a living person.
- His ownership is necessarily contingent, for he may never be born at all, but it is nonetheless a real and present ownership.
- The proprietary rights of an unborn child are fully recognized by Indian law.
- An unborn child is entitled for legal protection under the criminal law of India.
- Despite having a legal personality, an unborn child is generally considered in India as having no separate existence from the mother. Recognition of the status of an unborn child would go a long way in ensuring the girl child's survival, be it by moral guilt or legal guilt.

The basic concept of "abortion" contemplates that kind of conduct which leads to the expulsion of the foetus from the uterus before its full maturity[46] Foetus refers to the period from the 57th day, ending of birth. That means "morning-after pill" is not a species of abortion.[47]

45. Under the English law, such expectant mothers were sentenced to life imprisonment instead of death under the Sentence of Death (Expectant Mothers) Act, 1931.
46. This is the gist of the definition of "abortion" as given in the Oxford Concise Medical Dictionary (Oxford Reference Series, 1992). Macmillan's Concise Encyclopedia (1998) supports this meaning. See Bakshi, P.M., "Contraception and Abortion: Some Legal Issues", *The Lawyers Collective*, Vol. 11, No. 1, p. 22, January (1996).
47. *Ibid.*, Bakshi, P.M, The Pill has to be taken within 72 hours of unprotected sex; it prevents egg from being fertilized. Recently, the Government of India announced its decision to allow over the

(G) RIGHT TO ABORTION OF MOTHER V. RIGHT TO LIFE OF UNBORN/FOETUS

There can be arguments for and against. Religious, moral, and cultural sensibilities continue to influence abortion laws throughout the world. The right to life, the right to liberty, and the right to security of person are major issues of human rights that are sometimes used as justification for the existence or the absence of laws controlling abortion. Many countries in which abortion is legal require that certain criteria be met in order for an abortion to be obtained, often, but not always, using a trimester-based system to regulate the window in which abortion is still legal to perform. In this debate, arguments presented in favor of or against abortion focus on either the moral permissibility of an induced abortion, or justification of laws permitting or restricting abortion.

Arguments on morality and legality tend to collide and combine, complicating the issue at hand. Abortion debates, especially pertaining to abortion laws, are often spearheaded by advocacy groups belonging to one of two camps. Most often those in favor of legal prohibition of abortion describe themselves as pro-life while those against legal restrictions on abortion describe themselves as pro-choice. Both are used to indicate the central principles in arguments for and against abortion: "Is the fetus a human being with a fundamental right to life" for pro-life advocates, and, for those who are pro-choice, "Does a woman have the right to choose whether or not to have an abortion?"

I. A Woman has a Right to Abortion

- The continuance of the pregnancy would involve risk

---

counter (OTC) sale of Emergency Contraception (EC) or the 'morning after pill' in order to prevent accidental pregnancies (viz. on account of unprotected sex, contraception failure, coercive sex or rape) and unsafe abortions. A doctor's prescription will not be needed to buy it. The EC (taken in more than 100 countries) gives a woman the right over her sexuality and fertility. See *The Hindu*, New Delhi, September 10 (2005).

to the life of the pregnant woman greater than, if the pregnancy were terminated.

- The termination is necessary to prevent grave permanent injury to the physical or mental health of the pregnant woman.
- The continuance of the pregnancy would involve risk, greater than if the pregnancy were terminated, of injury to the physical or mental health of the pregnant woman
- The continuance of the pregnancy would involve risk, greater than if the pregnancy were terminated, or injury to the physical or mental health of any existing child of the family of the pregnant woman.
- There is substantial risk that if the child were born it would suffer from such physical or mental abnormalities as to be seriously handicapped.
- Or in emergency, certified by the operating practitioner as immediately necessary: to save the life of the pregnant woman or to prevent grave permanent injury to the physical or mental health of the pregnant woman.

2. Medical Termination of Pregnancy Act, 1971

The Medical Termination of Pregnancy Bill was passed by both the Houses of the Parliament and received the assent of the President of India on 10th August, 1971. It came on the Statute Book as the "The MTP Act, 1971". This law guarantees the Right of Women in India to terminate an unintended pregnancy by a registered medical practitioner in a hospital established or maintained by the Government or a place being approved for the purpose of this Act by the Government. Not all pregnancies could be terminated.

Section 3 of the said Act, says that pregnancy can be terminated:

- *As a Health Measure*: when there is danger to the life or risk to physical or mental health of the women;
- *On Humanitarian Grounds*: such as when pregnancy arises from a sex crime like rape or intercourse with a lunatic woman, etc., and

- *Eugenic Grounds*: where there is a substantial risk that the child, if born, would suffer from deformities and diseases.

Thus, under the provision of the Act, pregnancies up to 20 weeks can be terminated under the certified opinion of one or two registered medical practitioners depending upon the period of gestation. Pregnancy termination can be performed on humanitarian, eugenic, medical and social grounds.

A woman's right in this respect is doubtful because her right is dependant on certain conditions: proof of risk to her life or grave injury to her physical or mental health, substantial risk of physical or mental abnormalities to the child if born and a situation where abortion could only save her life, all to be arrived at by the medical practitioners. Can a woman request a medical practitioner to perform an abortion on the ground that she does not want a child at that time? Where the liberty of the woman is fully dependant on certain other factors, such are quest cannot be said to be just and reasonable. The M.T.P. Act also does not classify the pregnancy period so that the woman's interests and the state's interests could be given predominance in one's own spheres.

3. Arguments in Favour of Abortion

Indian law allows abortion, if the continuance of pregnancy would involve a risk to the life of the pregnant woman or grave injury to her physical or mental health. Abortion was being practiced earlier by many. Because it was illegal, it was practiced in a clandestine manner. The passing of the Act made medical termination of pregnancy legal, with certain conditions for safeguarding the health of the mother.

Following are the arguments in favour of legalizing abortion:

- The first argument is of Bodily Sovereignty. Each woman has the sole right to make decisions about what happens to her body—no one should force her either to carry or terminate a pregnancy against her will. Most abortions are carried out on the grounds of safeguarding the woman's mental health.

- Other are situations where abortions is done to safeguard the life of a fetus, as it would involve risk if pregnancy is carried, it might damage the fetus resulting in danger to the life of the mother.
- If abortion is banned, or just more restricted, we would return to the days of 'back-street abortions'. In the past this has been accompanied by wild claims of the risk to women's health from these procedures. The women resort to some unhygienic measures to abort the fetus.
- Act of performing an abortion to save the mother's life when occurs, however, the rationale is not that the fetus is seen to have less value than the mother, but that if no action is taken both will die. Aborting the fetus at least saves the mother's life.
- If suppose abortion is banned, a woman does not want to carry her pregnancy, she would carry it and then abandon the new born child. This would be more dangerous to the life of the baby. Thus, it is better to terminate the pregnancy at an earlier stage.
- Although in ancient and primitive times there were widespread practices of abortion and infanticide among savage, semi-civilized and even sophisticated races, the later period provided a better status to the unborn children. This is evident from the punishment and compensation provided in Old Testament for hurting a pregnant woman. The unborn was treated as equal to human being at least for the purposes of its protection. But as times have brought about revolutionary changes, each person has a right to bodily sovereignty and Human rights instruments protect such rights internationally. Thus, it becomes important to secure the right to abortion to every woman.

4. Arguments against Abortion

Following are the arguments which favour prohibition of abortion by the pro-life activists:

- The issue of the fetus' life, which raises the question

of whether one person's desire for autonomy can extend to ending another's existence.

- The killing of innocent is a crime and the fetus is also an innocent life.
- Many women suffer significant emotional trauma after having an abortion.
- There is also some evidence that having an abortion may increase a woman's risk of breast cancer in later life. Some other complications include damage and/or infection to the uterus and the Fallopian tubes making a woman infertile. Menstrual disturbances can also occur.
- Aborting fetuses because they may be disabled sends an implicit message of rejection to people with disabilities.
- Another argument is that an embryo (or, in later stages of development, a fetus) is a human being, entitled to protection, from the moment of conception and therefore has a right to life that must be respected. According to this argument, abortion is homicide.

International Efforts to Combat Vices of Sex Determination Test

It has become evident that despite important success in the comprehension and manipulation of many phenomena the prevailing scientific and technological approach is showing important deficiencies in the management of problems of organized complexity typical in the field of sustainable development.

The theme was also the focus of the World Conference on Science that under the rubric "Science for the Twenty-first Century", met in Budapest in mid-1999 (ICSU 1999). The documents of the conference emphasized the need for a new relationship between science and society, for a reinforcement of scientific education and cooperation, the need to connect modern scientific knowledge and traditional knowledge, the need for inter-disciplinary research, the need to support science in developing countries, the importance of addressing the ethics of the practice of science and the use of scientific knowledge, and other important issues.

In 19th century in England, infanticide was very rampant throughout the country. In fact, a debate over how to correct the problem was carried out in the media. In Greece of 200 BC, the murder of female infants was so common that among 6000 families living in Delphi, not more than one percent had two daughters.

There are evidences of sexism in Arabia before the time of Mohammad during 570-632 AD. The females were generally seen as an undesirable burden to a family in the Persian world. However, Mohammad introduced reforms and outlined the wrongfulness of infanticide in various sections of the Holy Scripture.

There are instances that show acceptance to gender discrimination and infanticide in the western world as well. Female child abortions has been reported from the South Asian Diaspora in Britain, the USA and Canada, over the last over 15 years.

Although there have been prevalence of gender selective abortions in many cultures over the globe, the extent of this problem has been in brightening proportions in the "Third World" countries mainly China and India. At least 60 million females in Asia are missing and feared dead. Estimates indicate that 30.5 million females are "missing" from China, 22.8 million in West Asia, 6,00,000 in Egypt and 2,00,000 in Nepal.[1]

(A) INTERNATIONAL CONVENTIONS RELATED TO SEX DETERMINATION TEST

Various international conventions and instruments provide for the right to life, survival, health, etc. in favour of women and children, and thus implicitly recognize the right of an unborn child. There is, however, no explicit recognition. India has also ratified various United Nations Conventions and treaties on human rights to secure equal rights of women.

1. Singh, D.P., "Female Foeticide in Punjab—Causes and Consequences", Paragon International Publishers, New Delhi (2007).

The Supreme Court of India has held that 'once signed and international treaty or convention will be treated as a part of law unless otherwise stated. The Indian government is thus bound in its obligation to implement any convention or treaty that is signed.

Right to life is protected from the moment of its conception by Article 6(1) of the ICCPR, Article 2 of the European Convention of Human Rights and Article 4 of the African Charter of Human and People's right. But they are silent on the issue of when does life begin. But the interpretations have forced us to believe that the child is not to be protected from the time of its inception. The right to life of the fetus has to be balanced with the rights of the mother.

International courts and tribunals have not addressed the difficult philosophical issue of when life begins, but have focused on the meaning of the language used in the relevant treaties. They have generally held that the references to every human being or everyone or every person do not include an unborn foetus. Following are the international conventions which recognise the rights of women and children.

1. Universal Declaration of Human Rights (UDHR), 1948

The Universal Declaration of Human Rights, 1948 opens with an assertion of the equal inalienable rights of all members of the human family to inherent dignity and the recognition of the aspiration of the common people for a world that is free from experiences of barbarous acts which have outraged with conscience of humankind.[2] Articles 1, 2, 3, 7, 16(3), 22, and 25(2) are specifically relevant to the present purpose, addressing questions of entitlement to dignity and freedom without distinction of race, colour, sex, etc.

2. Convention on the Elimination of All Forms of Discrimination Against Women (CEDAW), 1979

The Convention on the Elimination of All Forms of Discrimination against Women (CEDAW), adopted in 1979, is

2. Kannabiran, K., "Gender Cleansing: Female Foeticide or Crime against Humanity—State Liability", Combat Law, pp. 24-25, August-September (2003), available at http://indiafemale foeticide.org.

the most extensive and widely-ratified international agreement promoting the rights of girls and women. The CEDAW is considered to be equivalent to an international bill of rights for women, defining what constitutes discrimination and providing an agenda for action. It states the negative consequences of female discrimination and seeks full equality between men and women in all fields of political, economic, social and cultural life.[3] States that have ratified CEDAW must take concrete steps, such as enacting laws, establishing women's rights commissions and creating conditions to ensure that the human rights of girls and women are fulfilled. Their progress is monitored by the UN Committee on the Elimination of Discrimination against Women.

The Convention on the Elimination of All forms of Discrimination against Women (CEDAW), 1979, obligates State parties to eradicate all kinds of discrimination against women "in effect", in all walks of human activity.[4] The SAARC countries, of which India is a member, announced the year 1990 as "SAARC Year of the Girl Child" and to observe "SAARC Decade of the Girl Child" from January 1991, so as to create the right environment to secure a rightful place for female children.

The Supreme Court of India has discussed the impact and value of international instruments of human rights domestically in its case *Vishaka v State of Rajasthan*.[5] The court held that international conventions and norms that are in keeping with fundamental rights can be used for interpretation of those rights, particularly in the absence of domestic legislation on these issues. The judgment directed the government to rely on CEDAW to construe its guidelines on sexual harassment in the workplace.

3. United Nations Convention on the Rights of the Child (UNCRC), 1989

The International Conference on Population and

---

3. UN—Committee and Convention on the Elimination of Discrimination against Women.
4. The Convention entered into force on September 3, 1987. India Ratified the Convention on July 9, 1993.
5. (1997) 6 SCC 241.

Development recognized, the Programme of Action, which provides[6] that full attention should be given to the promotion of mutually respectful and equitable meet the educational and service needs of adolescents to enable them to deal in a positive and responsible way with their sexuality. Taking into account the rights of the child to access to information, privacy confidentiality, respect and informed consent, as well as the responsibilities, rights and duties of parents and legal guardians to provide, in a manner consistent with the evolving capacities of the child, appropriate direction and guidance in the exercise by the child of the rights recognized in the Convention of the Rights of the Child, 1989 (CRC), and in conformity with the Convention of the Elimination of All forms of Discrimination against Women, 1979.

The convention on the rights of the child recognizes that states parties shall respect and ensure the rights set forth in the present convention to each child within their jurisdiction without discriminations of any kind, irrespective of the child's or his or her parent's or legal guardian's race, colour, sex language, religion, political or other opinion, national ethnic or social origin, property, disability, birth or status.[7] In all actions concerning children, the best interests of the child shall be a primary consideration. Among the other rights of the child under the CRC one of the main high lights of the convention is that every child has the inherent right to life, and the states shall ensure, the maximum child survival and development. Therefore, right to take birth is the inherent right of the unborn child under the convention.

The U.N. Convention on the Rights of the Child, 1989, contains a set of universal legal standards or norms for the protection and well-being of children. Every child has the 'Right to survival'; 'Right to protection;' 'Right to development'

---

6. Report of the International Conference on Population and Development, Cairo, 5-13 September 1994 (United Nations Publication, Sales number E.95 XIII 18) Chap. I, Resolution 1, Annex I.
7. General Assembly Resolution 44/25, Annex Article 2, Para 2.

and, 'Right to participation'.[8] The Convention prohibits discrimination on the basis of sex.

Article 1 to the U.N. Convention on the Rights of the Child, 1989, gives the definition of the age of the child: "For the purpose of the present Convention, a child means every human being below the age of 18 years unless under the law applicable to the child, majorities attained earlier". No minimum age is defined. This was done to avoid debate over abortion, which could have threatened the acceptance of the Convention.[9]

UN Secretary General Kofi Annan has stated, "Gender equality is more than a goal in itself. It is a precondition for meeting the challenge of reducing poverty, promoting sustainable development and building good governance".

'The right of a woman to her private life has been the basis on which a number of international bodies have upheld the right of a woman to have an abortion. The right to freedom of expression and access to information has been used to argue for the right of women to receive information about abortion options. The right to access abortion may also be based on the right of a woman to decide freely and responsibly on the number and spacing of her children.

In the industrialized counties (Europe, USA, Japan), for example, there are, on an average, 106 women for every 100 men; in Sub-Saharan Africa, there are 102 women for every 100 men, and, in South-East Asia, 101 women for every 100 men.[10] In India, on the contrary, there are 93 women for every 100 men in the population.[11] Discrimination against girl children, female

8. The Government of India ratified the Convention on 12 November 1992. Article 6 of the U.N. Convention provides for the right to life, survival and development. Article 2 Convention provides for the right to life, survival and development. Article 2 contains provision relating to non-discrimination. Article 3 provides for the best interest of the child and Article 12 for the views of the child.
9. Bajpai, A, Child Rights in India—Law, Policy and Practice, OUP, New Delhi, p. 19 (2003).
10. Jain, Ashok Kumar, The Saga of Female Foeticide in India, Socio-Legal Offshoots, Ascent Publications, Delhi (2006).
11. Misra, P., "Female Infanticide: A Threat to Posterity", *NISD Journal*, pp. 24, 28 (2002).

foeticide and girl infanticide are in direct violation of Universal Declaration of Human Rights (UDHR), the international Convention on the Elimination of all Forms of Discrimination against Women (CEDAW) and the UN Convention on the Rights of the Child (UNCRC).

(B) SEX SELECTION AND ABORTION LAW IN VARIOUS COUNTRIES

1. Abortion Law in United States of America

In the United States tradition of jurisprudence, there are a number of sources of law that could be applied directly or by analogy to the problems involved in sex selection. The first is common law. The courts have articulated principles of common law within the context of tort and contract law and some of these principles may be applicable of solutions of the issues raised above. The second source can be found in the statutes enacted by state and local government's issues of sex selection. A last source of law can be found in the federal and state constitutions. Constitutional law is most important because it sets the overall tone of the legal environment and provides a backbone of legal principle upon which all of the other sources of law can build and grow.

In 1965 the United States Supreme Court found that the logical implications of six amendments to the United States Constitution the First, the Third, The Fourth, the Fifth, the Ninth, and the Fourteenth combine to imply a constitutional right of privacy that insulated the marital relationship from interference by the state in the form of laws prohibiting the practice the birth control.[12]

The role of privacy has been further refined in the subsequent cases of *Roe* v. *Wade*[13] and *Doe* v. *Bolton,*[14] Roe and Doe combined to form the constitutional cornerstone of the legal principles that govern many of the issues raised by prenatal sex selection. In this light, it is instructive to review the rationale of these cases in some detail to discover what the

12. Griswold *v.* Connecticut, 38 U.S. 479.
13. 410 U.S. 113.
14. 410 U.S. 179.

current state of the law is and to postulate how it may be further extended and/or modified.

Another body of litigation has developed that focuses on the avenues by which a pregnant woman can gain access to abortion.[15] These cases involve restrictions on the federal funding of abortion through Medicaid. It is now established that the federal government is not required to pay for abortions. Further, the policy of excluding payment for abortion services from Medicaid was held to be constitutionally permissible because it was an indirect rather than a direct, method of outlined the substance of its approach in the case of *Maher* v. *Roe*[16] by concluding that a Connecticut statute that prohibited Medicaid for abortions that were not medically necessary, but also allowed Medicaid payments for medical services incident of childbirth, was constitutional. The court wrote:

> "An indigent woman who desires an abortion suffers no disadvantage as a consequence of Connecticut's decision to fund childbirth; she continues as before to be dependent on private services for the service she desires. The state may have made childbirth a more attractive alternative, thereby influencing the woman's decision nut it has imposed no restriction on access to abortions that was not already there. The indigency that may make it difficult and in some cases perhaps impossible for some to have abortions is neither created nor in any way affected by the Connecticut regulation".[17] These developments in the constitutional foundations of the right of privacy as it applies to abortion cases indicate that the principle is a qualified right that has exceptions (as in the case of a minor seeking abortion) and also indicate that access to the exercise of the principle can be modified by indirect governmental intervention (as in the case of Medicaid funding for abortion). The combination of these two

15. Harris *v.* McRae, Supreme Court Opinion 79-1268; Williams *v.* Zbarez, Supreme Court Opinion 79-4.
16. 432 U.S. 464.
17. Maher *v.* Roe, 432 U.S. at 474.

developments creates an uncertain legal environment regarding the extent to which the right of privacy will be further accepted and modified.

In USA, Foetus is a "person" within the language and meaning of the "due process clause" of the Fourteenth Amendment to the United States Constitution. Like Indian Constitution (Art. 21—Right to life), there is however, no explicit recognition. In *Rosen* v *La, State Board of Medical Examiners,*[18] the court announced that embryonic and foetal to survive, on the basis of equality with human beings generally, the State is not violating the rights of the mother.

In America, the Law of Torts abounds in decisions where a child has been allowed to maintain action for injury sustained before its birth at any time during the entire period of gestation and it is now firmly established that any injury caused to the foetus is to be regarded as personal injury to the child. Life beyond death may still be an enigma, philosophical or otherwise. But life before birth in the mother's womb is a physiological phenomenon.[19] In an English case *R.* v. *Tait,*[20] (1989) 3 WLR 891, the Court of Appeal quashed the conviction of a burglar on the ground that 'threat to kill a foetus' is not an offence directed against the 'another person'.

Roe v. *Wade*[21] became one of the most politically significant Supreme Court decisions in history, reshaping national politics, dividing the nation into "pro-choice" and "pro-life" camps, and inspiring grassroots activism. This is a landmark United States Supreme Court decision establishing that most laws against

18. 380 F. Supp. 1217 (ED La 1970). In Abele *v.* Markle (1972), the court, however, invalidated a statute protecting human life from the moment of conception by failing to find a compelling State interest in it, reasoning on the basis of the mother's right to privacy. In Roe *v.* Wade (1973), the US Supreme Court refrained form resolving the difficult question of 'when life begins' and said that when those trained in the respective disciplines of medicines, philosophy and theology are unable to arrive at any consensus, the judiciary, is not in a position to speculate as to the answer.
19. Jane Roe *v.* Henry Wade, (1973) 410 US 113.
20. (1989) 3 WLR 891.
21. See, 410 U.S. 113 at 139 (1973); 93 S Ct 706 (1973).

abortion violate a constitutional right to privacy, thus overturning all state laws outlawing or restricting abortion that were inconsistent with the decision. Jone Roe, the plaintiff wanted to terminate her pregnancy because she contended that it was a result of rape. Relying on the current state of medical knowledge, the decision established a system of trimesters that attempted to balance the state's legitimate interests with the individual's constitutional rights. The Court ruled that the state cannot restrict a woman's right to an abortion during the first trimester, the state can regulate the abortion procedure during the second trimester "in ways that are reasonably related to maternal health", and in the third trimester, demarcating the viability of the fetus, a state can choose to restrict or even to proscribe abortion as it sees fit.

In response to *Roe* v. *Wade*, several states enacted laws limiting abortion, including laws requiring parental consent for minors to obtain abortions, parental notification laws, spousal consent laws, spousal notification laws, and laws requiring abortions to be performed in hospitals but not clinics, laws barring state funding for abortions, laws banning most very late term abortions. The Supreme Court struck down several state restrictions on abortions in a long series of cases stretching from the mid-1970s to the late 1980s.

In *Roe* v. *Wade*, Jane Roe brought a class action challenging the constitutionality of the Texas criminal abortion laws, restricting, procuring or attempting to procure abortion on medical advice for the purpose of saving the mother's life.[22] The petitioner pleaded that the state criminal abortion laws, were unconstitutionally vague and that they abridged her rights of personal privacy, protected by the First, Fourth, Fifth Ninth and Fourteenth Amendments to the USA Constitution.

The State of Texas on the other hand, argued that the state's determination to recognize and protect parental life from the after conception constitutes "a compelling state interest" and that the foetus is a "person" within the language and meaning of the "due process clause of the Fourteenth Amendment to the United State's Constitution".

22. S. Texas Criminal Law in Articles 1191 to 1196 lays down the law relating to criminal abortion.

In the case of *Planned Parenthood of South Eastern Pennsylvania* v. *Casey*[23] handed over by the Supreme Court of USA on 30 June 1992 upholding most aspects of restrictive Pennsylvania Abortion Control Act of 1982 has aroused a lot of controversy.

At this issue there were five provisions of the Pennsylvania Abortion Control Act 1982, which were added by the 1988 and 1989 amendments to the Act. The said provision: (i) require that a woman seeking an abortion must give her informed consent prior to the procedure, and specified that she be provided with certain information's at least 24 hours before the abortion is performed;[24] (ii) mandate the informed consent of the one parent for a minor (expectant mother) to obtain an abortion, but provides a judicial bypass process; (iii) command that, unless certain exceptions apply, a married woman seeking an abortion must sign a statement indicating that she has notified her husband;[25] (iv) define a "medical emergency" that will excuse compliance with the foregoing requirements;[26] and (v) impose certain reporting requirements on facilities providing abortion services.

The five abortion clinics and a physician representing himself and a class of doctors who provided abortion services, filed a suit seeking a declaratory judgment that each of the provision, namely, informed consent, parental consent, spousal notice, reporting requirements and public disclosure of clinics were violative of the Fourteenth Amendment of the United States Constitution.[27] The district court held all the provision unconstitutional and granted an injunction restraining their enforcement. The court of Appeal affirmed in part and reversed in part the Amendments, striking down the husband notification provision but upholding the others.

The Supreme Court of USA perhaps in one of the most emotional and politically explosive cases in years, by a majority of 5 to 4 affirmed the Court of Appeal's verdict and refused to

23. (1992) 120 L. Ed 2nd 674.
24. Pennsylvania Abortion Control Act, 1982, Section 3205.
25. *Ibid.*, Section 3209.
26. *Ibid.*, Section 3203.
27. *Ibid.*, Sections 3207(b), 3214(a), and 3214(f).

discard its 19 years landmark decision in *Roe* v. *Wade*[28] that made abortion legal as law of the land.

While the conservative dominated court controlled by justices chosen by Bush and Reagan, the former Presidents of USA, upheld the women's limited right to abortion recognized by roe, it also sought to accommodate by a bench of 7 to 2 the state's interest in potential life and said restriction could be allowed as long as they do not place an "undue burden on a woman's right". The court accordingly upheld most parts of the controversial Pennsyania law that make it more difficult for a woman to obtain an abortion.

2. Abortion Law in United Kingdom

At common law procuring or attempting to procure termination of pregnancy before "quickening" was not an indictable offence.[29] It was only after quickening that the abortion was punishable as an offence. By UK's first criminal abortion statute, Lord Ellen borough's Act 1803. The crime of abortion was pushed back to commencement of the pregnancy and distinction between an abortion before and after quickening abolished. In 1861 the Offences Against the Person Act 1861 in sections 58 and 59 made procuring or attempting to procure abortion a felony (offence) repealing the Act of 1803.

Section 58 of the Act of 1861 (subject to Abortion Act, 1967 and Human Fertilization and Embryology Act, 1990, section 37) prohibits attempt to procure miscarriage from any time after the conception of the child until its birth.[30] The section covers two situations, first, where a pregnant woman administers to herself any poison or noxious thing or uses any instruments or other means to procure her own miscarriage and second, where any one else unlawfully procures abortion whether the woman

28. See, the Due process Clause of the Fourteenth Amendment to the United States Constitution.
29. Blackstone, I.W., Commentaries, 129-30: E. Coke, Institutes III 50. The common law fixed the time of animation (vivacity), at the time of quickening when the foetus moved in the womb. An event that usually occurs about half-way through the pregnancy (around 20th week).
30. See Offences against the Person Act, 1861, Section 58.

is or is not pregnant. Punishment under the section on conviction may extend up to imprisonment for life.

Section 59 punishes supply or procuring of noxious drugs or an instrument knowing it to be unlawfully used for causing abortion with imprisonment which may extend up to five years[31] allied to the crime of miscarriage is the statutory offence—the Infant Life (Preservation) Act 1929. The Act is aimed at protecting the destruction of child. Section 1 of the Act as amended by the Criminal Justice Act 1948 states:

> Any person who, with intent to destroy the life of a child capable of being born alive, by any wilful act causes a child to die before it has an existence independent of its mother, shall be guilt and shall be liable on conviction to imprisonment for life.

Owing to the close proximity between the offence of miscarriage (Act of 1861) and child destruction (Act of 1929) the two offences may overlap at times. For instance, procuring a miscarriage so as to kill a child capable of being born alive may fall under the Act of 1861 as well as the Act of 1929. To overcome such an eventuality, sub-section 2 to section 2 of the Act of 1929 provides that where upon the trial of any person for (i) the murder or manslaughter of any child[32] or (ii) infanticide,[33] or (iii) an offence under section 58 of the Offences Against the Person Act 1861, the jury are of opinion that the person charged is not guilty of any of the offences mentioned therein, but it is shown by the evidence that accused is guilty of the offence of child destruction, he may be convicted accordingly.[34]

31. See *Ibid.*, Section 59.
32. Offences against the Person Act, Section 10 provides for trial of murder and manslaughter.
33. The Infanticide Act 1929 provides for punishment for causing death of child under the age of twelve months.
34. Smith and Hogan, Criminal Law 364 (6th ed. 1988), See Seaborne Davies, "The Law of Abortion and Necessity". Mod L.R. (1938-39). 58 LQR 472: J.W.C. Turner, Kenny's Outlines of Criminal Law 197-8 (9th ed. 1966).

A seemingly notable development in the English law was the case of *Rex* v. *Bourne*[35] in which the court apparently answered in the affirmative the question whether an abortion necessary to preserve the life of the pregnant woman was exempted from criminal liability under the Act of 1861. In the impugned case a girl under fifteen, who was criminally assaulted in the most revolting circumstances, became pregnant. Bourne, an eminent obstetrics, surgeon and gynecologist, thought that the operation ought to be performed in view of the age of the girl and the fact that she had been raped with great violence and so he terminated the pregnancy. Bourne was charged under section 58 of the Offences against the Person Act 1861[36] for unlawfully procuring the abortion of the girl.

While construing the provisions of section 58 of the Act of 1861, the court referred to the Infant Life (Preservation) Act of 1929 which provides punishment for child destruction. Section 1(1) of the Act of 1929 makes an intent to destroy the life of a child capable of being born alive[37] and cause it by any wilful act to die before it has an existence independent of its mother liable on conviction to imprisonment for life, unless it is proved that the act which caused the death was not done in good faith for the purpose only of preserving the life of the mother.

Justice Mac Naughten who delivered the judgment observed, that though the law with regard to procuring of an abortion under section 59 of the Act of 1861, under which the accused was charged, did not expressly incorporate the words, i.e., 'for the purpose only of preserving the life of the mother', they represent the common law and were implicit by the words "unlawful" occurring in the impugned section Justice Mac Naughten accordingly, said:

> The court further held that the phrase 'for the purpose of preserving the life of the mother' is wide and should be liberally interpreted to cover the acts that are dangerous to the health of the mother and will shorten the life as 'the

35. Held, All therapeutic abortions are lawful.
36. Section 58 : Offences Against the Person Act, 1861.
37. S. 1(2) : Infant Life (Preservation) Act, 1929.

life depends upon health and health may be so gravely impaired that it may result in death'. If the doctor performs the operation terminating pregnancy under such circumstances, it would be presumed that he acted in good faith for the purpose of preserving the life of the mother.

Since the crown in the impugned case failed to comply with the obligation of discharging the burden of proving that the operation was not procured in good faith for the purpose of preserving the life of the mother, the jury gave a verdict of acquittal.[38] But if a doctor is found to have acted in bad faith, he would be liable to conviction for procuring illegal abortion.[39]

The Court of Appeal held that a verdict of bad faith where there is no evidence as to professional practice and medical probabilities is often likely to be regarded as unsafe. However, it depends upon the nature of evidence and other factors.

(i) Abortion Act, 1967

In course of time it was realized that the strict provision of the law of abortion contained in sections 58 and 59 of the Offences Against the Person Act, 1861 was doing more harm than good. The attitude of medical profession was hostile and tragic cases continued to occur. Women who had been raped, deserted by their husbands, and overburdened mothers living in poverty with large families failed to get a medical abortion. Of course, the abortions could be bought but with a heavy price. As a result most of the women would go to back street abortionists' wielding a knitting needle, syringe, or stock leading to a great risk to their life. At times unwilling mothers used dangerous methods on themselves or committed suicide.

It was also noticed that although illegal abortions were taking place in thousands, as in the case of India before the passing of the medical Termination of Pregnancy Act of 1971, yet convictions were negligible. The police would not look

38. See, R *v.* Lobell, (1957) 1 All E.R. 734: Wilmington *v.* D.P.P. (1935) A.C. 402.
39. Cogan and Leak, (1975) 2 All E.R. 1059.

upon abortion as real crime. As these evils were beginning to be realized, a stone opinion grew that a woman had a right to control her own fertility and that the abortion should be legalized. At the same time a powerful religious lobby basing itself upon their "sanctity of life" was opposed to any move for change in the law. As a compromise measure the Abortion Act 1967[40] was passed which substantially liberalized the law of abortion though it did not concede all the demands of the pro-abortionists.

The Medical Termination of Pregnancy provides that a person shall not be guilty of an offence under the law relating to abortion,[41] when a pregnancy is terminated by a registered medical practitioner if two registered medical practitioners are of the opinion, formed in good faith.

To bring the act of termination of pregnancy within the purview of the exception clause to section 1(4) of the Act of 1967 the risk of injury feared from allowing the pregnancy to continue must be "greater than if the pregnancy were terminated".[42] The Act for the first time allows the interest of the children of the family to be taken into consideration while deciding the desirability of termination of a pregnancy. The protection of the interest of the children of the family would thus be a valid ground for termination of a pregnancy.

The termination of a pregnancy on eugenic grounds is basically justified upon the ground that the child if born would be seriously handicapped and would be a burden to the welfare of the parents and the society at large.

An important feature of the Act of 1967 is that it does not permit termination of a pregnancy on grounds of rape as in the case of India.[43] However, the fact of rape could influence the decision of the doctors in invoking the health grounds. Similarly, the failure of any device or method used by a married couple for the purpose of limiting the number of children cannot justify termination of a pregnancy as under the

---

40. The Act (c 87 of) 1967 is a small Act consisting of seven sections. The Act does not apply to Northern Ireland vide S. 7(3) of the Act.
41. Section 6, Abortion Act, 1967.
42. Section 1(a), Abortion Act, 1967.
43. Section 3, Medical Termination of Pregnancy Act, 1971.

Indian law.[44] Perhaps the ground of health of the children could be invoked to terminate unwanted pregnancy in such a situation.

(ii) Human Fertilization and Embryology Act, 1990

As suggested by the Lane Committee, the Human Fertilization and Embryology Act 1990 amended section 1 of the Abortion Act 1967.

To safeguard the interest of the pregnant woman section 1 of the Act has provided three procedural safeguards. Contravention of the provisions would make termination of a pregnancy illegal and contrary to law.[45] These safeguards are:

- (i) The pregnancy must be terminated by a registered medical pracititoner.[46]
- (ii) Two registered medical practitioners must have formed opinion in good faith that the abortion is necessary.[47]
- (iii) The treatment for the termination of pregnancy must be carried out in a National Health Service Hospital or in an approved nursing home, by the Secretary of the State.[48] However, the last two procedural safeguards do not apply where the doctors are of the opinion formed in good faith, the termination of pregnancy is immediately necessary to sage the life or to percent grave permanent injury to the physical or mental health of the pregnant woman.[49]
- (iv) Termination of Pregnancy by Medical Practitioners *vis-à-vis* Nurses.

In *Royal College of Nursing of the United Kingdom* v. *Department of Health and Social Security,*[50] in 1981 an important

44. Section 3, Medical Termination of Pregnancy Act, 1971.
45. Section 5(2), Abortion Act, 1967.
46. See, Medical Act, 1983 S. 56(1) for Definition of Registered Medical Practitioner.
47. Section 1(1), Abortion Act, 1967.
48. *Ibid.*, Section 1(3).
49. *Ibid.*, Section 1(4).
50. (1981) 1 All E.R. 545.

question as to legality of the role of nurses in termination of pregnancy by medical induction was being dated before the House of Lords.' There are two stages in medical induction, the first being the insertion of catheter by means of a pump or drip apparatus and second, the administration of fluid. The first stage was carried out by doctors and the second by nurses under the doctor's instructions but in his absence, although he would be on call. The causative factor in inducing labour and thus in terminating the pregnancy was the administration of fluid, which was done by the nurse and not the doctor.

The Department of Health and Social Security issued a circular to the nursing profession stating that no offence was committed within Section 1(1) of the Abortion Act, 1967 by nurses who terminated the pregnancy by medical induction. If a doctor decided on the termination, initiated it and remained responsible throughout for its overall conduct and control. The Royal College of Nursing disputed the contention and brought a declaration against the Department of Health and Social Security in the court that the advice was wrong and that the act carried out by the nurses in terminating a pregnancy by the induction method contravened the provision of Section 1(1) of the Abortion Act of 1967.

The lower court upheld the department's contention. The college appealed to the Court of Appeal which reversed the decision of the lower court holding that the whole process of medical induction had to be carried out by a doctor and not merely under a doctor's instruction if it was to come under Section 1(1) of the Act of 1967. The department appealed to the House of Lords against the decision.

The House of Lords by a majority of three to two set aside the unanimous verdict of the Court of Appeal and restored the verdict of the lower court. The court held that if a doctor prescribed the treatment for the termination of a pregnancy, remained in charge and accepted responsibility throughout, and the treatment was carried out in accordance with his directions, the pregnancy was terminated by 'a registered medical practitioner' for the purposes of Section 1(1) of the Act of 1967, and any person taking part in the termination was entitled to the protection afforded under the Act. But if the doctors were to direct the whole procedure by correspondence or over telephone, the operation would presumably be unlawful.

Section 4(1) of the Act of 1967 gives the right to a person to object and refuse to participate in any treatment relating to termination of a pregnancy, if his conscience does not permit him to do so as in the case of Singapore.[51] However, one cannot refuse to participate in treatment which is necessary to save the life or to prevent grave injury to the physical or mental health of the pregnant woman.[52] A secretary or clerk however, wills not the benefit of section 4(1) of the Act, if he or she refuses to type a letter arranging an abortion as the act does not amount to counseling or procuring the termination of a pregnancy.[53]

3. Sex Selection, Abortion and Law in Indonesia

The dominant religion in Indonesia is Islam and the legal traditions tend to reflect these religious values. At present, Indonesia has cautiously entered into a family planning program, but abortion is strictly forbidden (Sodhy, Metcalf, and Wallach, 1980). Laws relating to the family environment favor the male as was the case in India (El-Kammash, 1971). This produces as strong incentive to produce male offspring and a patrilineal and patrilocal family. Islamic law provides conflicting prescriptions concerning family planning generally (El-Kammash, 1971) and would probably make it very difficult to practice sex selection even if abortion were available.

In Indonesia abortion is illegal and termination of a pregnancy is not permitted under any circumstances. Even to save the life of the mother is not an excuse for termination of a pregnancy. The Penal Code of Indonesia of 1915 in articles 346 to 349 provides for punishment for offences relating to induced abortion.

Article 346 of the Code make a woman guilty of an offence if she with deliberate intent causes or lets another to cause the drifting off or the death of the fruit of her womb, and

51. Section 6, Termination of Pregnancy Act, 1974.
52. Section 4(2), Abortion Act, 1967.
53. Salford Health Authority, exp. *The Times*, 5th Jan. (1988) C.A. (Civ Dic.).

is liable on conviction to imprisonment which may extend to four years.[54] Article 347 holds a person guilty of a offence, if he causes the drifting off or the death of the fruit of the woman without her consent and is liable on conviction to a maximum period of twelve year of imprisonment,[55] and it it results in the death of the woman punishment may extend to imprisonment of fifteen years.[56] Article 348 provides for the lesser punishment in case the drifting off or the death of the fruit of womb takes place with the consent of the woman, which may extend to imprisonment of five years and six months,[57] and if it results in the death of the woman punishment may extend to seven year of imprisonment.[58]

Article 349 of the Code makes a physician, midwife or pharmacist guilty of an offence, if he or she is an accomplice to one of the crimes described in articles 347 and 348 and liable to punishment which may be enhanced to one-third of the punishment prescribed for the offences under the respective articles and may also be deprived of the exercise of the profession in which he or she commits the offence.

4. Sex Selection, Abortion and Law in Ireland

Art. 40(3) of the Irish constitution recognizes the right to life of the unborn. It was added vide Amendment to the Constitution in 1982, it says:

> "The State acknowledges the right to life of the unborn, and with regard to the equal right to life of the mother, guaranteed in its laws to respect, and as far as practicable by its laws to defend and vindicate that right".[59]

54. Penal Code of Indonesia, Article 346.
55. *Ibid.*, Article 347(1).
56. *Ibid.*, Article 347(2).
57. *Ibid.*, Article 348(1).
58. *Ibid.*, Article 348(2).
59. Ireland is one of the few countries that do not permit abortion under any circumstances. As per Sec. 7(2), Abortion Act, the termination of pregnancy is illegal and punishable under the law. See Gaur, K.D., The Indian Penal Code, Universal Law Publishing Co., Delhi (2004).

In Ireland, under The Civil Liability Act of 1961 law relating to wrongs would apply to a child in the mother's womb for its protection as if the child was born.

Abortion is illegal in Ireland.[60] The unlawful killing of an unborn child is a criminal offence under the provisions of sections 58 and 59 of the Offences Against the Person Act 1861carrying a maximum punishment of penal servitude for life. The protection given to the unborn child applies from the date of conception.[61]

In the case of *Attorney General of Ireland* v. *X*,[62] which evoked considerable debate in Ireland on the subject of abortion, in public and legal experts, a vexed question of law and fact as regards the right to life of the unborn and right to the life of the mother was involved. The facts of the case are very pathetic. A fourteen year old school girl who discovered in January 1992 that she was pregnant as the result of an alleged rape by the father of her friend in the month of December 1991 was not permitted under the Irish law to get her pregnancy terminated.

The girl and her parents accordingly decided to obtain an abortion in UK. But in the meantime the Attorney General obtained an interim injunction in the High Court restraining the girl and her parents from, (i) interfering with the right to life of the unborn; (ii) leaving the jurisdiction for nine months; and (iii) procuring or arranging an abortion within or outside the country.

Rejecting the defence plea that psychological damage to the girl of carrying a child would be considerable and that the damage to her mental health would be devastating, if the termination of pregnancy is not allowed, the High Court granted permanent injunction. A reference was made to sub-section 3 to section 3 of article 40 of the Constitution to vindicate the right to life to the unborn. The said sub-section says:

---

60. Section 7(3), Abortion Act, 1967.
61. Attorney General (SPVC) *v.* Open Door Counseling Ltd., (1988) I.R. 593 at 598.
62. (1992) 1 I.R., 1: *The Times*, 7 March 1992 (Lond).

> The State acknowledge the right to life of the unborn and with regard to the equal right to life of the mother, guaranteed in its laws to respect and as far as practicable by its laws to defend and vindicate that right.[63]

While referring to the above constitutional provisions the court observed that the right to life of the unborn is guaranteed under the Constitution and that it was the duty of the various organs of the government including judiciary to defend and vindicate that right. Judging the magnitude of the danger to the child and danger that exists to the life of the mother, the court said:

> "The risk that the defendant may take her own life if and order is made (prohibiting termination of pregnancy) is much less and is of a different order of magnitude than the certainty that the life of the unborn will be terminated if the order is not made. . . . The young girl has the benefit of the love and care and support of devoted parent who will help her through the difficult months ahead. . . . Having had the regard to the rights of the mother in this case, the court's duty to protect the life of the unborn requires it to make the order sought".[64]

However, the Supreme Court of Ireland by a majority of 4 to 1 allowed the appeal against the order of High Court and discharged the injunction issued against the defendants. The court observed that the Constitution requires that its provisions be interpreted harmoniously and that the rights thereby given to the unborn and the mother be interpreted in concert. Since there I was a real and substantial risk to the life of the mother by self-destruction as depicted by her suicidal tendency, which can only be avoided by termination of her pregnancy, the court observed that the defendant is permitted to obtain abortion in

---

63. Art. 40(3)(3) was added vide Eighth Amendment to the Constitution in 1983.
64. (1992) 1 I.R., 1: *The Times*, 7 March 1992 (Lond.) at 12.

Ireland.[65] It may however be noted that the judgment of the Supreme Court setting out its reasons for lifting in injunctions granted by the High Court have not set the law of abortion in Ireland in a satisfactory state. The law is in a most unsatisfactory state of uncertainty as before.[66] It is high time a suitable legislation be enacted in this important area of social concern affecting the right of the woman to privacy and freedom to decide to bear a child or not.

5. Sex Selection, Abortion and Law in Canada

The Canadian law recognizes legal personality of an unborn child. In the historic case of *Montreal Tramways Co.* v. *Leveille,*[67] a claim was made by female infant against the tramway company for the deformity caused to her while in her mother's womb due to defendant's negligence. The court awarded damages. The Irish Court, had, however, denied damages to an infant child under the similar circumstances.[68] The court rules that the railway company owed no duty of care towards a person whose existence was unknown to them. But the court did not specifically say that unborn child has no right to claim damages for personal harm.[69]

Significantly, Paton (a noted jurist) does not recognize a child in the mother's womb as a legal person because he is without rights. In his view, legal personality is conferred on a child only after he is born alive and completely separated form is mother's womb. It is, however, submitted that this view is

65. Attorney General (SPVC) *v.* Open Door Counseling Ltd., (1988) I.R. 593 at 55.
66. See, "Democracy and Distrust: Abortion Law in Ireland", Irish Law 57 (1992): James Kingston and Anthony Whelan, "The Protection of Unborn in Three Legal Order-Part-I, Part-II, Part-III, *Irish Law Times* 93-6, 104-8: and 166-70: 279-283 (1992). Roderick J.O. Hanlon, "The Attorney General *v.* X: Reg. *v.* Dudley and Stephens Reconsidered. *Irish Law Times,* April (1992) p. 86: Mel Cousin, "Abortion and E.C. Law on Social Security for Person moving within the Community", *Law Times,* 244 (1993).
67. [1933] 4 DLR 337 (Canada).
68. Walker, *v.* Great Northern Rly. of Ireland (1890) 28LR Ire. 69.
69. Paranjape, N.V., Studies in Jurisprudence and Legal Theory, Central Law Agency, Allahabad, India, p. 316 (2001).

not tenable, as many legal systems of the world have incorporated provisions in their laws extending legal protection and safeguarding the contingent rights of an unborn child.[70]

In the leading case of *Morgentalor Smoling and Scott* v. *R.* (1988) 44 DLR (4th) 385, the Court focused on the bodily security of the pregnant women. The Criminal Code of the country required a pregnant woman who wanted an abortion to submit an application to a therapeutic committee, which resulted in delays. The Supreme Court found that this procedure infringed the guarantee of security of a person. This subjected the pregnant woman to psychological stress.

6. Sex Selection, Abortion and Law in Singapore

The law of abortion in Singapore would reveal that it is one of the most progressive legislations on the subject n as much as it gives absolute immunity and freedom to a woman to decide about her own life and to chose to bear a child or not. In other words, the Act (Termination of Pregnancy Act, 1974) confers on a woman the right to privacy of her life.[71]

In the Republic of Singapore until 1970 the law relating to abortion was contained inspections 312 to 315 of the penal Code of Singapore[72] as in the case of India, Pakistan, Bangladesh, Sri Lanka and Malaysia. However, in 1970 the Abortion Act, 1970 was passed in order to soften the rigorous of the strict provisions of the draconian law of miscarriage. The Act, inter alias, provides for the establishment of a board to authorize treatment to terminate pregnancy by a registered medical practitioner in certain circumstances without the authority of the board. Since the life of the Act of 1970 was

70. *Ibid.*
71. A unique feature of The Singapore Act is that it confers the right to freedom not to participate in the process of termination of pregnancy, if one has a conscientious objection. It grants immunity to the doctors who because of their faith and conscientious objection do not want to participate in the treatment of termination of pregnancy, unless the treatment is absolutely necessary to save the life or to prevent grave permanent injury to the physical or mental health of a pregnant woman. In such cases, the doctor will be under a legal duty to participate in the treatment.
72. Abortion Act 1970 Section 2.

limited to four years only[73] in 1974 the Abortion Act of 1974 was passed repealing the Act of 1970. In 1980 the Abortion Act 1974 was amended vide Abortion (Amendment) Act, 1980 and eventually it was named as the Termination of Pregnancy Act.

The Termination of Pregnancy Act, 1974 is a small Act consisting of 11 sections.[74] The act legalizes termination of pregnancy and lays down the conditions under which it would not attract criminal sanction. Sub-section I to section 3 of the act which is the operative section states.

7. Sex Selection and Law in People's Republic of China

In contrast to the approach of examining legislative decree taken with respect to the Soviet Union, one must examine party action an its effect on private, social networks in the People's Republic of China. Understanding the operation of Chinese law is always most difficult for western analysts, especially those in the Anglo American tradition. This is because Chinese law operates in an opposite way from that of the West. Rather than have courts discover and formalize principles that govern private interactions in the form of court opinions, which is a large part of the United States tradition, Chinese law starts with general notions of party policy, which are given meaning through an informal sociopolitical network.

Modern Chinese law must be understood against the background of ancient Chinese custom. The central concept of ancient tradition is the cult of ancestor worship, in which it was absolutely necessary to provide male heirs in order to continue the line of one's ancestors and provide a proper level of worship (Luk, 1977). In this tradition, parents were given extraordinary powers over their offspring. In fact, a fetus did not become a complete person until birth, which contributed to a legal environment that provided light penalties for abortion and then only to protect the mother's interest (Luk, 1977). When the communist Party took power in 1949, induced abortion was initially prohibited following a Western oriented tradition. However, this policy was reversed in the 1950s and

73. *Ibid.*, Section 16(1). The Act consisted of 16 Sections.
74. The Termination of Pregnancy Act 1974 was amended by the Act of 1980.

there is evidence that abortion is now generally available on demand (Lee, 1973, p. F2). Because of the constraints of medical facilities available, abortions are encouraged as early as possible, many times in informal settings by "barefoot" doctors or midwives. The lack of facilities and the preference for early abortion would seem to be a factor greatly constraining to the use of selective abortion for prenatal sex selection. However, there does not seem to be any formal impediment to using abortion for those purposes.

A new population policy, officially adopted on a national basis in 1981, features a strong incentive system aimed at producing small, preferably one child, and families. Party leaders have acknowledge that ancient traditional practices favoring large families and male children still persist in rural areas and clash with the policy goals of the party. Party officials have announced steps to overcome these ancient traditions.

The steps operate informally through the local leadership, have the force of law, are attempting to create a gender neutral environment in which there is equal pay for equal work regardless of sex and in which families not producing male offspring are not put at an economic or social disadvantaged (Population Council, 1981). This is partly a legal attempt to eradicate the effects of male preference existing in a large portion of the population. Given the difficulty of overcoming these ancient traditions, it would seem that the legal environment would embrace technology that would allow families to realize their son preference and still maintain small families.

However in the absence of this type of technology, the legal environment in China is moving quickly to dampen the social and economic incentives attendant to the sex preferences of rural populations that also contribute to large families. The general principles of this approach were articulated by the marriage law of 1980, which attempted to give gender neutral content to the laws regulating marriage, divorce, and the obligations between parents and children (Population Council, 1981).

8. Sex Selection and Law in Australia

In 1974, the Austrian constitutional Court was confronted

with the question as to whether Art. 2 of the European Convention for the Protection of Human Rights and Fundamental Freedoms, which provides that everyone's rights to life shall be protected by law, is applicable to unborn life. The court refused to included unborn life in the definition of the term 'everyone' as pleaded by the Austrian government, because some member-States did not recognize a right to life for beings yet unborn, and held that the term 'everyone' is limited to born human beings. It was illogical to include protection of unborn life in the Convention, since the Convention provides in certain specified cases for the deprivation of life.[75]

9. Sex Selection and Law in Rome

The Rome Statute of the International Criminal Court, in Article 7 defines "Crimes against Humanity" as any of the following acts when committed as part of a widespread or systematic attack directed against any civilian population, with knowledge of the attack:

- Rape, sexual slavery, enforced prostitution, forced pregnancy, enforced sterilization, or any other form of sexual violence of comparable gravity; and
- Persecution against any identifiable group or collectivity on political, racial, national, ethnic, cultural, religious, gender, or other grounds that are universally recognized as impermissible under international law.

Extermination through systematic murder of newborn female infants and through abortion of female Foetuses [under clause (g) above] is part of the persecution of women as a class [clause (h) above]. In accordance with the Statute then, female foeticide meets the definition of a Crime against Humanity strictly construed and not by analogy.[76]

75. Bonda, "The Impact of Constitutional Law on the Protection of Unborn Human Life: Some Comparative Remarks", 6 Human Rights, 223, pp. 234-235 (1977), in Gaur K.D., The Indian Penal Code, Universal Law Publishing Co., Delhi, p. 502 (2004).
76. *Ibid.*

10. Sex Selection and Law in Germany

In West Germany, while abortion on the ground of rape would be permissible without any strict limit of period, abortion on the ground of saving the mother's health would be permissible only if two requirements are satisfied which are :

- that such abortion should be performed within 12 weeks of the commencement of pregnancy, and
- that the woman should have pre-abortion counseling.[77]

The attitude of the people, influence of religion and various other social, economic and moral factors influence the lawmakers in a country to permit abortion with qualifications, etc. The countries can broadly be classified into four categories, viz.[78]

First, countries that do not permit abortion under any circumstances are Indonesia, Philippines and Ireland where termination of pregnancy is illegal and punishable under the law. Second, countries like Bangladesh, Pakistan, Sri Lanka, and Malaysia permit abortion only to save the mother's life. Third, countries like India, United Kingdom, and United States of America permit induced abortion under prescribed conditions. Fourth, countries like Singapore which permits abortion at the discretion of the woman with no restriction of any sort except that a registered medical practitioner in a hospital or clinic approved by the government should perform it.

---

77. Bakshi, P.M., The writer observes: In India, as in Germany, the Constitution guarantees the right to life. But are both countries, after guaranteeing it, the Constitution does not proceed to define the moment when life begins and the moment when it ends. The question arose in Germany as to how far statutes permitting abortion were constitutional. Ultimately, the judiciary settled on what may be called a compromise and now the German Parliament has responded by reforming the law.
78. Gaur, K.D., The Indian Penal Code, Universal Law Publishing Co., Delhi, pp. 507-08 (2004).

11. Abortion Law in Malaysia

The law of abortion in Malaysia, as stated earlier is contained in sections 312 to 315 of the Malaysian Penal Code Section 312 of the Code punishes causing miscarriage as in case of section 312 of IPC. In 1989 section 312 was amended[79] and an exception clause was added in order to permit termination of pregnancy in certain limited cases, such as when it involves risk to the life or physical or mental health of the pregnant woman. Section 312 of the Code reads.

Whoever voluntarily causes a woman with child to miscarry shall be punished with imprisonment for a term which may extend to three years, or wit fine, or with both; and if the woman be quick with child, shall be punished with imprisonment for a term which may extend to seven years, and shall also be liable to fine.

The section 312 does not extend to a medical practitioner registered under the Medical Act, 1971 who terminates the pregnancy of a woman if such medical practitioner is of the opinion, formed in good faith, that the continuance of the pregnancy would involve risk to the life of the pregnant woman, or injury to the mental or physical health of the pregnant woman, greater than if the pregnancy were terminated.[80] The Exception clause softens the strict provision of law of abortion. It allows termination of pregnancy by a registered medical practitioner, if he is of the opinion formed in good faith that:

(i) The continuance of pregnancy would involve risk to the life of the pregnant woman; or
(ii) Injury to the mental or physical health of the pregnant woman.

12. Abortion Law in Philippines

The Revised Penal Code of Philippines of 1932 in articles

79. S. 5(a) "if such miscarriage be not caused in good faith for the purpose of saving the life of the woman." Was deleted from Section 312 of the Malaysian Penal Code with effect from 5.5.1989.
80. Exception clause was added in S. 312 of the Malaysian Penal Code vide Act A 727/89 S. 9(a) with effect from 5.5.89.

256 to 259 has made induced abortion punishable. Article 256[81] makes intentional abortion and article 257[82] unintentional abortions punishable. Article 258[83] provides punishment in case of abortion practiced by the woman herself or by her parents; and article 259[84] is attracted when abortion is practiced by a physician or midwife who, taking advantage of their scientific knowledge or skill shall cause an abortion or assist in causing the same. In such a case the penalty would be the same as provided under article 256 for intentional abortion. Any pharmacist who, without the proper prescription from a physician, shall dispense any abortive shall be liable to punishment under article 259 of the Code, for arrestor mayor and affine up to 1,000 pesos (Philippines currency).

The Philippines Penal Code like the Penal Code of Indonesia does not permit termination of pregnancy even to save the life of the woman. It is perhaps because of strong influence of Catholic Church which is opposed to and does not allow abortion under any circumstances.

13. Abortion Law in Pakistan and Bangladesh

In Pakistan and Bangladesh 'causing miscarriage' is punishable under section 312 of the respective Penal Codes, as in the case of India. The relevant provisions are contained in sections 312 to 316 of the Penal Codes of Pakistan and

---

81. Art. 256—International abortion : Any person who shall intentionally cause an abortion shall suffer:
    (i) The penalty of reclusion temporal, if he shall use any violence upon the person of the pregnant at woman.
    (ii) The penalty of prison mayor, if without using violence, he shall act without the consent of the woman.
    (iii) The penalty of prison correctional in its medium and maximum periods, if the woman shall have consented.
82. Article 257—Unintentional abortion: The penalty of prison correctional in its minimum and medium periods shall be imposed upon any person who shall cause an abortion by violence, but unintentionally.
83. Article 258, Penal Code of Philippines of 1932.
84. Article 259 provides punishment for abortion practiced by a physician or midwife and dispensing of abortive without proper prescription.

Bangladesh.[85] No serious efforts have been made to liberalize the law of abortion in these countries as a positive step to control the unprecedented explosion of population.

In Bangladesh the population has crossed 110 million in 1993. Bangladesh is perhaps having the highest density of population per square kilometer in the world. Pakistan is similarly facing a population crisis and is unable to control its rise. Thought the policy-makers are aware of the need for liberalization of the law of abortion, it is difficult for the government in these countries to go ahead with any legislation permitting abortion even in limited cases because of the great opposition by fundamentalists and religious leaders.

14. Abortion Law in Sri Lanka

In Sri Lanka abortion is punishable under sections 303 to 307[86] of the Ceylon Penal Code of 1885. The provisions are similar to those contained in sections 312 to 315 of IPC. In Sri Lanka also abortion is permissible only to save the life of the mother as in the case of Malaysia, Pakistan and Bangladesh. It appears that no serious efforts have been made to liberalize the law of abortion in Sri Lanka as yet.

15. Abortion Law in Pennsylvania

The Pennsylvania law requires, (i) a 24 hour waiting period; (ii) approval for minor by a parent or judge; (iii) doctor's telling women about foetal development and alternatives, such as, adoption; (iv) detailed reports by doctors to the government on each abortion performed; and (v) pre-abortion notification of the husband. The court only struck

85. Pakistan Penal Code and Bangladesh Penal Code have incorporated the provisions of the Indian Penal Code dealing with causing miscarriage.
86. Penal Code of Ceylon 1885 is based on the Indian Penal Code 1860 S. 303 provides punishment for causing miscarriage: S. 304 for causing miscarriage without the consent of the woman: S. 305 punishes when death is caused by an act done with intent to cause miscarriage an S. 307 deals with causing death of a quick unborn child by an act amounting to culpable homicide S. 306 holds a person guilty for an act done with intent to prevent a child being born alive or to cause it to die after birth.

down the husband notification provision as undue burden and approved the rest of the provisions. Thus, the Supreme Court allows the states to sharply restrict but no outlaw abortions.

16. Sex Selection and Law in India

In India under the Hindu Law, a son in entitled to have reopened the partition of the ancestral property taking place while he was in the mother's womb without keeping any share reserved for him. In the Law of Wills, both in India and in England, a child in the mother's womb is considered to be in existence and Section 99(1) of the Indian Succession Act, 1925, clearly provides that *"all words expressive of relationship apply to a child in the womb who is after wards born alive"*. The distinction made in the IPC (Section 312 and 316) between *woman with child, and a woman quick with child, and between the unborn child and quick unborn child,* goes to show that a woman is with child during the entire period of her pregnancy, and lexically as well as logically, a child is a person having life. This was pointed out by the Madras High Court in a decision as early as in 1886 in *Queen Empress* v. *Ademma.*[87] The English expression *'pregnant'* means to be with child and the Indian equivalent *'antaswatt'* unmistakably means to have life within.

Modern law relating to sex determination test and abortion has been dealt with in ensuing chapter.

87. Queen Empress *v.* Ademma, (1886) ILR 9 Mad 360.

Laws Pertaining to Sex Determination Test and Abortion in India

There are many constitutional provisions and legislative enactments regarding sex determination test. It ensures not only gender equality in its preamble and recognized as a fundamental right but also empowers the state to adopt measures of positive discrimination in favor of women by ways of legislation and policies.[1]

(A) CONSTITUTIONAL PROVISIONS

Part III of the Constitution of India guarantees various human rights and freedom of the Universal Declaration of Human Rights, 1948 and in the International Covenant on Civil and Political Rights, 1966. Recognition of the human dignity of the individual is elevated to the status of the fundamental

1. Preamble of the Constitution of India, 1950.

Rights. In fact, Part III of the Constitution is characterized as Magna Cart of India. Part III embodies and sanctifies certain fundamental, individual, justifiable rights which are primarily meant to protect and promote the basis human rights of the people and protect the individual against the state action by imposing negative obligations. They are limitations upon all the powers of the government, legislative as well executive and they are essential for the preservation of human right.

The declaration of fundamental rights in the Constitution serves as reminder to the government in power the certain liberties and freedoms essential for all the people and assured to them by the fundamental law of the land are to be respected. Speaking about the importance of fundamental rights, Bhagwati, J. (as then was) observed:

> "These fundamental rights represents the basic valued cherished by the people of this Country (India) since the Vedic times and they are calculated to protect the dignity of the individual and create conditions in which every human being can develop his personality to the fullest extent. They weave a 'pattern of guarantees' on the basic structure of human rights, and impose negative obligations on the State not to encroach on individual liberty in the various dimensions".[2]

However, absolute and unrestricted individual rights do not, and cannot exist in any modern State. Unrestricted liberty and freedom tends to become license and jeopardizes the liberty and freedom of others. The result would be chaos, ruin and anarchy. On the other hand, if the State has the absolute power to determine the extent of personal liberty the result would by tyranny.

Hence, it is very important to make a just balance between conflicting interests of the individuals and of the society. The Constitution of India permits the "reasonable restrictions" to impose on individual's liberty in the interest of the society. Thus, the State can limit the freedom and liberty of

2. Maneka Gandhi *v.* U.O.I., A.I.R 1978 S.C. 597 at 620.

the individuals on those grounds which are prescribed in the Constitution. Anything beyond that will be ultra virus of the Constitution.

I. Right of Equality

According to natural rights theory all human are equal and every human being should get equal opportunity for his/her development. The Constitution of India clearly and fairly provisions the equality under articles 14-18. The right to equality is the faith and creed of our democratic republic. It forms the foundation of socio-economic justice. Article 14 embodies the idea of equality as expressed in the preamble. The succeeding articles 15, 16, 17 and 18 lay down specific application of general rule laid down in article 14 of the Constitution.[3]

This provision is like the provisions of articles 1 and 7 of the universal declaration of human Rights, 1948. Articles 2(2) and 3 of the International Covenant on Economic, Social and Cultural Rights, 1966 also talk about equality among men and women. Articles 3 and 26 of the International Covenant on Civil and Political Rights also mention about the equal rights of men and women and equality before law and equal protection of laws respectively.

The reference to the principles of equality and non-discrimination is also found in the Charter of United Nations. Other basic instruments adopted by the United Nations and specialized agencies which expressly provide for equality and the prevention of discrimination are, International Covenant on the Elimination of All forms of Racial Discrimination; and the Declaration on the Elimination of Discrimination against women.

The principle of equality as enshrined in the Constitution of India is not merely guideline or recommendation but a strict and fundamental provision which imposes on the judiciary the obligation to find out if the legislative, executive and administrative authorities have respected the equality of all individuals.

3. Article 14 provides: *"The State shall not deny to any person equality before the law or equal protection of the laws within the territory of India"*.

However, equal protection of the laws guaranteed under Article 14 of the Constitution does not mean that all the laws must be general in character. In certain cases the States are obliged to adopt laws or take administrative measures which differentiate between individuals and they cannot be said to be discriminatory. Here, Article 14 permits reasonable classification but prohibits class legislation. It must always be remembered that the classification must not be arbitrary, artificial or evasive but must be based on some real and substantial distinction having rational relation with the object to be achieved.

2. Prohibition of Discrimination on Ground of Sex

Applying the general principle of equality, article 15 of the Indian Constitution specifically prohibits discrimination on grounds of religion, race, caste sex or place of birth. This above fundamental right is available to all the citizens of India. The corresponding provision to article 15(1) of the Indian Constitution can be found in article 2 of the universal Declaration of Human Rights, 1948; article 2(1) of the International Covenant on Civil and Political Rights, 1966 and article 2(2) of the international Covenant on Economic, Social and Cultural Rights, 1966.

Once the principle of equality is accepted, it becomes impossible to discriminate against any person or group of person. The principle of non-discrimination is based on equality and dignity. Discrimination can be said to be the denial of the fundamental and universally accepted rights of all human beings to persons or groups of persons who are excluded. In the fast changing world, new grounds for discrimination may also appear, for example, HIV/AIDS infection. Such new grounds have to be tackled carefully without violating the principles of equality.

Indian constitution has conferred equality of status and opportunities to all citizens, whether men or women, including the right to take birth. Article 15(3) provides that special treatment of women on account of the peculiar special position of women in India is justifiable and it is not violative of Article 15(1).

The Constitution guarantees the rights to equality before the law and equal protection of the law[4] The Supreme Court of India has, however, held that differential treatment could be given to people or objects if such differential treatment was based on reasonable classification.[5] The Constitution specifically bars any classification on the ground only of religion or caste or race or sex or place of birth.[6] Therefore, no classification can take place on the ground of sex. But there is a distinct provision which says that the State may make special provisions for the benefit of women and children.[7] This means that classification can be made on the basis of sex which is for the benefit of women.[8]

Article 16 prohibits discrimination on grounds of race, caste, sex or place of birth in any public employment. Right to life and personal liberty is most fundamental of all fundamental rights. Article 21 of the Constitution secures this right to all persons. It provides: "No person shall be deprived of his life or personal liberty except according to procedure established by law". This article advances the object of article 3 of the universal Declaration of Human Rights. Similar provision is also found in article 6 of the International Covenant on Civil and Political Rights.

3. Right to Personal Liberty

The right guaranteed under article 21 is available to both the citizens of India as well as to non-citizens. To begin with, the Indian Supreme Court interpreted the words "personal liberty" narrowly to mean nothing more than the liberty of the physical body, i.e. freedom from arrest and detention, from false imprisonment or wrongful confinement.[9] But in the later years the Supreme Court gave the widest possible meaning to

4. Art. 14, Constitution of India, 1950.
5. Chiranjit Lal *v.* Union of India AIR 1951 SC 41.
6. Arts. 15(1) and (2), Constitution of India, 1950; see also Article 16(2).
7. Art. 15(3), Constitution of India, 1950.
8. Sathe, S.P., "Gender, Constitution and the Courts," Engendering Law—Essays in Honour of Lotika Sarkar (Eds. Dhanda, A. and Parashar, A.), EBC, Lucknow, India, p. 123 (1999).
9. A.K. Gopalan *v.* State of Madras, A.I.R 1950 S.C. 27.

the expression "personal liberty" so as to include within itself all the varieties of rights which go to make up the personal liberty of man other than those dealt with in article 19(1) of the Constitution.

In other words, while article 19(1) deals with particular species or attributes of the freedom, "personal liberty" in particular species or attributes of that freedom, "personal liberty" in article 21 takes in and comprises the residue.[10] In *Maneka Gandhi* v. *Union of India,*[11] Bhagwati, J. (as he then was) while expanding the scope and ambit of article 21 observed:

> "The expression 'personal liberty' in Article 21 is of the widest amplitude and it covers a variety of rights which go to constitute the personal liberty of men and some of them have been raised to be status of distinct fundamental rights and given additional protection under Art. 19".[12] He was further of the opinion that the attempt of the Court should be to expand the reach and ambit of the fundamental rights rather than attenuate their meaning and content by a process of judicial construction.[13]

The Supreme Court has also given very wide interpretation to the expression "life" in article 21 of the Constitution of India. The right to "livelihood" has been held to be implicit in the expression "life" in article 21 of the Constitution. In *Olga Tellis* v. *Bombay Municipal Corporation,*[14] the Supreme Court Observed:

> "The sweep of the right to life conferred by Article 21 is wide and far reaching. It does not mean merely that life cannot be extinguished or taken away as, for example, by the imposition and execution of death sentence, by the imposition and execution of death sentence, except according to procedure established by law. An equally

10. Kharak Singh *v.* State of U.P., A.I.R 1963 S.C 1295.
11. A.I.R 1978 S.C. 597 at 620.
12. Kharak Singh *v.* State of U.P., A.I.R 1963 S.C 1295 at 622.
13. Pathuma *v.* State of Kerala (1978) 2 SCC1.
14. AIR 1986 SC 180 (1985) 3 SCC 545.

important facet of that right is the right to livelihood because; no person can live without the means of living, which is the means of livelihood. If the right to livelihood is not treated as a part of Constitutional right to life, the easiest way of depriving a person of his right to life would be to deprive him of his means of livelihood to the point of abrogation. Such deprivation would not only denude the life of its effective concept and meaningfulness but it would make life impossible to life".[15]

Recently, the Supreme Court of India in the case of *Mohini Jain* v. *State of Karnataka*[16] has interpreted the "right to education" as implicit in the right to life under article 21 of the Constitution. The Court observed: *"Right to life" is the compendious expression for all those rights which the Court must enforce because they are basic to the dignified enjoyment of life. The right to education flows directly from right to life. The right to life under article 21 and the dignity of an individual cannot be assured unless it is accompanied by the right to education"*.[17] Women have been finding place in local governance structures, overcoming gender biases. Over one million women have been elected to local panchayats as a result of 1993 amendment to the Indian Constitution requiring that 1/3rd of the elected seats to the local governing bodies be reserved for women.

In fact neither Article 21 nor any other law confers right to life. Article 21, as its marginal note clearly indicates, gives protection against the deprivation of life. The marginal note mentions; "Protection of life is a basic human right and the absence of which renders all the other rights meaningless, useless and worthless. In today's scenario, this right has received a global recognition and it has been incorporated in almost all the Human Rights legislations all over the world. Of late, the horizon of the right of life[18] has been widened by

15. Delhi Development Horticulture Employee's Union *v.* Delhi Administration, Delhi (1992) 4 SCC 99 at 110.
16. (1992) 3 SCC 666.
17. Unni Krishnan *v.* State of A.P. (1993) 1 SCC 645 at 680-81 where the Supreme Court has limited the right to education up to the age of 14 years as implicit in Article 21 of the Constitution.
18. Article 21 of the Constitution of India, 1950.

judicial interpretation and today it encompasses all the elements which one can thick of as an aspect for leading a complete, clean, healthy and dignified life.[19]

When the right to life is analyzed in the present context, it raises certain thought provoking questions, to which legal responses are to be sought in a comprehensive way. Some of the important questions to ponder are:

(A) Whether foetus is a 'person' and is the right to life under Article 21 extended to an unborn person also?
(B) Has an unborn person right to life protected under article 21 and whether it has a right to be born?
(C) Does a woman have a right over her reproductive organs and to choose whether or not to give birth to a child in the name of her right to privacy under Article 21?

Under the present law, i.e. Medical Termination of Pregnancy Act, 1971, (hereinafter referred to as MTPA, 1971) right to choose whether or not a give birth to a child, has been conferred upon her of course, under specified limited conditions. The MTPA, 1971 has legalized abortion in certain cases which was considered illegal under the Indian Penal Code, 1860. Though the MTPA 1971 indirectly recognizes the right to privacy of a pregnant woman to terminate her right comes in conflict with the unborn person's right to be born.

(i) Is Foetus a 'Person'?

'Foetus' means according to Oxford English Min Dictionary a developed embryo in a womb or egg and 'embryo' means something in an early stage of development. Different views are expressed as to when does life really commence. According to Catholic Church, life commences from the moment of fertilization. Another view is that life beings with zygote's implantation into the uterine wall which occurs six or seven days after fertilization.[20]

---

19. *Ibid.*
20. Ramsey, Reference Points in Deciding about abortion, in the Morality of Abortion Ed. by Noonan, J. (1970), 69-70.

The third view as expressed and adopted by the West German Constitutional Court is that, "life in the sense of the historical existence of a human individual exists according to a definite biological—physiological knowledge in any case from the 14th day after conception".[21]

According to Issac M. Quimby, who wrote in the Journal of the American Medical Association (Aug. 6 1987), on "Introduction to Medical Jurisprudence". This fallacious idea that there is no life until quickening takes place has been the foundation of and formed the basis of and has been the excuse to ease or appease the guilty conscience which hassled to the destruction of thousands of human lives". The American Congress introduced the Human Life Bill in 1981 the premise of which was that, "the life of each human being begins at conception and that 14th Amendment to the US constitution protects all human beings.

The US Supreme Court in *Roe* v. *Wade*[22] held that under the fourteenth amendment, a woman has a privacy right to terminate her pregnancy in the absence of a compelling state interest. In this case an unmarried pregnant woman who wished to terminate her pregnancy by abortion instituted an action in the US District Court for the Northern District of Texas, seeking a declaratory judgment that the Texas criminal abortion statutes which prohibited abortion except with respect to those procured or attempted by medical advice for the purpose of saving the life of the mother were unconstitutional.

The medical termination of pregnancy thus does violence to the right to life of the foetus. It can be said to be violative of article 21 of the constitution as the term life may include potential human life and as life beings at or near conception, the term person may be interpreted to include unborn person also. Since life of the unborn person is deprived or destroyed without procedural due proves under the Medical Termination of the Constitution and makes it unconstitutional.

21. Kommers, Abortion and the Constitution, The cases of the United States and West Germany in Abortion: New Directions for Policy Studies, 94 (Mainer, E., W. Liu and Solomon, D. eds. 1977).
22. 410 US 113 (1973).

The questions as to when does life being and what is the nature of obligation of the State to protect potential human life were not discussed or debated at all in the Constituent Assembly at the time of making of the constitution nor such questions were considered at the time of enacting Medical Termination of Pregnancy Act 1971. The architects of the MTPA 1971 have not taken into consideration the fundamental right, if any of the foetus to be born. It is submitted that life exist in the foetus while in the womb of the mother and in this context Article 21 of the Constitution of India is applicable to unborn person as well.

As 'life' beings at or near conception and the obligation of the Sate to protect such life being from the moment of conception under Article 21 the State cannot permit the deprivation or destruction of such life without the authority of law and without following just fair and reasonable procedure under such law. Foetus is a separate and distinct legal entity existing in the womb of the pregnant mother and its destruction without following the provisions of article 21 under a law like MTPA 1971 would tend to make such law unconstitutional, invalid, illegal and null and void.

The Medical Termination of Pregnancy Act, 1971 provides the substantive aspect for the deprivation of life which exists in foetus, but it fails to provide procedural aspect required under Article 21 for such deprivation of life.

In order to save the MTPA, 1971 from being unconstitutional what is needed is an amendment of Article 21. The existing Article 21 may be mentioned under Clause (1) of Article 21 and clause (2) may be added to article 21 to the following effect. Article 21(2) "Nothing in this Article shall prevent the Parliament from making any law or shall affect the operation of nay existing law depriving an unborn person of its life by termination of pregnancy by a woman if the continuance of pregnancy would involve a risk to the life of the pregnant woman or of grave injury to her physical or metal health or if there is a substantial risk that if the child were born, it would suffer from such physical or mental abnormalities as to be seriously handicapped".

Thus the effect of Clause (2) would be to save the MTPA 1971 from being unconstitutional as it would operate as an exception to article 21(1) and thus the constitutional validity of the MTPA 1971 would not be jeopardized in any way. 'Right to life' includes right of an unborn child to be born, as unborn child is also a person having legal personality.[23]

This will result in an enhancement of the status of an unborn child. When the parents themselves want to get rid of an unborn child, the State acting as parens patriae can claim such right on behalf of the unborn child.[24] Further, the State providing early childhood care and education for all children of 0-6 age group[25] is significant in the context of practice of female infanticide still prevalent in many parts of the country.

In the light of Article 21 of the Indian constitution, female foeticide, by bringing about a physical destruction of an entire class of persons by actively preventing births of members of that class, is a direct infringement on the right to life, dignity and security of person for surviving members of the class.

Sex selection for non-medical reasons violates the basic principles of equality. Devaluation of one sex in favour of another would encourage gender discrimination from the earliest stage of human development. The Indian Constitution forbids any form of discrimination based on sex and thus sex selection violates the fundamental tenets of the constitution.[26] It may be noted that fundamental freedoms granted to an individual under the Indian Constitution are subject to "reasonable restrictions" on the grounds of public good,

---

23. Jain, Ashok Kumar, The Saga of Female Foeticide in India, Socio Legal Offshoots, Ascent Publications, Delhi (2006).
24. *Ibid.*
25. The Constitution 86th Amendment (2001) added a new Art. 21-A after Art. 21 making the 'right of education' of children of the age of 6-14 years a fundamental right It also substitutes a new Article for Art. 45 (directive principles): "the State shall Endeavour to provide early childhood care and education for all children until they complete the age of 6 years".
26. *Ibid.*, The Constitution of India guarantees the rights to equality before the law and equal protection of the law (Art. 14). Articles 15(1) and 15(2) prohibit discrimination on the ground of religion, caste, sex, etc. At the same time, Art. 15(3) give power to the State to make special provision for women and children. Art. 16(2) prohibits discrimination on the ground of religion, caste, sex, place of birth, etc. in respect of any employment or office under the State.

decency, morality, etc., so reasonable restriction on right to abortion in PNDT. The Constitution of India, 1950, guarantees non-discrimination of gender and enjoins upon every citizen a duty to renounce practices that are against the dignity of women:

> Thus, we find that the Constitution of India is an Umbrella over the Human Rights of the citizens of the India. It is in fact the protector of the rights of the people.

The Indian Penal code, 1860, penalizes miscarriage; the Medical Termination of Pregnancy Act, 1971, permits abortion only in certain cases and disallows those which are based on gender; and the Pre-natal Diagnostic Techniques (Regulation and Prevention of Misuse) Act, 1994, penalizes the misuse of pre-natal diagnostic procedures for sex detection. The Act has been amended in 2002 to include cases of pre-conception sex selection. There are also other statutory provisions which prohibits gender discrimination and sex selective test and abortions.

(B) THE MEDICAL TERMINATION OF PREGNANCY (MTP) ACT, 1971

Abortion was legalized in India in 1971 after a 1965 UN mission to India recommended this step to strengthen the population policy. Although the stated reasons for passing the Medical Termination of Pregnancy (MTP) Act were humanitarian (to 'help' victims of sexual assault), health-related (to provide an alternative to those whose contraceptive measures failed) and eugenic (to reduce the number of 'abnormal' children born), there was a strong population control motivation underlying the passage of the Act. During the last thirty years many countries have liberalized their abortion laws. The worldwide process of liberalization continued after 1980. Today only 8% of the world's population lives in countries where the law prevents abortion. Although the majority of countries have very restricted abortion laws, 41% of women live in countries where abortion is available on request of women.

The Abortion Law in India prior to the passing of the Medical Termination of Pregnancy Act, 1971 was given Under Section 312 of Indian Penal Code. The word "miscarriage" used in the section includes not only abortions but also expulsion of viable foetus before the normal birth. The only exception is in case of a miscarriage caused in good faith for the purpose of saving the life of the mother. A demand for the liberalization of the stringent laws on abortion has, therefore, arisen all over the world and most countries have liberalized their laws relating to induced abortions.

I. History of the Act

The need for liberalizing the law relating to induced abortions has also been felt in India because the number of induced abortions in India has been estimated at 65 lakhs per year. The central Family Planning Board, at its meeting held on the 25th August, 1964 expressed anxiety on the reported increase in the number if induced abortion under in sanitary conditions affecting the health and life of the pregnant woman. The Board considered that the question was complex and recommended that a Committee may be formed to examine the question.

(i) Shantilal Shah Committee

Pursuant to the said recommendation of the General Family Planning Board, the General Government appointed in 1964 a Committee with Shri Shantilal Shah, Minister of Law, Health and Judiciary, in the State of Maharashtra, as the Chairman thereof.

After considering the evidence tendered before it and after considering the law on the subject in other countries, the committee submitted its report on the 31st December 1966, recommending, *inter alia* the liberalization of the law relating to induced abortions. The Committee recommended that abortion by qualified medical practitioners acting in good faith, should be permitted not only for saving the life of the pregnant woman but also:

(a) When the continuance of the pregnancy would involve serious risk to the life, or of grave injury to the health, whether physical or mental or the pregnant woman, whether before at or after the birth of child; or

(b) When there is a substantial risk that if the child were born, it would suffer from such physical or mental abnormalities as to be seriously handicapped in life; or

(c) When the pregnancy resulted—
   (i) From rape;
   (ii) From intercourse with an unmarried girl under the age of 16, or
   (iii) As a result of intercourse with a mentally defective woman.

The Committee further recommended that the following conditions should be complied with n connection with the treatment for the termination of pregnancy that is to say—

(a) Induced abortions can be performed only by a person who holds a qualification granted by an authority specified or notified in any of the Schedules to the Indian Medical Council Act, 1956;

(b) The treatment must be carried out in a place for the time being approved for the purpose by the government of India or the State Government;

(c) The opinion must be certified in writing by the medical practitioner who carried out the termination of pregnancy before the treatment is begun;

(d) There has been, before the treatment, the consent in writing by the pregnant woman or if under 18 years of age, the pregnant girl and on of her parents or of the pregnant girl or her guardian for the termination of the pregnancy. But no consent or certification of opinion for the termination of the pregnancy would be necessary for saving the life of the pregnant woman:

   Provided that where the medical practitioner is of opinion that the termination of pregnancy is immediately necessary in order to save the life of the pregnant woman (and certifies his opinion in writing either before or after the treatment) conditions (b) and (d) will not be compiled with.

(ii) Recommendation Regarding Intimations to be given

The Committee also recommended that the Government should prescribe rules requiring qualified medical practitioner, who terminates pregnancy, to give intimation of such termination and such other information relating to the termination as may be prescribed by regulation within such period as may be prescribed and with respect to disposal of certificates. The information so furnish shall not be made public or divulged to any person other than a police officer especially authored to obtain such information or under order of a court of law.

2. Analysis of the MTP Act, 1971

Passing of in pursuance of the recommendations of Shantilal Shah Committee, the Minister for health and Family Planning introduced the Medical Termination of Pregnancy Bill, 1969, in the Rajya Sabha on the 17th November 1969. The Bill was referred to a Joint Committee of both Houses of Parliament, consisting of 33 members (1) from the Rajya Sabha and 22 from the Lok Sabha). The Joint Committee after considering 21 memoranda received by it and the evidence of 26 witness examined by it, amended the Bill and recommended the consideration of the Bill, as amended by it. The amendments which were made by the Joint Committee have ushered in certain anomalies in the Act.

The anomalies have been pointed out at the appropriate place. The Bill, as reported by the Joint Committee, was further amended during its passage through Parliament and the Bill was passed by Parliament and assented by the President on the 10th August, 1971. On receipt of the assent of the President, the Bill became an Act of Parliament but it did not come into force in view of the provisions of sub-section (3) 1 of the Act. The Act came into force on the 1st day of April 1972.[27]

Implemented rules and regulations were again revised in 1975 to eliminate time consuming procedures for the approval

27. Vide Notification No. G.S.R. 285.

of the place and to make services more readily available. One example is the manner in which abortion became legal and available in India—not in response to women's demands but those of the population control lobby. The 1971 law was enacted by a government committed to reducing birth rates, and does not even acknowledge women's right to control their fertility. Abortion is used to promote the government's interests without any concern for the woman's psychological or physical health, or her rights.

The MTP Act, 1971 preamble states, "an Act to provide for the termination of certain pregnancies by registered medical practitioners and for matters connected therewith or incidental thereto".[28] The preamble is very clear in stating that termination of pregnancy would be permitted in certain cases. The cases in which the termination is permitted are elaborated in the Act itself.

Moreover, only a registered medical practitioner who is defined in Sec. 2(d) of the Act as "a medical practitioner who possess any recognize medical qualification as defined in Cl. (h) of sec. 2 of the Indian Medical Register and who has such experience or training in gynecology and Obstetrics as may be prescribed by rules made under this Act" is permitted to conduct the termination of pregnancy. Also other matters connected there with the incidental thereto are incorporated, for example, the question of consent of termination of pregnancy, the place where the pregnancy could be terminated, the power to make rules and regulations in this behalf.

3. Grounds for Termination of Pregnancy

Subject to the provisions of Act pregnancy may be terminated by a registered medical practitioner.

- Where the length of the pregnancy does not exceed 12 weeks if such medical practitioner is, or
- Where the length of the pregnancy exceeds 12 weeks but does not exceed 20 weeks, if not less than 2

28. Bhatt, R.V.; Social Implications of the MTP Act, Manual on Medical Termination of Pregnancy "An Update", 3rd edition, p. 25, FOGSI Publications.

registered medical practitioners are of opinion, formed in good faith that;

- The continuance of the pregnancy would involve a risk to the life of the pregnant women; or
- A risk of grave injury to the her physical or mental health; or
- If the pregnancy is caused by rape; or There exist a substantial risk that, if the child were born it would suffer from some physical or mental abnormalities so as to be seriously handicapped; or failure of any device or method used by the married couple for the purpose of limiting the number of children; or
- Risk to the health of the pregnant woman by the reason of her actual or reasonably foreseeable environment.

The Act does not permit termination of pregnancy after 20 weeks. The medical opinion must of course be given in "good faith". The term good faith has not been defined in the Act but Sec. 52 if the IPC defines good faith to mean as act done with 'due care and caution'. It is important to note that certain loopholes exist in the provisions. Firstly, nowhere has the Act defined what would involve a risk or a grave injury to her mental health.

Where any pregnancy is alleged by the pregnant woman to have been caused by rape, the anguish caused by such pregnancy shall be presumed to constitute a grave injury to the mental health of the pregnant woman. Therefore, rape *per se* is not an indication. It is the mental anguish following pregnancy due to rape, which is the main indication. In other words, mental anguish is to be taken into consideration; proving rape and affecting her character is not necessary. Her allegation that she has been raped is sufficient. Further proof of rape like medical examination, trial, and judgment is not necessary.

Where any pregnancy occurs as a result of failure of any device or method used by any married woman or her husband for purpose of limiting the number of children they anguish caused by such unwanted pregnancy may be presumed to constitute a grave injury to the mental health of the pregnant woman.

The Act says that mental anguish due to pregnancy due to contraceptive failure in a married woman is an indication. Can an unmarried woman avail of this clause? She cannot use this, but she can get abortion under the general clause of mental indication. In determining that whether the continuance of a pregnancy would involve such risk of injury to the health as is mentioned in sub-sec. (2), account may be taken of the pregnant woman's actual or reasonable foreseeable environment.

The provision provides the doctors with a yardstick for a broad interpretation of the basic concept of the potential injury to the mental health of the pregnant woman. The rest of the matters come in the case of mental indication where abortion is allowed and continuation of pregnancy would involve grave injury to her mental health. This is a subjective indication and commonly restored one.

Finally it may be noted that the M.T.P. Act does not protect the unborn child. Any indirect protection it gains under the Act is only a by-product resulting from the protection of the woman. The rights provided as well as the restrictions imposed under the statute show that the very purpose of the state is to protect a living woman from dangers which may arise during an abortion process. It is the protection to the mother that protects the unborn.

4. Qualification of Doctors

According to the Act, 'a medical practitioner who possess any recognized medical qualification as defined in clause (h) of Sec. 2 of the Indian Medical Council Act, 1956 whose name has been entered in a state medical register and who has such experience or training in gynecology or obstetrics as may be prescribed by rules made under this Act is permitted to conduct the termination of pregnancy'. Allopathic doctors who are duly registered with the State Medical Council are authorized to do abortion. Other like homeopathic, ayurvedic, unani doctors and unqualified doctors like RMP, Quacks, *et. al.* are not entitled to perform abortion. Even among allopathic doctors, only those who satisfy one or the other of the following qualifications are eligible to do MTP.

Once a doctor satisfies the require qualifications, he automatically becomes eligible to do abortions. He need not apply for eligibility to any authority. A doctor cannot refuse to do abortions on religious grounds. If he does so, his name is liable to be erased from the Medical Council. If he is a Government doctor, he is liable for departmental action.

5. Consent for Abortion

The MTPA clarifies as to whose consent would be necessary for termination of pregnancy.[29]

(a) No pregnancy of a woman, who has not attained the age of 18 years, or who having attained the age of 18 years, is a lunatic, shall be terminated except with the consent in writing of her guardian.
(b) Save as otherwise provided in Cl (a), no pregnancy shall be terminated except with the consent of the pregnant woman.

It is important to note, in this section, that the consent of the woman is the essential factor for termination of her pregnancy. The husband's consent is irrelevant. Therefore, if the woman wants an abortion but her husband's objects to it, the abortion can still be done. However, if the woman does not wants an abortion but her husband wants, it cannot be done. However, the consent of the guardians is needed in the case of minors or lunatics.

Law also requires certain forms of consents and opinions to be filled in before an MTP, though it is rarely followed to the letter of the law, when a mishap occurs. Lawyers tend to dig out all details to show that the doctor was negligent. Hence, it is always better to at least make notes in proper format on the case paper regarding these matters. A proper consent is extremely important for MTP.

Consent in case of MTP is many times controversial. One thing is certain that an adult woman can give consent for her own MTP, and her spouse's consent is not required. However, it is wise to get either husband or any other adult person's

29. Section 3(4) of the MTP Act.

signature as a witness to the woman's consent. In case of an unmarried girl her boyfriend has no legal status and his consent is not valid in the yes of the law. A doctor got into trouble where a minor girl claimed herself to be a major and signed the consent. As in the eyes of law it is the doctor's responsibility to ensure the age of the patient and to take her guardian's consent if she is minor.

6. Where the Pregnancy can be Terminated

The Act specifies the place where, under MTP, a pregnancy can be terminated.[30] It stipulates that an operation must take place in either "a hospital established or maintained by the government" or in "a place which has been approved for the purpose of this Act by the government". However, exceptions are made for emergencies. Under section 5(1), a doctor may terminate a pregnancy if it is "immediately necessary to save the life of the pregnant woman". In such situations, the requisites relating to the length of pregnancy, the need for two medical opinions and the venue for operation do not apply. However, it needs to be pointed out that one aspect of this emergency clause tends to restricts rather than liberalize the old law. Section 312 of the IPC permitted abortions by anyone with the object of saving the life of the mother, but under MTPA only a doctor can terminate the pregnancy.

7. Mens Rea—Not to Apply

Under the English criminal law, a crime is not committed of the mind of the person doing the act is innocent. The maxim which is followed is *actus non-facit reum, nisi mens sit rea*, i.e. the intent and act must both be present to constitute the crime. The said maxim has however undergone a change. The existence of *mens rea* may be dispensed with by a statute. It has been held by the Supreme Court that where it is absolutely clear that the implementation of the object of the statue would otherwise be defeated that *mens rea* may, by necessary implication, be excluded from a statute[31] *Mens rea* would thus be excluded

30. Section 4 of the MTP Act.
31. Vide Nathulal *v.* State of Madhya Pradesh, A.I.R. 1966 S.C 43.

where any pregnancy is terminated in contravention of the provisions of the Act.

The Act has been so drafted as to give an assurance to the registered medical practitioner that if he terminates any pregnancy in accordance with provision of the act, he will not be committing any offence punishable under the Indian Penal Code.

A question may arise as to whether it is optional for the registered medical practitioner to terminate a pregnancy, even though he is of opinion, formed in good faith, that the termination of such pregnancy on one or more grounds specified in the act is necessary. The act being an enabling one it is difficult to tome a specific conclusion. It seems that if a registered medical practitioner pregnancy on one or more grounds specified in the act is necessary, omits to terminate such pregnancy, he may be hauled up on a breach of his professional conduct.

The next question which arises is whether a medical practitioner who, being of opinion formed in good faith that the termination of a pregnancy is necessary on one or more grounds specified in the act, omits to terminate such pregnancy may be used for damages in the event of the pregnant woman suffering grave injury physical at mental or giving birth to a deformed child. The answer to this question will be found in the law of torts. Section 8 of the act only gives immunity to the registered medical practitioner for anything done or intended to be done in good faith under the Act.

If a registered medical practitioner omits, after forming the opinion that the termination of the pregnancy is necessary on one or more of the grounds specified in the act, he may not be regarded as having acted in good faith. Consequently, the immunity specified in Sec. 8 will not, it seems extend to him and as such he may be successfully sued for damages in any injury to the life or physical or mental health of the pregnant woman is caused by such omission. The question whether the birth of deformed baby may also give rise to an action for damages is not however, free from difficult because the claim for damages by an infant on the ground of "wrongful existence" may not be allowed because there is no method of computation of compensation for a life with defect as against the utter void of non-existence.

The Act does not also provide for the disposal of the foetus or the care of the children born as a result of the termination of the pregnancies. These matters would, be it is presumed dealt with under the existing regulations relating to sanitation and care of children.

8. Social Implications of the MTP Act, 1971

The Government of India has enacted much social legislation since independence. In practice we find that this very good social legislation has remained in the books and the govt. is not able to implement these laws. Take for example, the *antidowry* bill or the Child marriage bill or the *antisati* bill. Child marriages still takes place.

The MTPA is the only social legislation that has found wide acceptance without any resentment. Unwanted pregnancy is a social stress in all societies. Before the MTP Act, unwanted pregnancy was managed by resorting to illegal abortion, infanticide or deserting the newborn in lonely places. Now with the MTP Act, the social fears are considerably reduced and the urban and the rural community have taken advantage of the Act.

The impact of the MTP Act should be judged in the context of changing social values and attitudes. The social implications of MTP in unmarried girls and MTP in married woman are different. MTP in married woman is not considered as a social stigma, whereas MTP in unmarried girls is not easily accepted and hence girls are taken to other distant places for MTP, and hence the girl's social future is not destroyed. This social legislation has certainly reduced incidence of suicide in these women because they can seek safe abortion under the law.

The health of the woman has also shown improvement because of the MTP facilities. The acceptance of the family planning methods after MTP has also increased. It is paradoxical that though the community is taking the advantage of MTP services, they want to maintain secrecy and not let the neighbor about it. How true are the words in context of the present situation in India? The Government must see that MTP is done by trained surgeons only and that to in a hospital set-up.

Gynecologist must also share some blame for MTP complications. The young girls and women come to the gynecologist at any time for MTP. This is because they do not want to inform the parents or other family members about it. Some deaths on operation table have been reported because of the practice of performing quick MTP without proper checkup. It is necessary that gynecologist do not perform MTP at unearthly hours and without proper facilities to fight complications if they do arise.

9. Ethical Issues related to Abortion in MTP Act, 1971

Ethical and legal debate regarding prevention of unwanted pregnancies has been continuing for many years throughout the world, and this has established an idea of legislation of termination of pregnancy within certain terms and conditions. In India MTP Act was passed in 1971 and implemented in April 1972 and revised in 1975.

Basic principle is that pregnancy can bet terminated when there are some maternal and fetal indications, and is to be done by 20 weeks. But in spite of legislative and judicial action, ethical controversies surrounding MTP still continues. Though many people believe that MTP is immoral but in today social context it is a reality. The ethical and legal issues regarding MTP currently revolve around the quality of service, right of the dependent minor to give her own consent for MTP, fetal viability and the coercion. A few of the ethical issues are highlighted here.

10. The Medical Termination of Pregnancy (Amendment) Act, 2002

An Act to amend the Medical Termination of Pregnancy Act, 1971. Be it enacted by Parliament in the Fifty-third Year of the Republic of India as follows:

1. Short title and commencement—(1) This Act may be called the Medical Termination of Pregnancy (Amendment) Act, 2002.

(2) It shall come into force on such date as the Central Government may, by notification in the Official Gazette, appoint.

2. Amendment of section 2—In section 2 of the Medical Termination of Pregnancy Act, 1971 (34 of 1971) (hereinafter referred to as the principal Act):

(i) in clause (a), for the word "lunatic", the words "mentally ill person" shall be substituted;
(ii) for clause (b), the following clause shall be substituted, namely:

(b) "mentally ill person" means a person who is in need of treatment by reason of any mental disorder other than mental retardation.

3. Amendment of section 3—In section 3 of the principal Act, in sub-section (4), in clause (a), for the word "lunatic", the words "mentally ill person" shall be substituted.

4. Substitution of new section for section 4—For section 4 of the principal Act, the following section shall be substituted, namely:

"4. Place where pregnancy may be terminated.—No termination of pregnancy shall be made in accordance with this Act at any place other than—

(a) a hospital established or maintained by Government, or
(b) a place for the time being approved for the purpose of this Act by Government or a District Level Committee constituted by that Government with the Chief Medical Officer or District Health Officer as the Chairperson of the said Committee:

Provided that the District Level Committee shall consist of not less than three and not more than five members including the Chairperson, as the Government may specify from time to time."

5. Amendment of section 5—In section 5 of the principal Act, for sub-section (2) and the Explanation thereto, the following shall be substituted, namely:

(2) Notwithstanding anything contained in the Indian Penal Code (45 of 1860), the termination of pregnancy by a person who is not a registered medical practitioner shall be an offence punishable with rigorous imprisonment for a term which shall not be less than two years but which may extend to seven years under that Code, and that Code shall, to this extent, stand modified.

(3) Whoever terminates any pregnancy in a place other than that mentioned in section 4, shall be punishable with rigorous imprisonment for a term which shall not be less than two years but which may extend to seven years.

(4) Any person being owner of a place which is not approved under clause (b) of section 4 shall be punishable with rigorous imprisonment for a term which shall not be less than two years but which may extend to seven years.

Explanation 1—For the purposes of this section, the expression "owner" in relation to a place means any person who is the administrative head or otherwise responsible for the working or pregnancy may be terminated under this Act, maintenance of a hospital or place, by whatever name called, where he.

Explanation 2—For the purposes of this section, so much of the provisions of clause (d) of section 2 as relate to the possession, by registered medical practitioner, of experience or training in gynecology and obstetrics shall not apply.

(C) THE MAHARASHTRA REGULATION OF PNDT ACT, 1988

A determined campaign against the misuse of amniocentesis and other such test was launched by a group of activities in Bombay, known as the Forum against Sex determination and Pre-selection. This group collected a lot of information on the use of this test and the consequent abortion on discovering that it is a female fetus. According to one report, between 1978 and 1983, 78,000 female fetuses have been aborted after a sex determination test. Many doctors openly justify this practice. They feel that in several parts of the country, if a woman gives birth only to female babies, the husband will either get married again or he, along with his parents, will totally neglect her and the children.

In view of the strong agitations and protests, the Govt. of Maharashtra decided to enact a law against this practice. Surprisingly, there was a lot of opposition to such a law from certain quarters. For those people who had flourishing business out of the practice, it was a question of "bread and butter". Ban on the test would mean loss of business. It was also argued that the government's policy of family planning would be adversely affected. A couple wishing to have a son would end up with many girls and with more females; there would be growth in population. On the other hand, reduction in the number of girls would further decrease the growth of population. These people looked at women as baby producing machines".

Another argument which was given by the opponents of the Act was that the medical termination of pregnancy Act, 1971 legalizes abortion and the same is being resorted to as a family planning measure. Since abortion is legal female foeticide is legal too according to them. The law was also opposed on the ground that those who want to go in for the test would in any case find a way out and goes ahead. The legal ban would only give a boost to private clinics that would raise their charges for the service. The result will be that the poor will suffer. Either they will spend a lot of money for the test which they can ill-afford or have a large family in the hope of getting a son, which again, they are not in a position to bring up.

The fundamental right argument was also advanced. It was argued that it was a woman's right to choose her off-spring and so a ban on the test would be a violation of her fundamental right. Despite all opposition however there was a tremendous pressure on the Government of Maharashtra to pass the law. Consequently, the Maharashtra Regulation of Pre-natal Diagnostic Techniques Act, 1988 was passed. Though the law has been passed it has not helped in solving the problem. This is because of the government's lack of determination and political will. The anti-law lobby also succeeded in getting its provisions diluted.

For example the initial proposal was that private clinics and laboratories should not be given licenses for any pre-natal tests as it would be difficult to exercise control over them but this was opposed and under the Act now, even private clinics and laboratories can get a license. Besides, the very nature of the test is such that control is not easy. The test is simple and does not require sophisticated equipment, etc. all that it requires is a qualified doctor to remove the amniotic fluid which can be tested by a geneticist in any pathological laboratory.

Besides, the Bill is applicable only to the State of Maharashtra and so anyone who wants to have the test done can go to another nearby state and get the test as well as abortion performed, in case of need, without any legal problem. The net result was that the tests continued, clinics flourished and female fetuses aborted thereby bringing down the female populations. The need for a central legislation with stringent provisions was strongly felt. Because of the various pressures on the union government, an expert committee was set-up to look into the matter and submit a report. After a lot of deliberations the committee submitted its report and present Bill is an outcome of that report.

(D) THE PNDT BILL, 1991

As its title shows, the bill has two aspects—regulatory and preventive. It seeks to regulate the use of prenatal diagnostic techniques for legal or medical purposes[32] and prevent misuse for illegal purposes. In order to look into various policy and implementation matters the bill provides for the setting up of bodies along with their composition powers and functions. These are the Central Supervisory Board[33] Appropriate authorities[34] and advisory committees.[35] All said the law is a

32. The Pre-natal Diagnostic Techniques (Regulation and Prevention of Misuse) Bill 1991 cls. 4 and 5.
33. *Ibid.*, cl. IV, cls. 7 to 16.
34. *Ibid.*, cl. V, cl. 17.
35. *Ibid.*, cl. 17(5).

welcome step which seeks to put an end to an atrocious practice of foeticide consequent to a sex determination test.

The Pre-Natal Diagnostic Techniques (Regulation and Prevention of Misuse) Act (the PNDT Act for short) came into being since 1996. This was as a result of a campaign in 1986 that included women's groups and health activists. The campaign resulted in the Maharashtra government appointing a committee, which followed formulation of an Act at the state level in 1988. Given the concern of the then Health Secretary of Maharashtra and other organizations this issue was taken up at the Central government level resulting in the formulation of the Pre-Natal Diagnostic Techniques (Regulation and Prevention of Misuse) Act, 1994 (PNDT Act), which was brought into force from Jan. 1, 1996.

The passing of Pre-natal Diagnostic Tech Act in 1994 also is a step in removing gender discrimination. This Act seeks to end sex-determination tests and female foeticide and prohibits doctors from conducting such procedures for the specific purpose of determining the sex of the fetus.

(E) THE PNDT ACT AT A GLANCE

An Act to provide for the regulation of the use pre-natal diagnostic techniques for the purpose of detecting genetic abnormalities or certain congenital malformations or sex-linked disorders and for the prevention of the misuse of such techniques for the purpose of pre-natal sex-determination leading to female foeticide, and for matters connected therewith or incidental thereto. It consists of six chapters which clearly define:

1. Preliminary.
2. The establishments that conduct these tests, i.e. genetic Counseling centers, genetic laboratories and genetic clinics.
3. Regulation of Pre-natal Diagnostic Techniques.
4. Central Supervisory Board.
5. The administrative structures that need to be set up for the effective implementation of this Act, i.e. the

Central Supervisory board and the State Appropriate Authority and Advisory Committee.

6. Procedure for registration of the establishments, grounds for cancellation or suspension of registration.
7. Offences and Penalties
8. Maintenance of records and power to search and seize records.

(F) THE PRE-NATAL DIAGNOSTIC TECHNIQUES ACT (PNDT), 1994

According to Section 2(k) the pre natal diagnostic test means ultrasonography or any test or analysis of amniotic fluid chorionic villi. Blood or any tissue of a pregnant women conducted defect genetic or metabolic or chromosomal abnormalities or congenital anomalies or hoemoglobinopathies or sex linked diseases.

The all pre-natal diagnostic test can only be conducted by a registered genetic counseling centre, genetic laboratory or Genetic Clinic and no medical geneticist, gynecologist, pediatrician, registered practitioner or no other person shall conduct or cause to conduct any such test without the authorization from the designated appropriate authority under the Act.[36] No laboratory or centre or clinic or any person will conduct any test including ultra-sonography for the purpose of determining the sex of the foetus.[37]

The PNDT test cannot be conducted to determine the sex of the foetus but can be conducted only to detect.[38]

(a) Chromosomal abnormalities
(b) Genetic metabolic diseases
(c) Hoemoglobinopathies
(d) Sex linked genetic diseases
(e) Congenital disease

36. Section 3 of The Pre-Natal Diagnostic Techniques Act, 1994.
37. "Pre-Birth Elimination of Females—A Handbook of Guidelines", by National Commission for Women, 2008.
38. Section 4 of The Pre-Natal Diagnostic Techniques Act, 1994.

(f) Any other abnormalities or disease as may be specified by the Central Government.

No prenatal diagnostic technique can be conducted unless the person qualified to do so is satisfied that any of the following conditions are fulfilled. Thus, such test can be conducted when any of the following conditions are fulfilled:[39]

(i) The Pregnant woman is above 35 years.
(ii) She has undergone of two or more spontaneous abortions or foetal loss.
(iii) The woman has been exposed to potentially teratogenic agents (e.g. radiations, drugs, chemicals, etc.)
(iv) The pregnant women has a family history of mental retardation of physical deformity such as spasticity or genetic disease
(v) Any other condition as specified by the Central Supervisions Board.

A pre-natal diagnostic technique cannot be conducted unless the person conducting the test—[40]

- has explained all known side and after effects of such procedures to the pregnant woman,
- has obtained the pregnant woman's written consent to undergo such procedure in the language she understands, and
- has given a copy of the written consent so obtained to the pregnant woman.

But the Act prohibits the person (authorized) conducting pre-natal diagnostic procedure not to communicate to the pregnant women the sex of the foetus by words signs or in any other manners. So, no person, including the one conducting pre-natal diagnostic procedures as per the law will,

39. Sec. 4(3): The Pre-Natal Diagnostic Techniques Act, 1994.
40. Sec. 5: The Pre-Natal Diagnostic Techniques Act, 1994.

communicate the sex of the foetus of the pregnant woman concerned or her relatives by words, signs or any other method.

Section 6 prohibits the determination of sex as following:

(a) No Genetic counseling centre or genetic laboratory or genetic clinic shall conduct or cause to be conducted in its centre Pre-natal diagnostic techniques including ultrasonography for the purpose of determining the sex of a foetus.

(b) No person shall conduct or cause to be conducted any pre-natal diagnostic techniques including ultrasonography for the purpose of determining the sex of a foetus.

(c) No person shall, by whatever means, cause or allow to be caused selection of sex before or after conception.[41]

(i) Enforcement Machinery of PNDT Act

The central and state supervisory board will have representatives of women welfare organizations, social scientists as well as medical experts.

Sec. 17: The Appropriate Authority (constituted by the state or central government) will have a women's organization representative. The authority will possess powers to summon any person in possession of any information relating to violation of the act. It can also issue search warrant for any place suspected to be indulging in sex selection techniques. Appropriate Authority is appointed by the Central Government under the PNDT Act to perform the following functions:[42]

- Grant, suspend or cancel registration of the Genetic Counseling Centre, Genetic Laboratory or Genetic Clinic.

41. Ins. by Act 14 of 2003, Sec. 9 (w.e.f. 14-2-2003).
42. "Pre-Birth Elimination of Females—A Handbook of Guidelines" by National Commission for Women, 2008.

- Enforce standards prescribed for the Genetic Counseling Centre, Genetic Laboratory of Genetic Clinic.
- Investigate complaints of breach of the rules and provisions of the Act, and take immediate action.
- Seek and consider the advice of the Advisory Committee on registration application and on complaints for suspension or cancellation of registration.

(ii) Penalties under PNDT Act

The Act totally prohibits determination of sex of foetus and its disclosure through medical tests. Violation of this act invites imprisonment from 3 years to 5 years and fine from Rs. 50,000 to Rs. One lakh. Any person who puts out an advertisement for pre natal and pre-conception sex determination facilities in the form of a notice circular, label, wrapper or any other document, or advertises through internet or other media in electronic or print from, or engages in any visible representation made by means of hoarding, wall painting, signal, light, sound smoke or gas, can be imprisoned for up to three years and fined Rs. 10,000.[43] Any medical geneticist, gynecologist, registered medical practitioner or any person who owns a Genetic Counseling Centre, a genetic laboratory or a Genetic clinic where the test is conducted can be imprisoned for up to three years and be required to pay a fine of Rs. 10,000. For any subsequent offence, the fine can go up to Rs. 50,000 and imprisonment to five years.[44]

The person who seeks the aid of a genetic or ultrasound clinic or medical geneticist for sex selection can face imprisonment for a three year period and be required to pay a fine of Rs. 50,000. For any subsequent offence, the fine can go up to Rs. 1,00,000 and imprisonment up to five years. However, the woman who was compelled to undergo such selection will not be fined or imprisoned. Additionally, the court will presume, unless otherwise proved that the woman was compelled by her husband or relatives to undergo pre-natal

43. Sec. 22: The Pre-Natal Diagnostic Techniques Act, 1994.
44. Sec. 23: The Pre-Natal Diagnostic Techniques Act, 1994.

diagnostic techniques.[45] Ultrasound machines, including mobile ones, have to be registered and records of all pre-natal diagnostic tests conducted to be maintained.[46]

(iii) Implementation of PNDT Act

In *Centre for Enquiry into Health and Allied Themes CEHAT* v. *Union of India*[47] the Supreme Court observed that it is apparent that to a large extent, the PNDT Act is not Government nor the Central Government has taken appropriate action for its implementation. The directions issued by the Court mainly emphasized to:

- Create public awareness against the practice of pre natal determination of sex and female foeticide.
- Implement the PDT Act and rules made thereunder with all vigor and zeal.
- Appoint fully empowered advisory committee to aid and advice the Appropriate Authority.
- Appoint advisory committee to aid and advise the Appropriate Authority
- Take prompt action against any body or person who issues or cause to issue advertisement as prohibited U/S 22.
- Take prompt action against such person or bodies who are conducting PNDT test without valid certificate. Appropriate bodies were also directed to furnish Quarterly reports/returns to the Central Supervisory Body about the implementation and working of the Act.

(iv) Flaws in the PNDT Act

Besides the ground realities noted in the functioning of the Act there are some flaws in the PNDT Act.[48] The 2002

45. Sec. 23(3): The Pre-Natal Diagnostic Techniques Act, 1994.
46. Sec. 29: The Pre-Natal Diagnostic Techniques Act, 1994.
47. (2003) 8 SCC 398.
48. Jain, Ashok Kumar, The Saga of Female Foeticide in India, Socio-Legal Offshoots, Ascent Publications, Delhi (2006).

amendment in the PNDT Rules, 1996, inserted two new categories of units—the "Ultrasound Clinics" and the "Imaging Centers". The Rules, however, provide no clear directives on what the requisites are for the registration of such units.[49] It may be noted that those clinics which do not conduct pre-natal diagnostic procedures may obtain registration under these two categories. Though such clinics require registrations, they do not have to keep records in the manner prescribed under the Rules (i.e. a strict referral system), unless the test is in any way related to pregnancy.

In respect of qualification to be possessed by medical professionals in registered unit (GCC, GC or GL), the Rules prescribe additional training/experience. However, it does not provide for a procedure for the certification for such training/ experience or identify institutes or persons who are eligible to provide such certification. Hence, the registering authorities, who are medical professional themselves, have the discretion to decide whether such training/experience are valid or adequate.[50]

The Central Supervisory Board has no statutory representation from radiologists or sonologists.[51] Neither the Act nor the Rules provide for a situation where the advice of the advisory committee is at variance with the opinion of the Appropriate Authority. There appears to be scope for conflict as the Advisory Committee rules prescribe that the advice tendered by the Advisory Committee "Shall be adopted".

However, since the decision making powers are vested in the Appropriate Authority; the final decision has to be taken by him/her. It must, however, be shown that the advice of the Advisory Committee was duly considered while arriving at a final decision.[52]

The Police have no role to play in the implementation of the Act. Hence the Appropriate Authorities have been entrusted with the role of investigation and inspection of units

49. Jaising I (Ed.), Pre-Conception and Pre-Natal Diagnostic Techniques Act—A Users Guide to the Law Publishing Co., Delhi, p. 18 (2004).
50. *Ibid.*, at p. 23.
51. *Ibid.*, at p. 42.
52. *Ibid.*, at p. 49.

as well as the search and seizure of offending objects. There has been apprehension expressed by Appropriate Authorities with regard to undertaking such activities. This is because they feel it is dangerous for a lone medical officer to raid the premise of a unit especially when the unit has political backing.[53]

Another concern often raised by Appropriate Authorities is that they have many other functions to perform and hence are unable to devote enough time to carry out their functions under the Act.[54] The penal provisions in the Act are not strong enough to act as a proper deterrent.

There had been no convictions under the PNDT Act so far. Since the foetus is done away with in secrecy, there is no one left to complain about this breach. There are no witnesses on whose statement a case can be registered. Further, such diagnostic techniques cannot be conducted unless the women who seeks the test should have been informed of the after and the side effects of the procedure and also that her written consent has been obtained.[55]

(G) THE PRE-CONCEPTION AND PRE-NATAL DIAGNOSTIC TECHNIQUES ACT (PCPNDT AMENDMENT OF 2003)

Medical Science is fast developing science. Whereas, the enforcement machinery failed to implement provisions of the PNDT Act, 1994 adequately, Medical Science came up with a new technique of preconception sex selection. The technique made possible selection of sex of the foetus before conception. The concept of Designer Baby became popular and Indian public bought the concept without any hesitation and delay.

Those who could afford started availing facility of prenatal sex selection techniques for conceiving baby of the sex

53. *Ibid.*, at p. 53. The appropriate Authorities could take a police person along with them, as the police have been vested with the responsibility of maintaining law and order under all conditions.
54. *Ibid.*, at p. 47. It is possible for Appropriate Authorities to authorize persons to conduct some functions on their behalf, such as inspections and investigations.
55. "Pre-Natal Diagnostic Techniques: A Source of Gender Bias" by *Kashmir University Law Review-X* (2003).

of their choice. The genes responsible for conception of a female foetus were identified and isolated from the semen before it was used for fertilizing the ovum. This made total exclusion of the girl child at the conception stage itself. This technique forfeited the purposes of the PNDT Act, 1994 and a need was felt to strengthen the law to take care of his new development in Medical Science.

The PNDT (Amendment) Act,[56] 2002 was enacted to take care of the pre-natal sex selection techniques in compliance of directions issued by the Apex Court in the case of *CEHAT* v. *Union of India*.[57] On 17 January 2003, India amended its Pre-natal Diagnostic Techniques (Regulation and Prevention of Misuse) Act, 1994 that was renamed Pre-Conception and Pre-Natal Diagnostic Techniques Act (PCPNDT) of 2003. It was amended after a PIL was filed by CEHAT, MASUM and Sabu George for the implementation of the PNDT Act.

The main law for prosecuting persons who are engaging in sex selective abortion is the Pre-Natal Diagnostic Techniques (Regulation and Prevention of Misuse) Act, 1994 (link with part CPCR/National/Legislation). This Act provides for the prevention of misuse of such techniques for the purpose of pre-natal sex determination leading to female foeticide.

It prohibits misuse and advertisement of pre-natal diagnostic techniques for determination of sex of foetus, leading to female foeticide. It permits and regulates the use of pre-natal diagnostic techniques for detection of specific genetic abnormalities or disorders and use of such techniques only under certain conditions and only by the registered institutions. It gives punishment for violation of the provisions given in the Act.

Now, sex selection and sex determination is crime under the law and is punishable with three years of imprisonment and a fine of Rs. 10,000, besides the fact that his/hers registration to practice as a doctor will also be cancelled. Even advertising about such methods amounts to a crime, punishable under the Act.

(i) Salient Features of the Amendment Act are as under:

56. No. 14 of 2003.
57. (2003) 8 SCC 398.

(1) New sections 3-A and 3-B were inserted after section 3 of the principal Act. Section 3-A prohibits sex selection on a woman or a man or on both or on any tissue, embryo, concepts fluid or gametes derived from either or both of them. Section 3-B prohibits sale of ultrasound machine, etc. to persons, laboratories, clinics, etc. not registered under the Act. Both these sections aim at preventing sex selection tests by restricting sale of required equipments to registered clinics and expert only. The term sex selection and other terms related to the techniques have been defined in the amendment to section 2 of the principal Act.

(2) After section 16 of the principal Act, a new section 16-A has been inserted to provide for constitution of state advisory Board and Union Territory Supervisory Board.

(3) A new section 17-A defining powers of appropriate authority has been added. The appropriate authority was empowered to summon any person, who is in possession of any information relating to violation of provisions of the Act and issue of search warrant of a place suspected to be indulging in sex selection techniques.

(4) Corresponding changing in several other sections required as a result of prohibition of sex selection techniques and sale of ultrasound machines in the amended act were also done by way of amendments in sections 2, 3, 4, 5, 6, 7, 14, 15, 16, 17, 18, 22, 23, 24, 28, 30 and 32 of the Act.

(5) The Central Government made amendments[58] to prenatal diagnostic Techniques (Regulation and Prevention of Misuse) Rules, 1996 also in order to provide for effective implementation of the amended Act.

58. Vide GSR 109 (E) dated 14th February, 2003, published Gazette of India, Extraordinary-Pt., Sec. 3(i), dated 14th February, 2003.

The 2003 amendment is designed to strengthen the provisions of the previous Act. It prohibits the causing of sex selection before or after conception. It enlarges the scope of procedures and tests that are prohibited and categories of clinics and laboratories that are subject to the provisions of the Act. It prohibits the sale of any ultrasound machine or imaging machine or scanner or any other equipment capable of detecting the sex of a foetus to any clinic or person not registered under the Act. It prohibits any procedure, technique, test or the administration of anything for the purpose of ensuring or increasing the probability that an embryo will be of a particular sex. It requires persons carrying out tests allowed by the Act to keep records.

It provides for imprisonment of up to five years and a fine of up to Rs. 1,00,000 for violators of the Act. It enlarges the powers of officials to enforce the provisions of the Act. It creates state boards to monitor the implementation of the Act. The Government has taken action on strengthening the Pre-Conception and Pre-Natal Diagnostic Techniques Act (PC and PNDT Act) as well as creating awareness on the issue through various IEC mechanisms.

Some of the steps taken by the Government to improve the CSR in the country are: Constitution of the Central Supervisory Board under the Chairmanship of Union Minister of Health and Family Welfare, whose function, *inter alia*, is to review and monitor implementation of the Act and Rules and Regulations made thereunder and recommend to the Central government changes in the said Act and Rules, where required, and to create public awareness against the practice of pre-conception sex selection and pre-natal determination of sex of foetus leading to female foeticide; constitution of the National Inspection and Monitoring Committee for undertaking field visits periodically across the country and constitution of the National Support and Monitoring Cell for effective implementation of the Act, training of Judiciary, publication of Annual Reports, Frequently Asked Questions (FAQs), On-Line Complaint facility on the Ministry's Website, organizing sensitization workshops/seminars, launching of 'Save the Girl Child' campaign, seeking cooperation from the NGOs/religious leaders, etc. Further, under the National Rural Health Mission,

Auxiliary Nursing Midwife (ANM) and Accredited Social Health Activist (ASHA) are being sensitized on the issue. Also, funds have been provided to all States/UTs under the Rural Child Health Programme for implementation of the Act and related activities.[59]

(H) OTHER STATUTORY PROVISIONS REGARDING SEX DETERMINATION TEST

I. Indian Penal Code, 1860

Even in modern criminal law, abortion is a serious crime. The Indian Penal Code however, nowhere mentions the word abortion. We find sections 312 to 316 dealing with miscarriage. In common parlance the two words are used interchangeably. However, in medical terminology, miscarriage technically refers to spontaneous abortion, whereas voluntarily causing miscarriage, which is an offence under the code, stands for criminal abortion. Medically, three distinct terms, viz. abortion, miscarriage and premature labour are used to denote the expulsion of a foetus at different stages of gestation.

Following provisions can be used to prosecute for Female Foeticide, Infanticide or sex selective abortions:

- Culpable Homicide and Murder (Section 299 and Section 300).
- Voluntarily cause a pregnant woman to miscarry the unborn baby (Section 312).
- Causing miscarriage without woman consent. (Section 313).
- Death caused by act done with intent to cause miscarriage. (Section 314)
- Act done with intent to prevent a child being born alive or to cause it to die after birth (Section 315).
- Causing death of an unborn child (Section 316).
- Exposing and abandoning of a child below 12 years (Section 317).

59. Smt. Panabaaka Lakshmi, Minister of State for Health and Family Welfare, written reply to a question in the Lok Sabha.

- Concealing the birth of a child by secretly disposing her/his body (Section 318).
- The punishment for these offences extends from two years up to life imprisonment, or fine or both.
- (Section 375).
- Section 376A, 376B, 376C, 376D.

When death of a pregnant woman or female foetus is caused by a person and the elements of Sec. 299 or Sec. 300 is proved then he will be liable for culpable homicide or murder. Section 312 of IPC defines, 'causing miscarriage' as follows: Whoever voluntarily causes a woman with child to miscarry, if such miscarriage be not caused in good faith for the purpose of saving the life of the woman, be punished with imprisonment of either description for a term which may extend to three years, or with fine, or with both; and, if the woman be quick with child, shall be punished with imprisonment of either description for a term which may extend to seven years, and shall also be liable to fine.

Explanation—A woman, who causes herself to miscarry, is within the meaning of this section.

To attract the provisions of section 312 of the code two elements must be satisfied, viz., (i) miscarriage should have been caused voluntarily; and (ii) miscarriage should not have been caused in good faith for the purpose of saving the life of the woman.

The framers of the Code have not used the word 'abortion', in section 312, which relates to an unlawful termination of pregnancy. This was perhaps done to avoid hurting the sentiments of traditionally bound and conservative Indian society. The section speaks of 'miscarriage' only, which has not been defined in the Code. However, miscarriage, in its popular sense, is synonymous with abortion and consists in the expulsion of the embryo-foetus at any time before it reaches full growth.

Miscarriage technically refers to spontaneous abortion, whereas voluntarily causing miscarriage, which is an offence under the Code, stands for criminal abortion. Legally miscarriage means the premature expulsion of the product of conception, an ovum for a foetus, from the uterus, at any time before the full term is reached. Medically, three distinct terms, viz., abortion, miscarriage and premature labour are used to denote the expulsion of a foetus at different stages of gestation.

The terms abortion is used only when an ovum is expelled within the first three months of pregnancy, before placenta is formed. Miscarriage is used when a foetus is expelled from the fourth to the seventh month of the gestation, before it is viable, while premature labour is the delivery of a viable child possibly capable of being reared, before it has become fully matured.[60] A distinction is made under section 312 of the Code between causing miscarriage when a woman is 'with child' and quick with child'. As per judicial interpretation, a woman is considered to be in the former stage as soon as gestation begins and in the latter stage when the motion is felt by the mother. In other words, quickening is apperception by them mother that movement of the foetus has started. It obviously refers to an advanced stage of pregnancy.

Sec. 312 of the Code permits termination of pregnancy on therapeutic (medical) grounds in order to protect the life of the mother. The unborn child in the womb must not be destroyed unless the destruction of the child is for the purpose of preserving the yet more precious life of the mother. The provision by implication recognizes that the foetus has the right to life.

The Explanation clause appended to section 312 of the Code makes it clear that the offender could be a woman herself or any other person. The desire of a woman to be relieved of her pregnancy is no justification for termination of pregnancy. As early as 1886 in Ademma,[61] a woman was charged under section 312 of the Code for causing herself to miscarry, though she had been pregnant for only one month, and there was nothing which could be called even a 'rudimentary', 'foetus' or 'child'. The lower court acquitted the woman taking a lenient view of the matter and held that as the prisoner had been pregnant for one month only, she could not be said to have

60. Modi Medical Jurisprudence 325.
61. Sarinattudnga *v.* Government of Mysore (1935) 13 May, L.J. 69, See Gaur, K.D., Criminal Law Cases and Material 499-504 (1985) for a detailed discussion on the subject.

been 'with child' within the meaning of section 312 of the Code. But the High Court held the acquittal bad in law emphasizing that it was the absolute duty of a prospective mother to protect her infant from the very moment of conception.

As stated earlier, S. 312 of IPC permits termination of pregnancy on therapeutic (medical) grounds in order to protect the life of the pregnant woman. It means the unborn child in the womb must not be destroyed unless the destruction of the child is for the purpose of preserving the yet more precious life of the mother. A careful perusal of the provisions of IPC reveals that the law on abortion was very harsh.

It was estimated that before the enactment of MTPA, 1971, as many as five million induced abortions were carried out in India every year, of which more than three million were illegal and approximately one-seventh of women who became pregnant were resorting to back street abortions at the hands of inexperienced and unqualified persons such as quacks and paramedical personnel like nurse, midwives, etc. in strict secrecy to avoid the horror of law, through a variety of crude and unhygienic methods for paltry sums of money ranging from Rs. 5 to Rs. 300, with all risks of morbidity and mortality. At times greedy doctors would exploit helpless victims by extorting a huge sum of money for terminating a pregnancy. A change in the existing law was advocated now and then by doctors, social workers, etc.

A person is also liable for attempt to commit a criminal abortion under Section 312 read with section 511 of IPC, even if he fails in his endeavor. For instance, the Calcutta High Court in *Queen* v. *Arunja Bewa*[62] where the term of pregnancy was almost complete, and an attempted abortion resulted in the birth of the child, set aside a conviction under section 312 and maintained conviction under section 312 read with section 511 of the Code for attempt to commit miscarriage.

In *Munah Binti Ali* v. *Public Prosecutor,*[63] (a case from Malaysia) the accused, who tried to procure an illegal abortion,

62. (1873) 19 W.R. (Cr.) 32.
63. (1958) 24 M.L.J. 159 (C.A. Malaysia) Penal Codes of India, Pakistan, Bangladesh, Malaysia and Singapore in S. 511 provide punishment for attempting to commit offences punishable with imprisonment for life or other imprisonment.

be inserting an instrument into a woman's vagina with the view thereby of causing a miscarriage was held guilty of an attempt to cause abortion by the lower court under section 312 read with section 511 of the Malaysian Penal Code and sentenced to three months' imprisonment, through the woman unknown to the parties was not pregnant. Dismissing the appeal against the conviction, the High Court of the Federation of Malaya by a majority of two to one held that in a charge of attempting to cause a woman to have a miscarriage, it is not necessary for the court to be satisfied that the woman is 'with child' before that court proceeded to convict.

On the other hand, in *Asgarali Pradhania* v. *Emperor*[64] the Calcutta high Court held the accused not guilty of an attempt to cause miscarriage under section 312 read with section 511, IPC as the material sought to be made use of for termination of pregnancy were not harmful.

In *In re Malayara Setthu*[65] the appellant was convicted by the lower court under section 312 of IPC for having caused miscarriage on or about 30.11.1952 to a girl Ammayya and sentenced to rigorous imprisonment of two years and a fine or Rs. 300. The child in this case was born alive and the pregnancy was beyond seven months. Setting aside the conviction of the appellant, the High Court of Mysore held:

> Medically this is a case of premature labour and not of miscarriage. Acts of doctors and nurses which facilitate or accelerate delivery cannot be treated as offences under the section only because the delivery otherwise would have been delayed and particularly when the child is born alive and no injury is caused to the mother of the child as the case may be.[66]

(i) Abortion on Therapeutic Grounds

As stated earlier, Section 312 of IPC Permits termination of pregnancy on therapeutic (medical) ground in order to protect the life of the mother. The unborn child in the womb must not

64. A.I.R. 1932 Cal. 893.
65. A.I.R. 1955 Mys. 27.
66. *Ibid.*, at p. 29.

be destroyed unless the destruction of the child is for the purpose of preserving the yet more precious life of the mother. The provision by implication recognizes the foetus has a right to life.

However, the Austrian constitutional courts in 1947 refused to recognize 'right to life' to unborn life.[67] The court was confronted with the question as to whether article 2 of the European Convention for the Protection of Human Rights and Fundamental Freedom, which provides that 'everyone's right to life' shall be protected by law is applicable to 'unborn life' or not. The court refused to include 'unborn life' in its definition of the term 'everyone' as pleaded by the Austrian Government, because some states did not recognize a right to life for human beings yet unborn, and held that the term 'everyone' is limited to 'born human beings'.

It was illogical to include protection to unborn life in the Convention, since it provides for the deprivation of life in certain cases.

To claim exemption from criminal liability on therapeutic grounds, the threat of life, however, need not be imminent or certain. If the act is done in good faith[68] the person is entitled to the protection of law. But good faith is deceptive and ambiguous enough to protect most therapeutic abortions so long as they are conducted ostensibly to preserve the mother's life. In fact, what constitutes good faith is not a question of law, but of is to decide in each and every case according to its facts and circumstances.[69]

(ii) Inadequacy of Law to Protect Illegal Abortions

A careful perusal of the provision contained in Section 312

67. Bonda, "The Impact of Constitutional Law on the Protection of Unborn Human Life: Some Comparative Remarks", 6, Human rights 223 at 234-5 (1977).
68. Penal Code, S. 52, says, 'Nothing is said to be done or believed to be done in "good faith" which is done or believed without the due care and attention, see. Royal College of Nursing *v.* Department of Health and Social Security, [1981] 1 AII E.R. 545 (H.L.).
69. See. Rex *v.* Bourne, Held all therapeutic abortions are lawful. R *v.* Smith, [1974] 1 AII ER 376 D.S. David, "The Law of Abortion and Necessity", L.R. 126 (1938).

to 316 IPC would reveal that the law of abortion in India, till the enactment of the medical termination of Pregnancy Act 1971, was very strict.[70] It was estimated that before the enactment of that Act as many as five million inducted abortions were carried out in India every year, of which more than three million were illegal[71] and approximately one-seventh of women who become pregnant were resorting to back street abortions at the hands of inexperienced and unqualified persons, such as quack and paramedical personnel, like nurses, midwives, etc., in strict secrecy to avoid the horror of law, through a variety of crude and unhygienic methods for paltry sums of money ranging from Rs. 5 to Rs. 300, with all the risks of morbidity and mortality.[72]

At times greedy doctors would exploit helpless victims by extorting a huge sum of money for terminating a pregnancy. The rigidity of legal provisions in seeking public men, doctors, social workers and social scientists who advocated deforms now and then, the changed attitude towards a liberalized law of abortion really came about only when the idea was mooted by the Central Planning Board of the Government of India in 1964 as a family planning measure.

The apathy on the part of the social reformers and government was perhaps because of the fear of opposition by fundamentalists, fanatics, anti-abortionist groups and conservative religious leaders against any circumstances. Religion, in a traditionally bound and conservation society like India, Malaysia, Indonesia, Pakistan, Bangladesh, Shri Lanka, etc., in fact, plays a dominant role and commands a major influence upon the social development and value orientation of the populace.

70. Section 3 of Medical Termination of Pregnancy Act, 1971 for grounds of termination of pregnancy.
71. See. Bahandur, K.P., Population Crisis in India 165-9 (1977): Menon, N.R. Madhava, "Population Policy: Law Enforcement and the Liberalization of Abortion: A Socio-Legal Inquiry into the Implementation of the Abortion, Law in India", 16 J. I.L.I. 626 at 632-3 (1974): see. Michel Arnold E., "Abortion and International Law", 22 J. Fam. L. 24 (1982).
72. Bose, Asit K., "Abortion in India: A Legal Study", 16 J.L.I. 53 (1974).

There was an unprecedented uneasiness in the Ministry of Health and Family Welfare over the large number of abortions taking place in the county.[73] The Government of India was much concerned about the unprecedented rise in population. India's population on 1 March 1991 stood at 846.30 million (439.23 million males and 407.07 females),[74] which has further gone up to 900.03 million as on 10 July 1994.[75] India's population has doubled itself since 1974.[76] With the present growth rate of population it is expected that it will cross the watermark of 1,000 million by the end of the twentieth century. As a consequence, whatever progress India has made in economic, scientific, technological, social and educational fields during the last hour and a half decades have been partly diluted and whittled down. In fact, the population increase alone had absorbed more than 50 percent of the economic growth, leaving the level of living in almost the same position as before the second largest county in the world, next only to China, India is the home of 16 percent of the world's population.[77]

(iii) Steps to Liberalize Law of Abortion

As stated above one of the most crucial problems India is facing today is the burgeoning population, which has been growing at an alarming rate. It is increasing by about 17 million per year. Such a rapid increase in population has very serious repercussion on socio-economic development. Visualizing the gravity and magnitude of the enormous increase in population and its adverse effect on the one hand, and hardships caused to

---

73. Gandhian Institute of Rural Health and Planning in the State of Tamil Nadu estimated that out of every 100 conceptions 25 were abortions, 15 induced and 10 spontaneous.
74. Ministry of Information and Broadcasting, Govt. of India, INDIA 1993: A Reference Manual 7.
75. B.B.C. World Service Broadcast dt. 11 July 1994 on world Population Day.
76. See, *Indian Express*, 19 Oct. 1992, p. 8.
77. Ministry of Information and Broadcasting, Govt. of India, INDIA 1993: A Reference Manual 7 at 215. India was partitioned in 1947 by the British into (present) India and West and East Pakistan. East Pakistan later separated from West Pakistan and is now Bangladesh.

women as a result of the draconian law of miscarriage on the other, the government of India in 1964 constituted a committee to study the question of liberalization of the law of miscarriage (abortion) contained in section 312 of IPC which makes induced abortions illegal except to save the life of the women.

After making a careful study of the pros and cons of the entire issue and taking a pragmatic view of the socio-economic and legal problems involved in cases of unwanted pregnancies, the committee recommended to the Government of India, amendment in the out-dated and outlived law of miscarriage contained in section 312 of IPC.

(iv) Hurdles in Implementation of MTP Act, 1971

Though section 3 of MTPA as explained earlier, has legalized termination of an unwanted pregnancy in a number of situations, there are many difficulties in the successful implementation of the provisions of the Act on various counts. According to the Explanation clause 1 to sub-section (2) to section 3 to the Act,[78] abortion is not permitted if the pregnancy is caused as a result of an illegal sexual connection other than rape. Hence termination of a pregnancy in such a case would be criminal and punishable under section 312 of IPC.

(v) Causing Miscarriage without Woman Consent

When the termination of pregnancy is caused without the consent of the woman, punishment may extend to imprisonment for life or imprisonment of either description for a term which may extend to ten years and fine.[79]

(vi) Death Caused by Act done with Intent to Cause Miscarriage

If the death of the woman is caused by an act done with intent to cause miscarriage with her consent punishment may extend to ten years of imprisonment and fine, and if it is done without her consent, imprisonment for life or ten years and fine.[80]

---

78. MTP Act 1971, S.3(2) Explanation.
79. Section 313 of The Indian Penal Code, 1860.
80. Section 314 of The Indian Penal Code, 1860.

(vii) Act done with Intent to Prevent a Child being Born Alive or to Cause it to Die after Birth

An act done with intent to prevent a child from being born alive or to cause it to die after birth is punishable up to ten years of imprisonment or fine or both.[81]

(viii) Causing Death of an Unborn Child

And the causing of death of a quick unborn child (advanced stage of pregnancy) by an act mounting to culpable homicide is punishable up to ten years of imprisonment and fine.[82]

Section 316 punishes the causing of death of a quick unborn child by an act amounting to culpable homicide.[83] Illustration appended to this section reads: A, knowing that he is likely to cause the death of a pregnant woman, does an act which, if it caused the death of the woman, would amount to culpable homicide. The woman is injured, but does not die; but the death of an unborn quick child with which she is pregnant is thereby caused. A is guilty of the offence defined in this section.

According to Sec. 317, exposure and abandonment of a child under 12 years in any place by parents or persons having care of the child with the intention of wholly abandoning it is an offence.[84] If the child does in consequence of the exposure, the offender will also be guilty of murder or culpable homicide as the case may be (Explanation to Sec. 317).

This section is intended to protect infants/children of tender years, who are unable to take care of themselves. In India, abandonment of a girl child is not an uncommon phenomenon. Cases of female infanticide could be covered under Sec. 317.

---

81. Section 315 of The Indian Penal Code, 1860.
82. Section 316 of The Indian Penal Code, 1860.
83. The punishment prescribed is imprisonment up to 10 years and fine. The offence (as under Sec. 315) is cognizable, non-bailable, and non-compoundable and is triable by a Sessions Court.
84. The punishment prescribed is imprisonment for 7 years, or with fine, or both. The offence is cognizable, bailable, and non-compoundable and is tribal by a Magistrate of First Class.

Intentional concealment[85] of (or endeavor to conceal) the birth of a child by secretly burying or otherwise disposing of the dead body of the child, whether such child dies before or after or during the birth, is an offence under Sec. 318.[86] The essential ingredient of this offence is that the culprit must secretly dispose of the dead body of a child. If he disposes of a living child, then Section 317 would cover the action of the culprit. The secret disposal of the body must be with the sole intention of concealing or attempting to conceal its birth. If it is a foetus only, then Sections 312 and 511 (Attempt) of the Code will apply.

This section has relevancy in cases where people try to hide their sinful acts of foeticide/infanticide (especially female) in order to escape liability under the provisions of the Code (Sections 312-317).

Karnataka is the only State that has authorized non-medical officers such as officials in the State Women's Commission to take action for non-registration of diagnostic machines and maintenance of records of all medically terminated pregnancies. In fact, the State Women's Commission has jointly worked with Vimochana (a forum for Women's rights, fighting the menace of female foeticide in Bangalore and Mandya districts) to conduct several raids on clinics and nursing homes suspected of conducting sex-determination tests and sex-selective abortions in Bangalore and Mandya districts.[87]

Section 375 of the IPC enumerates six situations under which sexual inter-course by a man a woman would amount to rape.[88] The gist of the offence consists in, (i) having sexual intercourse with a woman against her will; or (ii) without her consent; or (iii) when consent was obtained by putting her or any person in whom she is interested into fear of death or

---

85. Section 318 of The Indian Penal Code, 1860.
86. The punishment prescribed is imprisonment up to 2 years, or with fine, or both. The offence is cognizable, bailable, non-compoundable, and triable by a Magistrate of First Class.
87. Anonymous, "Karnataka in Grip of Son Syndrome", *The Times of India*, New Delhi, June 12 (2005).
88. S. 375 of the Indian Penal Code was amended in 1983 vide the Criminal Law (Amendment) Act, 1983.

physical hurt; or (iv) with her consent, when consent was procured under a misconception of fact that the man was her husband; or (v) with her consent, when, by person of unsoundness of mind or intoxication, etc., she is unable to understand the nature and consequences of that to which consent was given; or (vi) with or without consent when she is under sixteen years of age and is incapable of giving consent in law.

According to the principle of criminal jurisprudence, a man is presumed to be innocent, until his guilt is established in a court of law beyond reasonable doubt. Hence the question arises, as to whether the woman subjected to rape should postpone the termination of her pregnancy till the charge of rape is established in a court of law an the accused is found guilty, or get the pregnancy terminated during the pendency of the trail. In the latter case, if the man charged of rape is acquitted of the offence, the woman would be liable to punishment under section 312, IPC for causing illegal abortion.[89] And if the former course is adopted, no abortion could be possible, because a case would take a minimum of three to four years before it is finally disposed of by court of law.

According to sections 376B,[90] 376C,[91] and 376C[92] of (added vide Criminal Law (Amendment) Act 43 of 1983) sexual intercourse by, (i) a public servant with a woman in his custody, (ii) a superintendent of a jail, or remand home, etc., with any female inmate of such jail, remand home, or (iii) any member of the management or staff of a hospital with any woman employee in that hospital has been made an offence and punishable under IPC.

---

89. In such a situation the doctor procuring the abortion would also be guilty of causing miscarriage under S. 312 IPC.
90. S. 376B, IPC provides punishment for intercourse by a public servant with a woman in this custody.
91. S. 376C, IPC deals with interfuse by the superintendent of a jail and remand home, etc., with any female inmate if such institutions.
92. S. 376D, IPC makes intercourse by any member of the management staff of a hospital with a woman in that hospital punishable.

Sections 376-B to 376-D of IPC comprise a group of sections that create a new category of sexual offences which do not amount to rape, because the consent of the victim is given in such cases under compelling circumstances.[93] In fact, these offences are committed by those persons who happen to occupy a supervisory position an powers in the institution under their control and they take undue advantage of their authority and position an obtain consent of the woman by inducing or seducing her for sexual intercourse. For instance, if a senior officer has sexual intercourse with his junior taking advantage of his authority, the case will fall under section 376-B of IPC.

Likewise, if a sexual intercourse is committed by a superintendent of a jail, or remand home on a lady inmate or by a management staff of a hospital on a woman in the hospital staff, sections 376-C and section 376-D are attracted.

Thus, if a pregnancy is caused as a result of intercourse falling under sections 376B, 376C and 376D of IPC it will not amount to have been above cause by rape, which would entitle the woman to get the pregnancy terminated under section 3 of MTPA since consent of the woman for intercourse is implicit in the act.

Similarly, Section 376A.[94] IPC fails to take note of a special situation where the husband and wife are living separately under a decree of judicial separation by mutual consent. In such a case marriage subsists in law, and if the husband has sexual intercourse with his wife without her consent, the wife cannot for termination of pregnancy, should she become pregnant because sexual intercourse under such circumstances would not be rape within the meaning of section 375 of IPC to justify termination of pregnancy under section 3(2) of MTPA.

To obviate such a difficulty the following explanation clause may be added to section 3 of MTPA which would entitle

93. See, Gaur, K.D., A Text-book on the Indian Penal Code, Universal Law Publishing Co. pp. 539-41 (1992).
94. S. 376A, IPC makes intercourse by a man with his wife during judicial separation punishable with imprisonment up to 2 years and fine.

a woman to get her pregnancy terminated in the circumstances falling under section 376-A, 376-B, 376-C and 376-D of IPC.

2. Female Infanticide Act, 1870 (Act viii of 1870)

The evil of female infanticide was quite prevalent among Rajputs (western India) known for the fierce pride in their race.[95] There was extreme pressure of caste status in the marriage of Rajput girls. There were sanctions as to whom one could marry and pride prevented marriage to anyone except to an acknowledged equal, generally, of course, a superior. Although the Rajputs took many wives, they considered girl child a curse.[96]

Since the high status Rajputs were solely dependent on agricultural land to buttress their socio-economic status (they tried to avoid high dowries and land alienation through female infanticide), they practiced female infanticide to such an extent that British officials were horrified to find whole taluks and villages without even a single Rajput female child in peninsular Gujarat and the North-Western Provinces (later the United Provinces).[97]

In Punjab, among Jat Sikhs, the concept of "honour killings" of girls was prevalent. A critical study of the society reveals that the concept of individual rights has never been developed in Punjab though struggles for group rights have been exemplary. While the women are deprived of their rights, they are treated as the hallmark of the family's honour, though only to get targeted while settling family disputes.[98] The British assumed a moral high ground to condemn female infanticide

---

95. Jain Ashok Kumar, "The Saga of Female Foeticide in India, Socio-Legal Offshoots, Ascent Publications, Delhi (2006).
96. P. Misra, Female Infanticide: A Threat to Posterity", *NISD Journal*, pp. 23-25 (2002).
97. L.S. Vishwanath, "Female Foeticide and Infanticide", *Economic and Political Weekly*, September 1 (2001), available at www.epw.org.in.
98. Pandher, S., "Deep-rooted Evil", *The Hindu*, August 19 (2001). The concept of purity of identity and the evolution of the Sikhs as a "Marital race" have contributed to the practice of female infanticide, which has now metamorphosed into female foeticide. On the doorstep of the office of Akal Takht Jathedar in the Golden Temple complex in Amritsar, stand two 'Nishan Sahibs' where the 'kesari'

because unlike 'sati', they proved; it did not have any religious sanction. Wilson has extensively quoted from Puranas to show that infanticide was criticized even in the scriptures. Nor did it originate with the coming of Muslims.[99] The female infanticide Act, 1870 was thus enacted which made female infanticide an illegal practice. It was enforced on 17th April, 1871. It provided a system of compulsory registration of births, deaths, betrothals marriages and remarriages by a Registrar appointed for the purpose by the government. The Act was, however, difficult to enforce in a vast country like India. Most births were non-institutional and registration of births and deaths was uncommon. The high infant mortality rate due to natural causes could easily camouflage suffocation or poisoning of the infant girl. Furthermore, no one felt morally compelled to report such incidents for gear of getting embroiled in disputes and achieving nothing in the process.[100] The Act was repealed in 1906. However, the efforts of British officers did not prove totally in vain. With respect to infanticide practices a gradual disliking was strengthened due to growth of education.

Voluntary Health Association of India, available at http://indiafemalefoeticide.org. The national and State Governments announced various schemes of financial incentives to persuade families to save their daughters. The schemes suffer from the basic flaw that the poor are primarily escalating these practices.[101] The practice has become quite common in middle-income and also high-income groups.

---

cloth cover is changed every day. According to a recent study conducted by the Institute for Development and Communication (IDC), like at many other places all over the State, those who seek blessings for a male child sponsor 95 per cent of such activity.

99. Y. Snehi, Female Infanticide and Gender in Punjab: Imperial Claims and Contemporary Discourse", *Economic and Political Weekly*, October 11 (2003), available at www.epw.org.in

100. Chandra, S., "Female Foeticide: Causes, Laws and Preventive Strategies," Paper presented at a Symposium held at New Delhi, July (2005).

101. Krishnaji, N., Pauperizing Agriculture—Studies in Agrarian Change and Demographic Structure, OUP, New Delhi (1992), in Mazumdar, V., "Political Ideology of the Women's Movement's Engagement with Law", Engendering Law—Essays in Honour of Lotika Sarkar, EBC, Delhi, p. 359 (1999).

3. Hindu Marriage Act, 1955

The MTPA 1971 recognizes the free choice of woman to decide whether and when she will terminate her pregnancy and make guardian's consent irrelevant incase the woman is of the age of eighteen years or above. The question arises whether women can terminate her pregnancy without the consent and against the wishes of her husband and if so, whether such action on her part would amount to cruelty under section 13(1) (ia) of the Hindu Marriage Act, 1956 and would entitle the aggrieved husband to obtain a decree of divorce against her.

This question came for decision in *Satya* v. *Shri Ram*[102] in which the High Court observed, "In this sort of a case, the Court has to attach due weight to the General principle underlying the Hindu law of marriage and sonship and the importance attached by the Hindus to the principles of spiritual benefit of having a son who can offer a funeral cake and libation of water to the manes of his ancestors, and held that termination of pregnancy at the instance of wife but without the consent of her husband amounts to cruelty.

In this regard the *High Court of Delhi,*[103] 155, has observed that if however, a wife undergoes abortion with a view to spite the husband then it may in certain circumstances, be contended that the act of getting herself aborted has resulted in an act of cruelty.

In *Sushil Kumar Verma* v. *Usha,*[104] the court held that aborting the foetus in the very first pregnancy by a deliberate act without the consent of the husband would amount to cruelty. In this case, the wife, who became pregnant within one month of her marriage, got the foetus aborted the following month in a government approved pregnancy termination center with the help of a registered medical practitioner without consulting her husband.

The husband was kept completely in dark about the fact of pregnancy as also of its abortion. The husband being aggrieved filed a petition for the grant of a decree of divorce on the ground of cruelty, which was dismissed by the District

---

102. AIR 1983 P. and H 252.
103. Deepak Kumar Arora *v.* Sampuran Arora (1983) 1 DMC 182.
104. AIR 1987 Delhi 86.

Court, but the High Court granted it on appeal. Recently in *Samar Ghosh* v. *Jaya Ghosh*,[105] the Supreme Court ruled that if consent or knowledge of her husband, such an act of the spouse might lead to mental cruelty,[106] Therefore, to keep the matrimonial relation harmonious women may carry foetus obviously not out of her free consent.

4. Medical Council Act, 1956

Constituted by the Indian Parliament in the Medical Council Act, 1956, the relevant section of the Code of Medical Ethics states: "On no account, sex determination test shall be undertaken with the intent to terminate the life of a female foetus developing in her mother's womb, unless there are other absolute indications for termination of pregnancy as specified in the Medical Termination of Pregnancy Act, 1971. Any act of termination of pregnancy of normal female foetus, amounting to female foeticide, shall be regarded as professional misconduct on the part of the physician leading to penal erasure besides rendering him liable to criminal proceedings as per the provisions of this Act (Clause 7.6)".

5. Criminal Procedure Code, 1973

(i) Postponement of Capital Sentence on Pregnant Woman

If a woman sentenced to death is found to be pregnant, the High Court shall order the execution of the sentenced to be postponed and may, if thinks fit commute the sentence to imprisonment for life.[107]

(I) GOVERNMENTAL POLICIES AND EFFORTS TO CURB FEMALE FOETICIDE

In a country like India, a caring and protective environment for girl children does not develop easily. Failure to

105. Manu/Sc/1386/2007 and 2007(5) Scale 1.
106. Similarly, if a husband submits himself for an operation of sterilization without medical reasons and without the consent or Knowledge of his wife.
107. Section 416 Criminal Procedure Code, 1973.

ensure protection of the girl children entails their promotion, prevention and rehabilitation. However, many initiatives have been developed and legislation exits in theory to protect girl children. The ministry of Health and Family Welfare (G.O.I.) is well aware of the problem of female foeticide in India. Repeatedly the Government has expressed its policy,[108] both inside of the Parliament and outside of dealing effectively with this social malaise.

The Government policy is based on the constitutional guarantees that state shall not discriminate only on ground of sex in the matter of employment or appointment. The mandate contained in Arts. 15 and 16 of the Constitution would remain dead letters if a female child is not allowed to born and grow as a citizen to enjoy the constitutional rights.

With a view to educating the masses the Government has launched a programme of drawing the attention towards the social evil. The government has declared its policy that it shall not discriminate between male and female and that both have an equal status. The government is handling this problem both at social level and through law. It has thus enacted Pre-natal Diagnostic Techniques (Regulation and Prevention of Misuse) Act, 1994.[109]

I. Forum against SDT and Sex Pre-Selection in Bombay in 1986

The state government appointed committee commissioned me for the foundation for research in Community Health (FRCH), Bombay to conduct a short study of the pre-natal sex determination tests and female feticide in Bombay city. The study was conducted in November 1986 with objective:

(a) Determining the extent of the spread of sex determination Test (SDT) and female foeticide in Bombay city,

(b) Finding out other related aspects of this practice, and

(c) Knowing the views and perceptions of the doctors involved in this practice.

108. Arts. 15(1), 16(1) and 16(2), Constitution of India, 1950.

109. Pre-Natal Diagnostic Techniques (Regulation and Prevention of Misuse) Act, 1994.

A Plan of Action for the SAARC Decade of Girl Child 1991-2000 and National Plan of Action for Children was formulated in 1992 for the "Survival, Protection and Development of Children", including the girl child. Balika Samriddhi Yojana, 1997 was a major initiative of the Government to raise the overall status of the girl child.

2. National Population Policy (NPP) 2000

The new population policy of the Government of India does not talk of two-child norm. It was agreed that quality of the life be emphasized and that there would be no force, coercion, incentives or disincentives. India got out of its 'emergency model' family planning approach and introduced the target-free approach, following this up with the National Population Policy (NPP), 2000.[110]

NPP 2000 defined the overriding objective as improvement in the quality of life. There is no mention made in the policy of the two-child norm, or of targets and disincentives. The consultations that took place prior to NPP show that the two child norm with its package of disincentives was opposed due to its anticipated adverse impact on poor women, and hence omitted from the policy.[111] Yet, for breach of the two-child norm, several States have put together a package of punitive measures, such as exclusion from elections, ration cards, education in government schools to the third child and welfare programmes for SC/STs.

Research in Orissa, Rajasthan, Haryana and Madhya Pradesh indicates that the norm to disqualify candidates (having more than two children from the election) has led to the desertion of wives and families, demand for abortions, giving away children for adoption and initiation of new marriages by male elected members.[112]

The Government also announced the National policy for empowerment of women in 2001 to bring out advancement,

---

110. Gonsalves, C., "Population Phobia", *The Times of India*, New Delhi, October 30 (2004).
111. A section of population experts have argued against the use of coercive methods for population control.
112. *Ibid*.

development and empowerment of women. The Government has also drawn up a draft National policy for the empowerment of women which is a policy statement outlining the state's response to problems of gender discrimination. As persistent gender inequalities continue we need to rethink concepts and strategies for promoting women's dignity and rights.

Some exemplary district administrations have taken a lead in combating this problem. In a district of Andhra Pradesh, a system of methodically auditing all scan centers in the district was introduced. Details of the scans, the personal information of the families were noted and authorities were able to follow up on the cases until the birth of the children. The district handed out 361 notices, suspended 91 registrations, and seized 54 scan machines. Three suppliers were prosecuted for distributing the pre-natal diagnostic machines without proper registration.

In Haryana, the 'Ladli' scheme for the girl child was drawn up by the State Government to provide incentives to the family. Under this scheme, a sum of Rs. 5000 per annum for five years is paid to couples giving birth to a second girl child (Rs. 2,500 for each of the two girl children). This money is invested in Kisan Vikas Patras in the joint names of the second girl child and the mother. In case the mother is not alive, then this money is transferred to a joint account of the second girl child and father.

In Tamil Nadu, under the guidance of Chief Minister, Jayalalita several programs have been instituted to aid the lives of baby girls Dr. Manickavel to introduce a program where cradles were set-up in public places like hospitals so parents and women can leave their babies anonymously, knowing the government will take care of them, try to find a home.

In Tamil Nadu, the vice of female infanticide involves the cruelest methods of putting the child to death by smothering, poisoning and the use of violent means. People tolerate a first born female baby but not a second girl baby. In Tamil Nadu, gender imbalance increased over the years as there were 972 females per 1000 males in 1901, which has reduced to 929 females per 1000 males in 2001.

To combat these issues, various programmes are being implemented under the Mother and Child Welfare Project (MCWP) in Usilampatti. These are mother and child care counseling programme, women's development project, sponsorship for girl students, area intensive programme—Kalluthu, adolescent girls training programme, health care project, vocational training programme for women and girls, day care centers for children and reception centre for female babies. SIDA, Sweden also undertook a project covering Usilampatti taluka.

The major objectives of this Project were to abolish the practice of female infanticide in Usilampatti Taluk; improve the status of women in the community; and bring about a change in gender attitudes in the community. The ultimate goal of the Project being the protection of the girl child, it was necessary to assess to what extent this has been achieved in the past 12 years. Groups of women, making purposeful strides towards the bank or for their meetings have become a common sight in these villages.

The grassroots movement initiated by ICCW, Tamil Nadu towards economic, social, political and cultural development of the girl child and society as a whole has accomplished a creditable task.

Efforts in future to sustain and enhance positive gains and the attempt made by the Council (ICCW) prove that social change can be brought about against unhealthy practices. The recommendations were that all girls must go to school. Their education would make the whole family educated.

3. Other Strategies and Public Awareness

The Tenth Five year plan stresses on elimination of all forms of gender discrimination so as to enable women "to enjoy not only *de-jure* but also *de-facto* rights and fundamental freedom on par with men in all spheres, viz. political economic, social civil cultural, etc". and complete eradications of female foeticide and female infanticide through effective enforcement of the Pre-conception and pre natal diagnostic techniques (Prohibition of Sex Selection) Act, 1994.[113]

113. Jain, Ashok Kumar, "The Saga of Female Foeticide in India, Socio Legal Offshoots, Ascent Publications, Delhi (2006).

A comprehensive action plan should be launched throughout the country to educate people about the value of the girl child.[114]

(J) PARTICIPATION BY NON-GOVERNMENTAL ORGANIZATIONS (NGOS), INTERNET AND MEDIA TO CURB FEMALE FOETICIDE

The NGOs must work towards proper and effective implementation of the social welfare legislations particularly the laws relating the welfare of the girl child. Another important collaborative effort to be performed by the NGOs is to help the administration to catch and punish the culprits. There should be various roles of NGOs viz., empowering and educating women (63.34%) and generating awareness at the community level. The NGOs have an important role in sensitizing the media and exercise issued-based advocacy. Since most of the NGOs are community-based they can indeed help root out this evil more effectively.[115]

Non-governmental organizations (NGOs) have also organized campaigns, rallies and programs to raise awareness about female foeticide around the country. They work with various stakeholders including other NGOs, governmental agencies, media, medical professionals, opinion-makers, religious leaders, role models, youth icons and the communities.[116]

The efforts done by Voluntary Health Association of Punjab (VHAP) have been laudable. VHAP has been working at the grassroots levels to sensitive people against the growing trend of female foeticide since early 1990s. The organization has been organizing seminars, holding meetings, having consultation and counseling people ever since. VHAP also has started advocacy campaign with the media. It is due to the

114. Singh, S.C., "Pre-Natal Diagnosis and Female Foeticide", *Unreported Judgments Journal*, p. 58, 2002 (1).
115. Singh, D.P., "Female Foeticide in Punjab : Causes and Consequences", Paragon International Publishers, New Delhi (2007).
116. State of the World Mother, 2005: The power and promises of girl education. Save the Children 2005.

pursuance of VHAP that the Akal Takht issued a Hukamnama on 18 April 2001 calling upon the Sikhs not to kill their daughters.[117]

Another NGO called Upkar in Nawanshahr has also been able to change the mind set of the people to turn their back on female foeticide. Due to the initiatives of this small organization there has been a quantum jump in terms of male female sex ratio in the region. The man behind the scene was the then Deputy Commissioner of Nawanshahr Mr. Krishna Kumar, who launched a major drive to raise the female-male child ratio. The D.C. involved all sarpanches, students, anganwari workers and the NGOs for monitoring every pregnancy in the villages. With the initiative of Mr. Krishna Kumar 30 NGOs of the district came under one common umbrella called the Upkar coordination society. This society has initiated various girl friendly schemes which have proved very successful. This model as a whole has yielded good results and has been adopted by other districts as well.

Apart from these NGOs, various other NGOs like the Red Cross Lions International, Rotary International and various students' bodies have also been making noticeable efforts towards improving the gender imbalance in Punjab.

A core group of individuals and NGOs in Maharashtra, for instance, has been formed to provide direction and address various issues that would arise in the course of future advocacy. Sensitizing on gender issues (through collaboration with schools, colleges, youth festivals, etc.), dissemination of information available on the issue and coordination between various NGOs were identified as certain key areas of work.

An important tool helping the Government of India to accomplish their cherished goal of all together stopping female foeticide is a website solely dedicated to Female Foeticide-www.indiafemalefoeticide.org set-up by Datamation Foundation Charitable Trust. Nalini Abraham of Plan International inspired to start this portal and since then has been constantly providing technical inputs. Sarita Sharma from

117. Singh, D.P., "Female Foeticide in Punjab—Causes and Consequences", Paragon International Publishers, New Delhi (2007).

the Foundation with her rich community experience effectively leads the project.

This major ICT based campaigning and advocacy programme is to help prevent occurrences of selective sex tests and selective abortions of the female fetuses in India. Is modern India going gender-awry, especially as society seems to turn against the female baby and fetus? This volume raises the emotive issue of millions of girls in India who fail to appear on the social scene, not figuratively, but in real demographic terms. The contributors to this work, all distinguished demographers and/or social scientists, describe the political economy of sentiments and sexual mores that lead parents to kill unborn daughters. In doing so, they ably unravel the values, principles, and practices behind the depleting child sex ratio in India.

The work examines the ways in which reproductive technologies such as the ultrasound are misused at the family, community, and state levels. In this alarming scenario, it highlights both the participation and defiance of the various authorities dealing with reproduction, health services, and the problem of female feticide. Their engagement with the state is analyzed in the light of colonial policies, the law of adoption, health policies, family planning programs, and the Pre-natal Diagnostic Techniques (PNDT) Act of 1994 and its amendment in 2002.

Datamation Foundation is involved in active championing, and advocating complete ban and penal action against selective sex tests, working at the convergence of ICTs, and social as well as human development. Some of its main objectives includes sensitization and awareness generation about the Pre-Natal Diagnostic Act (PNDT) 1994, as well as its recent amendment passed by the Parliament that bans any form of sex selection tests; increasing compliance amongst the maternity and nursing homes, ultrasound clinics, radiologists for registering their ultrasound machines under the PNDT Act; exchange information, dialogue as well as communication amongst the interested stakeholders; and making technical material and resources available to all stakeholders online and also Building e-Governance modules that can help identify ultrasound clinics, nursing homes carrying on illegal sex determination tests.

I. Participation by Internet

For the urban community and interested stakeholders, ICTs have played a major role in capacity building and awareness creation, facilitated by the use of Internet and net-telephony. Through emails, till date the foundation has sensitized eight million people world wide on this issue. It is proposed to target the rural population, not enjoying Internet access through Internet radio and Internet video. Besides this, the Foundation staff and volunteers are going to rural areas to educate people about this crisis, using a portable computer mart called a 'computer thela', which has been taken to the Panchayat level for the dissemination of information about the site. The youth are targeted through the Internet centers and cyber cafes by pasting posters at appropriate locations, and also near private hospitals and nursing homes. Parliamentarians as well as the law-makers are targeted by means of giving them timely updates electronically.

The complaint lodging process protects the identity of the complainant, and yet provides an effective vehicle for booking the doctor, maternity home, ultrasound clinic or radiology clinic. The complaints are retrieved into a database format at Datamation from where they are handed over to the competent authority for re-addressal.

The response is also expected to be sent back to Datamation to enable updating of the database within a month's time, failing which an automatic reminder gets published for the competent authority to act upon the Female Foeticide complaints received. The website has a separate tracking process for the medical community and for the people in general. The complaints pertaining to the families, who have indulged in the crime, are forwarded to the regional voluntary groups proposed to be set-up for the management of these complaints by the Government and the competent authorities.

The interpretation of the law in form of demographic data is also put on the website. Another important platform for the website is the 'Pledge Support' page that highlights two features—Pledge Support and Information. Through the 'pledge support' feature one can enter the information regarding the type of the volunteer service the person or the organization is ready to offer, and the 'information' option allows one to enter the information about any ultrasound clinics, doctors, radiologists, etc. to enable database building.

Serving as a rich resource center is the 'what's new' page that includes the latest news, articles, interviews, reports and case studies pertaining to Female Foeticide. The attempt here is awareness generation and capacity building both amongst the community and the stakeholders. The 'Links/Resources' page contains the contact addresses of different NGOs and agencies working for the prevention of Female Foeticide, and gives data for state-wise, sex ratio and Female Foeticide and sex selection.

To enable sensitization through sound and visual media, radio and video links have also been added to the website. Indeed a war needs to be waged against the Female Foeticide in India. Many initiatives have been developed by government and non-government actors to protect more effectively the girl child by restricting misuse of SDT. There is a need for new kinds of institutions, incorporating new norms and rules that support equal and just relations between women and men. Today women are organizing themselves to meet the challenges that are hampering their development.

2. Participation by Media

Media highlighted the problem through investigative reports and articles; they launched widespread awareness campaigns in the form of video spots on national and private television stations. Despite all these, the practice of sex determination test and female foeticide continues to thrive in India. The reasons are many; incongruence of legislative provisions with governmental policies, shortcomings of existing legislations, ineffective implementation machinery, etc.

Legal and Ethical Issues and Judicial Response

Women are both worshipped and accorded a highly revered status in our Indian society, yet the progressive technological developments cannot hide one of the worst impending 'gender' crisis and the society is facing the rapid depletion of women population. In India, there are less than 93 women for every 100 men in the population (2001). For a poor family, the birth of a girl child can signal the beginning of financial ruin and extreme hardship. During 1800, the British Government found that there were no daughters in a village in Eastern Uttar Pradesh.

Class, race and sex biases of the ruling elites have crossed boundaries of human dignity. After almost five decades of revolution and socialist reconstruction, sex determination tests for female extermination continue to be popular even after government's promotion of two child norm and now also one family policy. Within the discovery of new technological tools, techniques and means the "Human Life" has been upgraded up to an extent but, on other hand, the misuse of the advanced technological aspects posed a great threat to "Human Ethical Values". It is beyond doubt that the Development of Science and Technology helped the world population up to a great extent. But, it is also a bitter truth that these inventions are being misused by the man.

Progress of science and technology is mandatory for the progress of a nation. So technological advancements should not be criticized, as what matters most is its manifestation and beneficial application. If doctors stop sex selection and sex determination, the dwindling sex ratio would be stabilized.

(A) LEGAL ISSUES

1. Medical Ethics

In order to regulate the medical practice pertaining to sex determination test, there are three keys legal obligations that must be fulfilled by a doctor,[1] which are:

- The obligations to possess and apply sufficient knowledge, training, and skill in the delivery of prenatal care.
- The obligation to counsel and communicate material information to the patient accurately, effectively, and in a timely fashion.
- The duty to respect and protect the rights of the patient.

2. Informed Consent

The patient's right to an informed consent is the other side of the physician's duty to inform. The essence of the legal doctrine of informed consent is to permit patients to make their own decisions regarding a proposed course of action after the risks, benefits alternatives, and any other information material to making such decisions have been carefully explained. Thus practitioners engaging in the delivery of prenatal care must

1. See Healey, J. (1980), The Legal Obligations of Genetic Counselors, in Genetics and the Law II (A. Milunsky and G. Annas, Eds.) Plenum Press, New York, pp. 72-73.

obtain the informed consent of each patient before performing diagnostic test or therapeutic treatments such as amniocentesis, ultrasonography, fetal therapy and abortion.

3. Confidentiality

The physician's duty to protect and respect the rights of the patient also encompasses the patient's right to privacy, one aspect of which is medical record confidentiality. Pre-natal practitioners have a duty to respect the privacy of a patient and to avoid disclosing information concerning the patient to any third party without the consent of the patient.

4. Medical Professional Misconduct

According to the Indian Medical Council (Professional Conduct, Etiquette and Ethics) Regulations, 2002, followings are treated as medical professional misconduct;

- Improper conduct/abuse of his position.
- Prescribing steroids/psychotropic drugs when there is no absolute medical indication.
- Selling Schedule 'H' and 'L' drugs and poisons to the public, except to his patient.
- Sex determination test with the intent to terminate the life of a female foetus.
- Issuing a certificate that is untrue, misleading or improper.

The physician shall observe the laws of the country in regulating the practice of medicine and shall also not assist others to evade such laws. He should be cooperative in observance and enforcement of sanitary laws and regulations in the interest of public health.

A physician should observe the provisions of the State Acts like Drugs and Cosmetics Act, 1940; Pharmacy Act, 1948; Narcotic Drugs and Psychotropic Substances Act, 1985; Medical Termination of Pregnancy Act, 1971; Transplantation of Human Organ Act, 1994; Mental Health Act, 1987; Environmental Protection Act, 1986; Pre-natal Sex Determination Test Act, 1994; Drugs and Magic Remedies (Objectionable Advertisement) Act, 1954; Persons with Disabilities (Equal

Opportunities and Full Participation) Act, 1995 and Bio-Medical Waste (Management and Handling) Rules, 1998 and such other Acts, Rules, Regulations made by the Central/State Governments or local Administrative Bodies or any other relevant Act relating to the protection and promotion of public health

The physician shall not aid or abet torture nor shall he be a party to either inflection of mental or physical trauma or concealment of torture inflicted by some other person or agency in clear violation of human rights.

5. Other Rules and Regulations Regarding Medical Ethics

There are many rules and regulations that regulate the conduct of doctor, especially regarding sex determination test, which are:

- Graduate Medical Education Regulations, 1997 (Summary).
- Teacher's Eligibility Qualifications, 1998 (Summary).
- Post Graduate Medical Education Regulations, 2000 (Summary).
- MCI Regulations 2000.
- Code of Medical Ethics Regulations, 2002.
- Eligibility Certificate Regulations, 2002.
- Screening Test Regulations, 2002.

6. Implementation of Sex Determination Test Laws

Sex selection in the present context is a complex issue for which doctors, social groups and the government machinery have serious concern. Each has to play their part to deal with it at various levels.

In October 1985, the Forum against Sex Determination and Sex-Pre-selection was formed in Bombay, its members were from the feminist, rational, health, human rights and people's science movements and also included doctors. Their object was more than a woman's issue and involved the question of social responsibility in the use of science and technology. Soon after, doctors within the group felt the need to form a sort of sub-group called "Doctors Against Sex Determination" to refute the charge that the Forum was anti-doctor and also to be able to lobby more effectively with various professional medical bodies.

In spite of the Forum's insistence to keep the private sector out, the law passed by the Maharashtra Government allowed private clinics to get licenses to perform the test, and there were no checks to prevent misuse of the test.

(B) ETHICAL ISSUES

Ethical considerations of sex selection tend to follow the economic paradigm very closely. The ethical paradigm is heavily influenced by the competing desires to protect both individual rights and collective rights. In balancing of the affected parties involved in a sex selection decision, it is constructive to sort out the interested parties, the decision makers, and the circumstances impinging on the sex selection decision.

Rules of law must evolve to identify the decision-makers involved in sex selection and to determine how all of the competing interest will be balanced in the decision proves. These legal structures must balance the competing interests will be balanced in the decision process. These legal structures must balance the competing individual interests of protecting social integrity and they must be developed within the existing cultural traditions of society. For example in the Anglo-American legal tradition there is a tendency to give a primacy to individual rights and impinge on individual decision-making only when necessary to protect key social institutions or to protect society from outcomes of the decision process that might accumulate to the significant detriment of society.

With regard to sex selection, it is possible that severe sex ratio imbalances could occur that would force social institutions like marriage and the family to adapt unusual ways. Also the use of technology to produce sex selection could possibly spin of into more general applications of positive and negative eugenics that significantly alter the structure of society in either a positive or negative way. In the Anglo American tradition, individuals would be given freedom to choose the sex of their children subject to the rules developed to provide for the protection of outside individual interest and the societal concerns mentioned previously.

In contrast to this approach would be the socialist tradition, which would reserve the priority of rights and develop rules governing sex selection that would best suit the interest of society subject to the needs of the individuals involved. For example, in an article on population control in the People's Republic of China. Deputy Prime Minister Chen Muhua outlined why the control of population growth as "an objective demand of the socialist system [Population Council, 1979, p. 224]". China has revealed targets for population that would produce zero population growth by the end of the century. In order to do this, they are attempting to eliminate large families and to popularize the one child family.

Earlier, the right to abortion was not permitted and it was strongly opposed by the society. The termination of pregnancy was termed to be a murder of the fetus. But due to the change in time and technology, nowadays this right has been legally sanctioned by most of the nations after the famous decision of *Roe* v. *Wade* by the US Supreme Court. But the oppositions are still present and people do believe that it should be legally prohibited.

The law most undoubtedly authorizes the man who is under reasonable apprehension that his life is in danger or his body in risk of grievous hurt to inflict death upon his assailant even when the assault is attempted or directly threatened by the apprehension must be reasonable and the violence inflicted must not be greater than is reasonably necessary for the purpose of self-defence. In this case the continuation of the existence of the foetus is looked upon as dangerous to the life of the mother. The balancing of one life against another life in such circumstances may be understood by some stretch of reasoning. The difficulty arises on the issue of balancing of one person's health against another person's life.[2] Here arise certain ingrained complexities. Life and health do not get equated on a common platform.

2. Shaw, S.P., Laws of Child in India, 2001 Edition, Alia Law Agency Goonesekere Savitri, Children Law and Justice, 2000 Edition, Allahabad Law Agency.

The fact that the women's health would be endangered if the pregnancy is carried to the full term was not (until fairly, recently) recognized as a justification for abortion. That step has not been taken but obviously it constitutes a greater inroad in the sanctity of life (of the foetus) than a provision intended to guard against danger to the women's life.

From the ethical and human rights perspective, female foeticide has led to a controversy surrounding the ethics of, and right to opt for, abortion. In India, the Medical Termination of Pregnancy (MTP) Act, 1971 permits abortions only under certain conditions, but these can be broadly interpreted and abortion can be carried out on demand. Here the question arises that if abortion is legal in our country, why should a democratic state interfere in a couple's decision to abort a female foetus[3] clearly, the right to abortion and the right to end female foeticide is in a complex interrelationship within feminist discourse.

It is argued that if abortion is a right over one's body, how are feminists to deny this right to women when it comes to the selective abortion of female fetuses? Women often condemn anti pre-selection activist by saying that they are unrealistic and do not understand the life of a common woman. Even many educated women are of the view that sex selective abortion is the lesser of two evils, compared to what a woman is going to face until the day she dies. One woman defended the act by saying it is better to be killed in the mother's womb than be burnt by the mother in laws.[4] Studies have shown that dowry demands and dowry deaths are one of the main reasons why parents do no desire to have daughters.

Sex determination clinics play on this fear, advertising these tests with attractive slogans, such as cheaper alternative to dowry and better pay Rs. 500 now than Rs. 5,00,000 later.[5] Here it may be noted that families who are relatively affluent and who can easily afford dowries also resort to foeticide.

3. Human Development in South Asia (Report), 2000, p. 123.
4. *Ibid.*
5. Bumiller Elizabeth, "May you be the Mother of a hundred Sons: A journey among the Women of India", Random House, New York, 1990, p. 115.

As noted above, abortion can be carried out easily under the Medical Termination of Pregnancy Act, 1971. Under this Act, a medical practitioner can cause abortion if there is substantial risk that, if the child was born, it would suffer from such physical or mental abnormalities, as to be seriously handicapped (eugenic ground). Again, the abortion is also permitted for social and economic reasons. These provisions in the MTP Act provide an ample opportunity for doctor's to avoid penal risk of sex selection test. So, sex selective abortions can easily be carried on under the pretext of detecting abnormalities in the fetuses. Today there are a large number of unregistered and illegal genetic laboratories and genetic clinics in almost all cities of India that openly carry out sex determination test under the coverage of MTP Act.

There are two risks to society and its institutions from disseminating the technology to make sex-choice decisions. First, the unharmful desire to plan or balance children in a family could result in harm to the ideal of equality between male and females if there are significant increases in first born males and decreases in second born females. Steinbacher (1980, p. 28) appropriately asks, "Will the second class status of women in the world be confirmed by choice? Male preference is still dominant in most societies to a greater or lesser degree, but it is by no means clear that male preference is indelible (Williamson, 1976) from the perspective of social justice, however, the interests of women in sharing equally in the benefits and responsibilities of citizenship and leadership could be damaged by a long-term trend of sex selection of first born males.

A second risk is a precedent for a reintroduction of some of the ideas of positive eugenic, defined historically by Lydmerer (1978, p. 458) as "the striving to increase wanted traits in the populations by urging 'worthy' parenthood". This dimension can be seen at work in the argument that sex choice would make children, especially girls, feel especially wanted. Williamson (1978 p. 28) refers to the benefit of wantedness in girls, citing the thought of Margaret Mead, in the context of a future method of sex selection that would be "foolproof and universally feasible".

The major negative effects that can occur when a pregnancy is forced on a woman inspite of today's liberal abortion laws. This can occur due to emotional pressure from the husband or from the senior member of the family. This can also occur due to misconceptions about safety of modern legalized abortions or enforced religious and moral; values. Several studies have emphasized the long-term harm that can occur to women mental health as a result of unwanted and mandatory motherhood. One should also not forget the fate of unwanted children who tend to be physically and mentally impaired.

In the first scenario, sex selection would be seen as a factor in achieving quantitative control over the population. Form an individual point of view, this would arise out of a desire to control the sex composition of the family in terms of the overall number of male children are born. Form the point of view of society, sex selection could be desire as and inducement to achieve smaller family sizes and ultimately a reduction of population growth. One could speculate that couples would seek to achieve a certain number is reached.

While the PNDT Act seeks to regulate and prevent misuse of pre-natal diagnostic techniques, it rightly cannot deny them either. The law permits ultrasound clinics, clinics for medical termination of pregnancies and assisted reproductive facilities as a routine matter and as a legitimate business.[6] Only diagnostic techniques are regulated under the Act and not abortion services. Anecdotal evidence suggests that strong competition has reportedly led to a reduction in charges for availing these services, which has worked to the advantage of potential clients. In *Javed and Others* v. *State of Haryana*[7] the Supreme Court took up this issue, which was enacted in the Haryana Panchayati Raj Act. The court upheld the legislation and ruled that it did not violate any fundamental right. The court stated, "population control assumes a central importance

6. Dani, A., "Death in the Womb-Sex Selection Law Fails to Check Foeticide", *The Times of India*, New Delhi, November 19 (2004).
7. (2003) 8 SCC 369.

for providing social and economic justice to the people of India".[8]

The gender discrimination dimensions of these societal problems are revealed in the *State of Haryana* v. *Santra.*[9] In this case, a woman sterilized under a government program nonetheless conceived after the operation and underwent delivery since abortion posed a risk to her life. She gave birth to a daughter who was also her eighth child. The Supreme Court awarded the mother damages that covered the child's expenses until the age of puberty. Its decision acknowledged the extra burden that an unwanted girl child posed, particularly in a country where population growth is a huge problem and are of government priority.[10]

The amendments to the PNDT Act to curb the practice of female foeticide were resisted strongly by a powerful lobby of the doctors, a question arises: 'Why do the doctors with good intentions not want regulations'? According to a senior cardiologist, some of the reasons for the presence of so many ultrasound clinics in a particular city were the following: Having an ultrasound machine was considered as a status symbol by doctors: it was an easy way to earn more in less time: local manufacture of ultrasound machines had reduced the basic cost[11] a qualitative study of women in Maharashtra showed that while regular abortion cost between Rs. 100 to 1200 depending upon whether it was a public or private facility, the cost went up to Rs. 5000 for a sex-selective abortion.[12]

---

8. Barot, S., "Assessing Reproductive Rights: Concern Areas and the Way Forward", *The Lawyers Collective,* New Delhi, p. 8, October (2004).
9. (2000) 5 SCC 182.
10. Barot, S., "Assessing Reproductive Rights: Concern Areas and the Way Forward", *The Lawyers Collective,* New Delhi, p. 8, October (2004).
11. "Darkness at Noon: Female Foeticide in India", Voluntary Health Association of India, available at http://www.indiafemale foeticide.org
12. Gupte, M., *et. al.* "Abortion Needs of Women in India—A Case Study of Rural Maharashtra", Reproductive Health Matters, May (1997), in R. Duggal, "Abortion Economics", Seminar 532, p. 50. December (2003)

Collusion between doctors and clients makes the situation worse the modus operandi of a sex selective abortion is as follows: A doctor from a city or even a small town goes to villages in Himachal Pradesh with his mobile ultrasound machine and in case the sex determination test shows a female foetus, gives the client an address in Pathankot City in Punjab and asks her to report on a Saturday evening when the abortions are conducted in secrecy. This makes it extremely difficult for the Appropriate Authority in Himachal Pradesh to trace (or apprehend) the doctors or the patients for violating the PNDT Act. There were cases in Punjab when the Police arrested some women for undergoing sex determination test while the doctors went scot free. This led to an agitation by several health activists and ultimately the women were set free.[13]

Doctors are generally aware of the PNDT Act. They know that it is illegal to conduct such tests and subsequent abortions. The question that arises is: in a situation where the clients are not aware of the legal status of these tests and yet theses tests are being conducted, the people cannot be blamed and the fault lies squarely with the doctors.

The fact remains that in most cases of female foeticide, the clients and doctors are on the same wavelength, in the sense that both support such tests and foeticide because of the great demand on the part of pregnant women to know the sex of unborn child and the tendency of doctors to male quick money. A health activist observed. "The clapping in real hard when both the hands clap together forcefully as is the case with female foeticide involving motivated doctors and equally motivated clients".[14]

The Council's Code of Ethics still does not recognize female foeticide or even sex determination tests as unethical. There is a collective responsibility of professional bodies like

13. "Darkness at Noon: Female Foeticide in India", Voluntary Health Association of India, available at http://www.indiafemale foeticide.org
14. "Darkness at Noon: Female Foeticide in India", Voluntary Health Association of India, available at http://www.indiafemale foeticide.org

the MCI and IMA, for derogatory practices by members on a mass scale targeting and entire class of persons, practices use of the professional training and qualifications that quality them for membership in these bodies.

The supreme court of India has asked the MCI to amend the medical code to prosecute erring doctors. The National Human Rights Commission (NHRC, India) has also asked MCI to examine the ethical aspects of sex determination tests which it too acknowledges are causing a high rate of female foeticide. The code and the PNDT Act should complement each other. And definitely the code should be amended. The revised Code of 2002, however, deems sex determination an offence only if intent to foeticide can be proved.

The medical fraternity is of the viewpoint that it is not the PNDT Act that is resented by radiologists but the difficulties of compliance which encourage graft and undue harassment. For every doctor who indulges in sex detection there is another who resolutely refuses to tell demanding individuals the sex of their child. But the PNDT official machinery looks at every radiologist as a criminal declared guilt who resolutely refuses to tell demanding individuals the sex of their child. But the PNDT official machinery looks at every radiologist as a criminal declared guilty until birded otherwise.

However, the liability of medical fraternity could not be negated by the honesty of few doctors. Medical professionals violating the Act should be held most responsible as they have the choice of not doing the test. On the decline in sex ratio, the Census Commissioner also observes that the alarming down slide could be attributed to the recent medical support in terms of sex determination test, and to social (an) cultural bias against the girl child.[15]

(C) THE ECONOMIC PARADIGM

Economic considerations frequently enter into legal analysis. It is therefore useful to examine an economic

15. Contractor, Q., "Sex Selection and the Law", Combat Law, p. 69, April-May (2002).

paradigm that may possibly be used to address the issues of sex selection. A commonly used approach is cost benefit analysis. Each individual is seen as making decisions based upon the expected benefits and costs attendant to the decision. Similarly, society makes divisions on the basis of the benefits and costs accruing to its choices. A problem arises when individuals and society must make a decision about the same thing. In these cases, private cost benefit calculations can deviate considerably from social cost benefit analyses. Laws are sometimes enacted to balance these opposing considerations. Situations of this sort often develop because private decisions produce effects on individuals not immediately involved in the decision.

These externalities can accumulate to produce a positive or negative effect on society; in the event that they are significant, society has an interest in inducing or compelling individuals to modify their decisions by doing more or of refraining from some activity. If the individual decision results in an activity that has a higher social benefit to cost ratio than private benefit to cost ratio, it is in society's interest to are individuals do more of that activity than they would be expected to do if they only considered their own situations. If the social benefit to cost ratio is less than the private, the reverse result obtains and society has an interest in curtailing the individual's activities.

When the discrepancy between private and social cost benefit calculations is sufficient to warrant governmental action, law may be developed either to change the parameters used by individuals in making those decisions so that resulting decisions are compatible with the social good, or to regulate individual activity so that individuals are forced to conform to the socially desirable conduct. For example, the state may require an individual to attend formal schooling to a greater extent than that person desires or may prohibit economic activity destructive to the environment.

Sex selection is a private decision that can produce significant externalities. The externalities touch every single member of the family, the offspring, and society in general. It certainly affects the texture of the relationship between parents and their offspring. In societies where sex roles are well defined, children born as a result of sex selection will have the course of their lives materially affected by that decision. Moreover, if sex selection materially alters the sex age affected. It is easy to imagine situations in which the externalities accruing to sex selection decisions would accumulate sufficiently to warrant social intervention, and depending on the situation, the intervention might be oriented toward encouraging sex selection of a given type or curtailing sex selection in general or of a specific type. In order to develop law suitable for such intervention, rules must evolve to identify those situations in which externalities are as considerable as to warrant social intervention and to develop a framework that will balance private *versus* social considerations equitably.

In analyzing the benefits and cost of sex selection one must always look for what is gained or lost, quantitatively and qualitatively, by enabling parents to choose the sex of their children. Quantitative aspects of the decision involve overall family size and the number and party of each sex. Qualitative aspects involve physical characteristics of the offspring and family investment strategies with respect to children of each sex. Becker and Lewis (1975) postulate that quantity-quality tradeoffs with respect to childbearing are natural concomitants of rising incomes and rising cost of child care. One might expect an increasing incidence of sex selection in societies characterized by increasing family incomes, child quantity could be expected in these situations.

One could also view child bearing as an investment process. In these cases parents will invest in raising children hoping for some from of return either to themselves or to society in the future. It is quite possible that the rates of return would vary considerably with respect to the cultural setting in which sex roles are defined. One must conclude that if the economic paradigm has relevance to childbearing then child quality *versus* quantity tradeoffs are natural parts of the decision proves involving childbearing and should be factored into every public and private regarding fertility, including sex selection.

(D) NEED OF STRICT LAWS AND POLITICAL WILL

It is easy but unrealistic to suggest that the government must frame laws which have teeth and then vigorously implement them to curb female foeticide and infanticide.[16] The reality seems to be that the government, whatever its political complexion might be, relies on the dominant castes for votes and support.[17] Further, it is difficult to take action against doctors because they have a powerful lobby and have close links with politicians. The governmental apathy is another major hurdle.

(E) ROLE OF EDUCATION

The impact of modernity and modern education is known to be complex. In states having a long history of female infanticide (now foeticide), education may not enlighten the castes which have been getting rid of their female offspring for generations. On the contrary, college or university education may enhance the groom price. Degree and job-oriented education, which our educational system provides, may not create the awareness of discrimination against females and other social evils. This does not mean that we should not have education. Literacy has very positive aspects and must be encouraged.

The point is that the potential of our formal educational system to remove gender bias and eradicate social evil is sometimes overstated. For example, high dowries are endemic among the Syrian Christian of Kerala though this state is often projected as a model which other states should try to emulate.[18] It is absolutely necessary to bring about an attitudinal change among castes and communities which resort to female foeticide and infanticide through a different kind of informal education

16. Jain, Ashok Kumar, "The Saga of Female Foeticide in India", Socio-Legal Offshoots, Ascent Publications, Delhi (2006).
17. Vishwanath, L.S., "Female Foeticide and Infanticide", *Economic and Political Weekly*, September 1 (2001), available at www.epw.org.in
18. Vishwanath, L.S., "Female Foeticide and Infanticide", *Economic and Political Weekly*, September 1 (2001), available at www.epw.org.in

in rural areas. This is a tall order as it calls for a radical restructuring of our educational system.

(F) CRIMINALIZATION OF FEMALE FOETICIDE

Recently, the Chinese government criminalized abortion and ultrasounds obtained for sex-selection purposes, in the hope that criminalization will prove more successfully in curbing these practices. A new Chinese law calls for prison terms of up to threes and fines for doctors and other health workers who assist in telling the gender of unborn babies, leading to abortions.[19] To kill someone because of his or her sex is, in some sense, a hate crime. It needs to be punished by the same "deterrent logic" as in the case of an ordinary murder, though the punishment need not be that severe. The punishment in case of foeticide could not be mild either.

Whatever punishment to be given, it should be effective. The problem with investigating a woman's reasons for abortion is, however, not that simple. Consider the enforcement of such a law. If police suspected a woman of having had a sex selection abortion, they could subject her to the sort of interrogation that might ordinarily wrongful abortion were found "innocent" after this investigation, the fact of her abortion would have become public knowledge, and she when have suffered the stigma that attaches to this procedure (even when obtained for medically sound reasons). Also because it may often be difficult for a person to establish her reasons for terminating a pregnancy, the prospect of a criminal accusation could place a serious chill on the exercise of the right to choice, even for women who have no preference for male or female offspring.[20]

Morally, the decision to terminate a pregnancy on the basis of a baby's sex may be an ugly decision that deserves no protection. But the reality is that the reproductive rights of women who would never abort on the basis of sex depend on the government's staying out of the decision altogether. We

19. Anonymous, *The Times of India*, New Delhi, December 27 (2005).
20. Colb, S.F., "Criminalization of Sex Selective Abortion in China", Find Law, available at http://indiafemalefoeticide.org

must hope. Instead, that women will prove worthy of the trust and responsibility that is placed in their hands, even as we refrain from finding out whether that trust is warranted.[21] According to some writers, criminalization of female foeticide works as a catalyst in the fire of social stagnation. What we need to realize is that female foeticide is not a result of criminal intent, but that of compulsion caused by circumstance caused by rapid victimization of female in the society.

An evil practice can be curbed not by cutting the stems growing on the trunk above the ground, but by eliminating the roots standing beneath.[22]

The above view is correct. However, not all crimes are committed with a criminal intent. Take the cases of violations of environmental and traffic regulations. The deterrent measures need to be used to 'discipline' the erring public and medical fraternity, along with social awakening measures. "We may have to for some time at least, revive the guilt of foetal murder.[23]

Families that seek "female foeticide services", but more importantly doctors and medical practitioners (and all categories of employees in establishments with ultrasound or other diagnostic or fertility treatment facilities) who use the facilities to either commit or aid in the commission of female foeticide, or, to use Satish Agnihotri's phrase 'Female Foeticide Service Providers" will be liable for punishment for perpetrating crimes against humanity under the provisions of the Rome Statute (International Criminal Court)[24] in far more serious ways than contemplated by the current legislation,

21. *Ibid.*, the author's views are in the context of legitimacy of sex selective abortions in USA. In the Indian context, where a woman's views and choices are conditioned in a patriarchal set-up, she need not be held guilty in all cases and her family members could be held liable.
22. Agarwal, M., "Female Foeticide: Law and its Effectiveness", available at http://www.indiafemalefoeticide.org
23. Sridhar, L., "Female Foeticide: The Collusion of the Medical Establishment", available at http://indiafemalefoeticide.org
24. Article 25 of the Rome Statute, available at http://www.indiafemalefoeticide.org

which imposes extremely mild punishment for the first offence and then step it up gradually.

(G) SEX DETERMINATION : WOMAN'S ISSUE

Thought sex determination has to be understood in the context of increasing violence against women, it has to be viewed as a social issue. The term 'sex-selective abortion' is in use in recent years and United Nations publications also use this expression. But if one's objective is to fight foeticide one must know how best to convey the message of condemning foeticide to the masses. From this point of view, the term 'female foeticide' is translated as 'bhrun hatya' and this term communicates the gravity of the problem; the term foeticide, akin to genocide, invokes a sense of guilt, anger and passion. It is a glaring case of social injustice. Thus, the term 'female foeticide' should be used to arouse the conscience of the people to fight a growing social malaise.

But when one talks of MTP, the entire subject is put in the arena of medical doctors. In the people's perception it is the doctor who has to decide whether the abortion should take place or not and whether it poses a danger to the life of the mother and/or the child. In short, a moral controversy has been tactfully transformed into a medical issue. That is why there is hardly and opposition, whereas in several western countries there is in intense controversy on the issue of abortion, which even has political overtones.[25]

(H) FAMILY PLANNING AND FEMALE FOETICIDE

As a result of 50 years of propaganda on the merits of a small family norm, there is today general awareness of family planning and the need for adopting a small family norm. Men and women in Punjab, Haryana and Himachal Pradesh do accept the idea of a two-child family and they are also aware

25. "Darkness at Noon: Female Foeticide in India", Voluntary Health Association of India, available at http://www.indiafemalefoeticide.org

of the technology of pre-birth sex determination tests. As in most parts of India, two sons constitute the cut-off point for accepting sterilization.

The people seem to be quite puzzled that while the government wants a small family norm to be practiced, it yet opposes the conduct of these tests and subsequent abortions. They argue that since every family wants at least one son, if not two, the best way to ensure a small family is to go for the test and act according to the results. In the eyes of the people, there is a dichotomy between the government's sustained advocacy of family planning and a small family norm, with legislation prohibiting the conduct of sex determination tests and sex-selective abortions. This mix-up is the creation of circumstances and neither the government nor the people can be blamed.[26]

(I) DOWRY AND GENDER VIOLENCE

There are multiple opinions regarding the dowry issue within the Indian women's movement. One view argues that dowry provides women with the only feasible avenue to claiming their share of parental property in a social climate that makes it difficult for daughters to enforce legal claims to other forms of inheritance (e.g. Kishwar, 1999).

Therefore, until other avenues to inheritance are ensured, dowry should not be entirely discouraged, but familial support structures that limit exorbitant demands and provide some security for women should be put into place. At the same time, families should begin to view daughters as capable of providing as effective old age support as sons, and value them accordingly.[27]

---

26. *Ibid.*
27. Kishwar, M., Off the Beaten Track—Rethinking Gender Justice for Indian Women, OUP, New Delhi (1999). She says that even when laws are passed (as in Andhra Pradesh) spelling out the rights of daughters as equal inheritors, the daughters sign away their inheritance, accepting dowries instead. People still believe that a woman "belongs" in her marital home and so must give up claims in her natal home after she receives the golden handshake—the dowry.

(J) STATE LIABILITY

Any enactment of national legislation on female foeticide must take cognizance of its occurrence in radically new terms in order to effectively combat it, but more importantly to put an end to impunity, which is the hallmark of this practice today. While it may be argued that the State has in fact taken steps to stop this practice through the enactment of the PNDT Act, the ineffectiveness of the Act in real terms translates into State liability, not "apathy" since we are not speaking of individual crime but of mass extermination, for which the mechanisms and the urgency of redressal cannot be a mild legislation like the PNDT Act alone. This is one more reason why India must ratify the Rome Statute (International Criminal Court).[28]

(K) CONSTITUTIONAL VALIDITY OF THE RESTRICTIONS

Since the MTP Act takes away the right of some of the medical practitioners, whether qualified or not, to terminate pregnancies, a question might arise as to whether these provisions of the Act are constitutionally valid because they impinge on the fundamental right conferred by Article 19 of the Constitution of India on a person to practice his profession. The fundamental rights conferred by the article are not absolute rights and reasonable restrictions may be imposed on such rights in the interests of the general public. Parliament is competent to specify by law the professional or technical qualifications necessary for practicing any profession or carrying on any occupation, trade or business [vide Art. 19(6)] of the Constitution these provisions of the Act appear to be constitutionally valid provisions.

28. Kannabiran, K., "Gender Cleansing: Female Foeticide or Crime against Humanity? State Liability", Combat Law, pp. 24-25, August-September (2003), available athttp://www.indiafemalefoeticide.org

(L) JUDICIAL RESPONSE TO LEGAL AND ETHICAL ISSUES

1. In *Queen Empress* v. *Ademma*[29] a women was charged for causing herself to miscarry, though she had been pregnant for only one month, and there was nothing which could be called a foetus or 'child'. The Madras High Court held that it was the absolute duty of a prospective mother to protect her infant from the very moment of conception. Thus, the High Court effectively used the provisions of the Code (IPC) to protect an embryonic life.
2. In *Emperor* v. *Cripps*[30] the mother of a newly-born child with a view to dispose of the child, secretly gave it to A, who carried it by a railway train and left it in a second class compartment. The child was carefully wrapped and its side left a bottle of milk. The mother was held guilty under Secs. 317 and 109 (Abetment), and under Sec. 317. The court observed that any person receiving an infant from its mother on the understanding that the mother never desired or wished to have it back again must be regarded as a person having care of it. A has, therefore, the care of the child.
3. In *Rex* v. *Bourne*[31] it was held that all therapeutic abortions are lawful. In this case, a girl under 15, who was criminally assaulted, became pregnant. The surgeon, who terminated her pregnancy, was prosecuted for causing abortion against the law. Justice Macnaghten opined that the bona fide object of avoiding the practically certain physical or mental breakdown of the mother will afford an excuse.
4. In *Satya* v. *Shri Ram*[32] *the Punjab and Haryana High Court Observed*: "In this sort of a case, the court has to attach due weight to the general principle underlying

29. (1886) ILR 9 Mad 369.
30. (1916) 18 bom LR 934.
31. (1938) 3 ALL ER 615.
32. AIR 1983 P&H 252.

the Hindu law of marriage and sonship and the importance attached by Hindus to the principle of spiritual benefit of having a son who can offer a funeral cake and libation of water to the manes of his ancestors".

5. In *Fowler* v. *Fowler,*[33] the court observed: "If a man takes contraceptive measures against the will of his wife . . . so as to prevent her having children without reasonable excuse for so doing, then it is easy to infer that he does it with intent to inflict misery on her. . . . But when a wife herself takes contraceptive measures, or asks her husband to take them, her conduct can often by attributed to fear for the consequences to herself, without any intention of injuring him. She fears the pains and risk of childbirth. This is very unnatural and unfortunate, but it is not cruelty unless she has also an intention to inflict misery on her husband".
6. In *Sushil Kumar* v. *Usha,*[34] the Delhi High Court opined that whether or not an abortion would amount to cruelty would also depend upon whether one of the parties desired a child and did not consent to it. The court further held that aborting the foetus in the very first pregnancy by a deliberate act without the husband's consent would amount to cruelty.
7. In *Planned Parenthood of Sough Eastern Pennsylvania* v. *Casey,*[35] the Supreme Court of the United States struck down the 'pre-abortion notification of husband' provision of restrictive Pennsylvania Abortion Control Act, 1982 (as amended by 1989 Amendments). The impugned provision commanded that, unless certain exceptions apply, a married

---

33. (1952) 2 TLR 143. See Kusum, Family Law Lectures, Butterworth India, p. 50 (2003).
34. AIR 1987 Del 86, The English Courts have also opined that a wife's refusal to have children would amount to cruelty. See Forbes *v.* Forbes (1995) 2 ALL ER 311; P. *v.* P. (1965) 2 ALL ER 456.
35. (1992) 120 L ED 2nd 674.

woman seeking an abortion must sign a statement indicating that she has notified her husband.[36] The court struck down the spousal notice provision as undue burden. In the context of sex selection abortions, the medical fraternity, which could make a difference, has remained largely unmoved and public officials are indifferent claiming it is difficult to implement the law. Yet, even one determined doctor or official could make a difference.

8. In *Dr. Nisha Malviya and Anr.* v. *State of M.P.*,[37] the accused had committed rape on minor girl aged about 12 years and made her pregnant. The allegations are that two other co-accused took this girl, and they terminated her pregnancy. So the charge on them is firstly causing miscarriage without consent of girl. The Court held all the three accused guilty of termination of pregnancy which was not consented by the mother or the girl.
9. In *Centre for Enquiry into Health and Allied Themes (CEHAT) and others v. Union of India and Others,*[38] two NGOs CEHAT, MASUM and Sabu George, an individual activist filed public interest litigation (PIL) in the Supreme Court. The PIL seeks to accomplish the following objectives—
   - To activate the central and state governments for rigorous implementation of the central legislation, and
   - To interpret the legislation and/or to demand amendments to ensure that the techniques that use pre-conception or during-conception sex selection are also brought under the purview of the Act.

The first positive step forward was a favourable interim

36. Sec. 3209: The Pennsylvania Abortion Control Act, 1982. See Gaur, K.D.: A Text-book on the Indian Penal Code, Universal Law Publishing Co., pp. 539-41 (1992).
37. 2000 CriLJ 671.
38. (2003) 8 SCC at 398.

judgment by the Supreme Court of May 4, 2001. The order called for all the state governments to take necessary steps towards the implementation of the Act. The government that is the Department of Family Welfare too got energized and they issued an advertisement in national dailies saying that it is a crime to carry out sex selection and also activated the Central Supervisory Board by calling a meeting.

The order also came heavily on the medical profession and their unethical practice. As a result the Indian Medical Association (IMA) at the national level made a turn around and issued a warning to its members. The Federation of Obstetrician and Gynecologist Societies of India (FOGSI) too showed some concern through its newsletter. The governments were also asked to conduct a survey of the existing bodies conducting these tests. The hearings henceforth have been follow-ups on the May 4th directive. There has been very poor compliance by the State Governments including Maharashtra.

Another major landmark in the course of the PIL was the hearing held on the 11th of December 2001. The Supreme Court called upon the Chief Health Secretaries of Punjab, Delhi, Bihar, Rajasthan, Gujarat, Haryana, Uttar Pradesh, Maharashtra and West-Bengal to remain present before the Court on the 29th of January 2002 for non-compliance of orders passed by the same.

The Supreme Court also directed companies manufacturing ultrasound machines to provide information about the individuals or groups to whom ultrasound machines have been sold during a period of last 5 years. Furthermore, the Customs and Import Department are directed to supply information on number of ultrasound machines sold to clinics or individuals as the case may be.

The court further observed that it is unfortunate that law which aims at preventing such practice is not implemented and therefore, non-governmental organizations are required to approach this Court for implementation of the Prenatal Diagnostic Techniques (Regulation and Prevention of Misuse) Act, 1994 renamed after amendment as "the Preconception and Prenatal Diagnostic Techniques (Prohibition of Sex Selection) Act" which is the normal function of the executive.

During hearing of the case, the Apex Court made

following observation on September 19, 2001 on implementation of the law:

> "At the outset, we may state that there is total slackness by the administration in implementing the Act. Some learned counsel pointed to that even though the Genetic Counseling Centers, Genetic Laboratories or Genetic Clinics are not registered, no action is taken as provided under section 23 of the Act, but only a warning is issued. In our view, those centers, which are not register, are required to be prosecuted by the authorities under the provisions of the Act and there is no question of issue of warning and to permit them to continue their illegal activities".

Directions to the Central Government

The following directions were issued on the basis of various provisions for the proper implementation of the PNDT Act in the CEHAT case:

- The central Government is directed to create public awareness against the practice of pre-natal determination of sex and female foeticide through appropriate releases/programmes in the electronic media. This shall also be done by Central Supervisory Board (CSB) as provided under section 16(iii) of the PNDT Act.
- The central Government is directed to implement with all vigour and zeal the PNDT Act and the Rules framed in 1996. Rule 15 provides that the intervening period between two meetings of the advisory Committees constituted under sub-section (5) of section 17 of the PNDT Act to advise the Appropriate authority shall not exceed 60 days. It would be seen that this rule is strictly adhered to.

Directions to the Central Supervisory Board

Following directions were given to the Central Supervisory Board:

- Meetings of CSB will be held at least once in six months [re proviso to section 9(1)] the constitution of CSB is provided under section 7. It empowers the Central Government to appoint ten members under section 7(2)(e), which includes eminent Medical Practitioners, including eminent Social Scientist and representative of women welfare organizations. We hope that this power will be exercised so as to include those persons, who can genuinely spare some time for implementation of the Act.
- CSB shall review and monitor the implementation of the Act [re section 16(ii)].
- CSB shall issue direction to all State/UT Appropriate authorities' to furnish quarterly returns to CSB giving a report on the implementation and working of the Act. These returns should *inter alia* contain specific information about:
    - o Survey of bodies specified in section 3 of the act.
    - o Registration of bodies specified in section 3 of the Act.
    - o Action taken against non-registered bodies operating in violation of section 3 of the Act, inclusive of search and seizure of record.
    - o Number and nature of awareness campaigns conducted and results flowing therefrom.
- CSB shall examine the necessity to amend the act keeping in mid-emerging technologies and difficulties encountered in implementations of the Act and to make recommendations to the Central Government (re Section 16).
- CBS shall lay down a code of Conduct under section 16(iv) of the act to be observed by persons working in bodies specified therein and to ensure its publication, so that the public at large can now about it.
- CSB will require medical professional bodies/ associations to create awareness against the practice of pre-natal determination of sex and female foeticide and to ensure implementation of the Act.

Directions to State Government

Following directions were given to State Government:

- All State Governments/UT administrations are directed to appoint by notification, fully empowered appropriate authorities at district and sub-district levels and also advisor committees to aid and advise the Appropriate authorities in discharge of their functions [re section 17(5)]. For the advisory committee also, it is hoped that members of the said committee as provided under section 17(6)(d) should be such persons, who can devote some time to the work assigned to them.
- All state Governments/UT Administrations are directed to publish a list of the Appropriate authorities in print and electronic media in their respective states/UTs.
- All State Governments/UT Administrations are directed to create public awareness against the practice of prenatal determination of sex and female foeticide through advertisement in print and electronic media by boardings and other appropriate means.
- All State Governments/UT Administrations are directed to ensure that all State/UT Appropriate authorities furnish quarterly returns to CSB giving a report on the implementation and working of the act.
- These returns should *inter alia* contain specific information about:
  - survey of bodies specified in section 3 of the act,
  - registration of bodies specified in section 3 of the act,
  - action taken against non-registered bodies operating in violation of section 3 of the act, inclusive of search and seizure of record, and
  - number and nature of awareness campaigns conducted and results flowing therefrom.

Directions to Appropriate Authorities

- Appropriate authorities are directed to take prompt action against any person or body, which issues or causes to be issued any advertisement in violation of section 22 of the Act.
    - o Appropriate authorities are directed to take prompt action against all bodies specified in section 3 of the Act as also against persons, who are operating without a valid certificate of registration under the Act.
    - o All State/UT Appropriate authorities are directed to furnish quarterly returns implementation and working of the Act. These returns should *inter alias* contain specific information about:
        - ❖ survey of bodies specified in section 3 of the Act,
        - ❖ registration of bodies specified in section 3 of the act including bodies using ultrasound machines,
        - ❖ action taken against non-registered bodies operating in violation of the section 3 of the Act, inclusive of search and seizure of records,
        - ❖ complaints received by the Appropriate authorities under the Act and action taken pursuant thereto, and
        - ❖ number and nature of awareness campaigns conducted and results flowing there from.

Despite the direction of the Apex Court in the CEHT Case, the enforcement of the Act has been slack and tardy.

In *Murari Mohan Koley* v. *The State and Others*[39] a woman wanted to have abortion on the ground that she has a 6 months old daughter. She approached the petitioner for an abortion. And the petitioner agreed to it for a consideration. But

39. (2004) 3 CAL LT 609(HC).

somehow the condition of the woman worsened in the hospital and she was shifted to another hospital. But it resulted in her death. The abortion was not done.

The petitioner who was a registered medical practitioner had to establish that his action was done in good faith (includes omission as well) so that he can get exemption from any criminal liability under section 3 of the MTP Act, 1971.

The Indian government enacted the pre-conception and pre-natal diagnostic tests (prohibition of sex selection) Act in 1994. Taking exception to it, couple Vijay Sharma, 42, and Kirti Sharma, 37, has approached the Bombay High Court, seeking permission to determine the sex of their third child. The Sharma's have two daughters, Smriti, 14, and Aishwarya, 6, and want to have a son this time. The couple has contended in court that the government had enforced the law in order to stop sex selective abortions, but the law should be amended for couples who already had children.

They have made it clear that they would have a third child only if it was a son. Having had two daughters, they wanted to experience raising a son as well, they said, and hence, should be given the liberty to determine the sex of their unborn child. The case filed in 2005 came up for hearing before a division Bench of Justice J.N. Patel and Justice S.C. Dharmadhikari.

It was, however, adjourned for two weeks for further arguments and the case is still pending in the honorable High Court of Maharashtra. The case has relied on a ruling of the Supreme Court, which says that a child conceived is entitled to full development irrespective of its sex.

However, Sharma's, the petitioners in the case, have contended that the legislature has enacted the medical termination of pregnancy Act, 1971, which legalizes abortions within 12 weeks of conception for limiting the number of children, and is equivalent to foeticide. They have further contended that the prohibition of sex selection Act, 1994 and further amendments made to it in 2002 were ambiguous as they imposed a blanket ban on sex determination tests which, the couple said, were closing doors on married couples wanting to use advanced medical facilities to their avail. The Sharma's have also said that although the law did not permit pre-natal diagnostic tests, people do get them conducted illegally and continue to choose the sex of their children. Activists however, were not convinced with their argument.

The two-child policy has got mixed up with female foeticide. The preference for at least one of two children to be a boy, often leads to the second girl born to a family being treated far worse than her older sister. Over the years it has become quite clear that if people are forced to limit the size of their families, they prefer to do so at the cost of the girl baby, even if it means that they have to "import" brides from outside their states or communities.[40]

In a victory for those fighting for the rights of the girl-child, the Bombay High Court upholds an amendment to the law banning sex-determination tests. A Mumbai-based couple had mounted a legal challenge to the constitutional validity of the amendment that bans pre-conception gender selection.

An attempt to amend the law banning pre-conception sex selection in India has been turned down by the Bombay High Court, which observed that allowing pre-natal sex selection in a country which has a definite bias against the girl-child would amount to sex-selective abortion.

The court was ruling on a controversial petition filed by Vinod and Kirti Sharma to allow parents with one or more children of the same gender to select the sex of the child before it was conceived.

The couple had challenged the constitutional validity of an amendment to the Pre-natal Diagnostic Tests (Regulation and Prevention of Misuse) Act of 1994—that then became the Pre-Conception and Pre-Natal Diagnostic Techniques Act, 2002 (PCPNDT Act)—that bans pre-conception gender selection on grounds that it violates the fundamental rights to life and the couple's liberty to choose the gender of their child before it is conceived.

In a strongly worded order upholding the provisions of the PCPNDT Act 1994, a division bench of Chief Justice Swatanter Kumar and Justice Ranjana Desai dismissed the petitioner's contention saying that in view of the skewed sex ratio in India, the provision was valid. In such a society, the

40. Indian Child available at http://www.indianchild.com

court observed, sex selection would be as good as sex-selective abortion.

The Mumbai-based couple wanted their third child to be a boy, after having had two girls. However, they were prevented by the law from doing so. Due to provisions in the existing Act that penalize medical practitioners and clinics for carrying out sex-determination tests, no clinic was ready to conduct the pre-conception sex selection procedure.[41]

Pre-conception sex selection should be allowed for those who have one child and want another child of the opposite sex, the Sharma's' petition said, so that couples could achieve their desire for a 'balanced' family.

Their reasoning, which Justice Desai called "shocking" in her judgment, was that the law-makers have not considered the "mental anguish" a mother experiences when she learns that the second child is of the same sex as her firstborn.

The Sharma's also argued that affluent couples who have the financial and social means should be allowed to choose, as opposed to couples who use such tests to have only male children. Kirti Sharma had even gone so far as to say that mothers like her, who had more than one girl-child, had played a role in righting the country's sex ratio that is heavily skewed in favour of males.

What the judges found most objectionable was the Sharmas' argument that it was better to have a male child in India as the country was not socially or economically ready to accept a female child. They argued that for a "less advanced society" like India, where a "patriarchal mindset exists" and where a "girl-child is not socially accepted", it is better that such children are not born.

The Sharma's contended that such a treatment—legally available in many advanced countries was different from female foeticide or infanticide as it did not involve killing the foetus. "There is nothing wrong with it; the motivating force behind it has been my mother. She wanted to pave the way for couples who already have one or two daughters", said Kirti Sharma.

---

41. A girl's right to live—Female Foeticide and Girl Infanticide. Working Group on the Girl Child report Dec 2007 available at www.advocacy/reports/2007.

Justice Desai said this argument alone reinforced the decision to uphold the ban on pre-natal sex-determination tests. "It is unfortunate that people should be under the influence of outdated notions regarding sons *versus* daughters. As long as such notions exist, the girl-child will be unwanted", the judgment said, noting the statistics provided by the Ministry of Health and Family Welfare on the low.

While this is not the first time the PCPNDT Act has been legally challenged, it is certainly one of the most keenly watched and high-profile cases. It has been closely followed by women, child and health activists across the country who are strongly opposed to any changes in the law.[42]

The PCPNDT Act seeks to curb the rampant practice of sex-selective abortion that has effectively resulted in millions of girls being killed before they are born. The law bans the determination of the sex of a foetus or the practice of pre-determining the sex of a fertilized egg before it is implanted in the womb.[43] A 2002 amendment to the PCPNDT banned pre-conception gender selection and it was this amendment that the Sharma's were seeking to have struck down by the courts.

"Sex selection is not only against the spirit of the Indian Constitution; it also insults and humiliates womanhood. It violates a woman's right to life. This is perhaps the greatest argument in favour of the ban on pre-natal sex determination tests in India", said the Bombay HC on Thursday as it threw out a petition pleading that couples with same sex children be allowed to conduct such tests to "balance their families".

The judgment came from a Division Bench comprising Chief Justice Swatanter Kumar and Justice Ranjana Desai but was written by the latter who is among the few women judges in the high court. The 32-page judgment rejected the challenge to the constitutional validity of provisions of the Pre-Conception and Pre-Natal Diagnostic Technique (Prohibition of Sex Selection) Act, which banned pre-natal diagnostic tests to verify the sex of an unborn child. The petition was filed by a couple, Vijay and Kirti Sharma, residents of Lokhandwala complex in Andheri, on grounds of alleged inequality between

42. *The Hindu*, September 7, 2007.
43. *The Telegraph*, September 7, 2007.

the provisions of the Pre-Natal Act and the Medical Termination of Pregnancy (MTP) Act.

The couple, who had two daughters and wanted a son to create a "balance" in their family, wanted to be able to conduct the pre-natal test so that they could choose a male child. Their reasoning, which Justice Desai said was "shocking", was that legislators have not considered the "mental anguish" a mother would be put to when she finds that the other child is the same sex as the first one.

The Sharma's also argued that affluent couples who have the financial and social means should be allowed to choose as opposed to couples who use such tests to have only male children. What the judges found most shocking was the couple's submission that for a "less advanced society" like India where a "patriarchal mindset exists" and where a "girl child is not socially accepted", it is better that such children are not born. Justice Desai said this argument alone reinforced the decision to uphold the ban on pre-natal sex determination tests and observed:

> "It is unfortunate that people should be under the influence of outdated notions regarding sons versus daughters. As long as such notions exist, the girl child will be unwanted", the judgment said, noting the statistics provided by the ministry of health and family welfare on the low sex ratio, especially in affluent areas of north India. "A stage may soon come when it would be difficult to make up for the missing girls", the ministry said. The court said in the most prosperous parts of Punjab, Haryana, Delhi and Gujarat, the ratio was already less than 900 girls for every 1000 boys.[44] In Kurukshetra district of Haryana, it was as low as 770 girls per 1000 boys".[45]

44. Female Foeticide, in Haryana and Punjab: a situational analysis, Shakti Vahini, 2003, p. 11.
45. The Status of Children in India: An alternate report to the United Nations Committee on the Rights of the Child on India's first periodic report, Asian Centre for Human Rights, 2003, p. 116.

The court said that while the MTP law was meant for certain cases where a mother's life and health, both mental and physical, might be endangered or where a child may be born with abnormalities, it in no way dealt with sex selection as a basis for a legal abortion.

Dr. Dahiya, a Civil Surgeon of Faridabad district in Haryana, who exposed two Clinics found violating the PNDT Act, faced the threat of transfer. His zealousness in booking the violators had perhaps ruffled some feathers in the political establishment of the state.

Likewise, the Collector of Hyderabad, Mr. Arvind Kumar, took upon himself to ensure that the provisions of the PNDT Act were actually implemented. He got the District Appropriate Authority (District Medical Officer) to check if the city's scanning centers had done the paper work required by the law. Predictably, records had not been kept at most centers. Where they existed, they were either incomplete or contained false information. The mandatory form that anyone undergoing a scan must fill includes information about the number and sex of the children the woman already has. In the majority of the forms, this vital piece of information was missing as also the foetus age at the time of the scan.[46] The Collector took action against clinics that do not keep a record by posting a government nurse outside to keep track of the number of pregnant women going in so that it could be tallied against the clinic's medical records.

Based on this information, show cause notices were issued to 361 Centers (93 percent of the all scanning centers in Hyderabad). The registration of 91 was suspended, 51 machines were seized (although 40 were returned after the owner had paid the fine) and three main suppliers of the scan machines were prosecuted for not following the law. Now the Collectorate plans to follow each woman having a scan until the point she delivers and compile a scan centre based 0-6 years' sex ratio.[47] The findings would be fascinating, particularly if they reveal a change in the trend. It is too early

46. Sharma, K., "Stop the Violence", *The Hindu*, New Delhi, December 11 (2005).
47. *Ibid.*

to tell now. But what it does illustrate is the kind of determined intervention that is needed to reverse the steady elimination of women in India.[48]

In a landmark judgment, the judicial magistrate (first class) Rajesh Kapate on Monday sentenced a doctor to three years' rigorous imprisonment (RI) and imposed a fine of Rs. 90,000 on him for carrying out a sex determination test (SDT) in a village near Karad in Satara district. This is perhaps the first sentencing in the state (Mumbai) under the Pre-Conception and Pre-Natal Diagnostic Techniques (Prohibition of Sex Selection) Act, 1994.

Thus, the case laws show that a woman has an absolute right to abortion and no one can take away this right from her. The Judiciary has been playing a vital role in securing these rights to women. Right to abortion is a fundamental right of privacy.

48. *Ibid.*

Conclusion and Suggestions

Science and technology have influenced the course of human civilization and has provided us remarkable insights into the world we live in. There is an awakening of modern science in India through the efforts of a number of outstanding scientists as a result of that India is now one of the developing countries in the world.

The key role of technology as an important element of national development is also well recognized. The Scientific Policy Resolution of 1958 and the Technology Policy Statement of 1983 enunciated the principles on which the growth of science and technology in India has been based over the past several decades. These policies have emphasized self-reliance and sustainable and equitable development. Today, due to scientific and technological developments, there is a sound infrastructural base in India. These include—research laboratories, higher educational institutions and highly skilled human resource, etc.

The invention of new medical tools and techniques has made the complicated operations/surgery easier. Due to invention of new medicines, the normal span of human life has been increased and death ratio had been decreased. In this way, the medical science has also contributed a lot in human life and improved the human health to a great extent. New techniques of treatment of cancer, T.B. and other diseases save the life of human beings.

But at the same time, we observe that gifts of the science and technology have been misused by the human society which yields gross violation of the human rights and posed challenges to Human Values like—moral, social, ethical, cultural as well as the legal aspects also. In these days, the advancement of medical science, especially, the Sex Determination Technology has made an adverse impact upon the progress of Human Rights. The advancement of Medical Science hampered the true spirit of law, medical science and Human Rights.

With the passage of time, the technique of sex determination test, which was developed for the noble cause for the benevolent of human beings, started to be misused by man and that has violated the human rights of the fetus even in mother's womb. In present scenario, this is one of the burning issues and it puts a question mark on the human rights of the fetus in the mother's womb. If doctors stop sex selection and sex determination test, the dwindling sex ratio would be stabilized in families.

Family is the basic unit of society in which Woman plays a critical and significant role therefore; there is always a need of protection and support to women. In different cultural, political and social systems, various forms of the family exist in which a woman make a great contribution to the welfare of the family and to the development of society but still her worth is not properly recognized and a result of that discrimination against women occurs.

It is rightly said that the discrimination against women starts in the womb of mother. In most of the families girl child is not preferred. Indian society is a male dominated one and it will remain so, if nothing happens to change it. The old age attitude of society to have a son has not changed due to non-recognition of the significance of maternity, motherhood and the role of woman in the family. The people still prefer son and for that they go to the extent to kill the female foeticide; consequently sex ratio in society is disturbed.

The decline in sex ratios is not restricted to the north of India or the economically vulnerable sections, as it is largely perceived, but affects the nation as a whole. The fall in sex ratios has been greater in economically prosperous states like Punjab where men now look for brides and there is a same position in Bihar and Jharkhand. Empirical approaches for the women empowerment made so far have not yielded desired results. Indeed, the country's social indicators and gender empowerment measures remain poor. It is time to call for government's attention for controlling child marriages, female infanticide, sexual harassment, especially, where sex ratio is declining rapidly.

In India and China this phenomenon has reached alarming proportions. Sex ratios in Europe, North America, Caribbean, Central Asia and the poorest region—sub-Saharan Africa are favorable to women as these countries neither kill/ neglect girls, whereas in South Asia, sex ratios are adverse for women because they do so; the lowest sex ratio is to be found in India. There is a strong linkage between declining sex ratio and the larger issue of violence against women in India. The task ahead is to change mindsets of doctors and clients and create a socio-cultural milieu that is conducive to the girl child's survival.

Declining Sex Ratio and violence against women-accompanied with neo-liberal economic policies have harmed the numbers and status of women every where. Under pressure to procreate sons women too are falling prey to the enticements of sex selection advertisements and medical establishments that offer sex selective abortions. Compounding the problem and denying women the right to their bodies is due to government's passive attitude. In particular, the Rural Health Mission and Tribal Health Project are having glaring anomalies. They have failed to take into account the larger social milieu, including the non-availability of services for health or population control, infrastructure or institutional lacunae.

An intense awareness campaign on declining sex ratios must be formulated; it is important to involve both women and men in the endeavor. The pronounced decline in sex ratio is indicative of violence against women. It needs to be countered by mobilizing all sections of the family, community, and society to act to end the practice and build popular pressure on the State to implement the existing policies. The corporate sector can address the challenge of declining sex ratios in multiple ways.

In Asian countries, globalization has facilitated easy import of new reproductive technologies leading to selective abortions of female foetuses. Prenatal diagnostic tests give women a choice to select the sex of a child. Choices are made within patriarchal compulsions to procreate sons. Sex-selective abortions of female foetuses in the states of Maharashtra, Gujarat, Bihar, Uttar Pradesh, Rajasthan, Madhya Pradesh, Punjab, Haryana and Tamil Nadu should be tackled immediately.

In Andhra Pradesh, Bihar, Gujarat, Haryana, Madhya Pradesh, Punjab, Rajasthan, Tamil Nadu and Uttar Pradesh (known for high rates of abortion) revealed a frightening fall-out of sex-selective abortions. This practice has increased particularly among those who want small families of one or two or a maximum of three children. Communities practicing female infanticides earlier have now shifted to using sex-selective abortions. National Family Health Surveys (NFHS) have to identify the reason for this fall to be sex selective abortions.

The reality is that an astounding sixty lakh female infants and girls are missing due to abuse of amniocentesis, chorionic villi Biopsy, sonography, and ultrasound and imaging techniques. Shortage of women in Haryana, Punjab, Bihar, Madhya Pradesh, Rajasthan and Uttar Pradesh have escalated forced abduction and kidnap of girls, forced polyandry, gang rape and child-prostitution.

Female foeticide is the result of an unholy alliance between the traditional preference for a son and modern medical technology, increasing greed of doctors and rising the demand for dowry that makes daughter financial burden.

It also shows up the ineffectiveness of the PNDT Act, the liberal Medical Termination of Pregnancy Act and the lack of any serious involvement of civil society in fighting this social menace. Those women who undergo sex determination tests and go for abortion must know that the foetus is female are actively taking a decision against equality and the right to life of the girls.

The issue of sex selection from a legal perspective emphasized that sex selective abortions are a violation of basic human rights mentioned in the Universal Declaration of Human Rights (UDHR) as well as the Convention on the Rights of the Child (CRC) to which India was signatory. So far as national legislation is concerned, there are various provisions in the Constitution, in the Indian Penal Code, etc., that deal with the problem of forced abortion.

In many cases, the women are not independent agents but merely victims of dominant family ideology based on preference for male children. The status of the women has much to do with the spread of his horrifying practice. The techniques (Amniocentesis) developed to discover birth defects are being used to determine the sex and therefore, the life and death of the child before birth.

This practice as is well known has arisen out of the social conditions in our country, under which a woman has a comparatively very low status. Often woman who gives birth to daughter only, is faced with a risk of being divorced or torture. In this situation, she has a difficult choice to make avoid sex selection test and unwanted abortion. She puts either her own life in a peril or perish a female child, whom she is about to give birth.

Abortion is an issue to be left to the decision of the mother. However, taking viability of a legal standard, necessary protection should be provided to the unborn. It is also beneficial to the mother, where the state or voluntary organizations are ready to take care of the unborn. There is no meaning in conferring a right to the mother to destroy the foetus. Her right is limited to have a termination of pregnancy.

The law has to take care of the liberty of the mother as well as the unborn. As a hospitable community we should seek ways of providing support for lonely and frightened mothers, and for lonely and abandoned babies. We need to offer women with unplanned pregnancies as much love and support as they require and to assist them in finding compassionate alternatives to abortion.

Women need to be given equal rights, opportunities and the freedom to formulate their choices so as to ensure gender equality. The view that men are superior and women are subordinate to them must be discarded at it has become out dated notion the mission of women empowerment should be prompted and strengthened.

Real empowerment of women will occur, only when there is an enabling environment in the country where women can exercise their rights both within and outside their homes. Legislation alone will not be able to ensure this. Communities as a whole including religious leaders, teachers, elected representatives of local panchayats, etc. have to take sincere efforts in this regard. Their efforts to curb discrimination and sex selective abortions must be accompanied by programmes on literacy, gender empowerment and building of women's rights within the community so that there is collective bargaining for basic needs and participation in decision-making and planning.

For a social change in attitudes, it is necessary to involve large numbers of people. The aim should be to spread awareness on the issue pertaining to violence against women through mass mobilization to use public education events and to use of communication material like posters, kits and comics to bring about changes in social attitudes and influence people to adopt gender-just practices have been extraordinarily successful.

There are many methods devised by unscrupulous doctors to circumvent the law which bans sex determination of an unborn child under the PNDT Act to prevent the female foeticide just by registering sonography machines. Unless the state makes some example by taking severe action against erring doctors, nothing will happen. It is necessary to involve both men and women both to prevent, and ultimately to end, abuse against women.

The South Asia campaign has been launched to end violence against women, especially in Bangladesh, Sri Lanka, India, Nepal, Pakistan and Afghanistan. A coalition of 400 organizations is trying to deal with the problem of violence in the region through a community 'awareness-to-action programme'.

By 2011, the campaign aims to reach and influence 50 million ordinary men and women across South Asia to stop violence against women. By doing this, it may save approximately 50 million 'missing women' in the region due to discriminatory practices and violence.

It is strongly recommended for sensitization of the medical fraternity for better monitoring systems with linkages to grassroots level health workers and NGOs to check mushrooming of ultrasound facilities; scaling up advocacy efforts and a six-monthly or annual monitoring of birth-related statistics for formulating strategies.

A presumption as in dowry deaths must be taken in favour of female infanticide. The law Pre-natal Diagnostic Techniques (Regulation and Prevention of Misuse Act, 1994) is a welcome step which seeks to put an end to an atrocious practice of foeticide consequent to a sex determination test.

The government has also failed to address the threat of emerging techniques to select the sex of the child prior to conception; the poor rate of conviction makes it clear that the law is being flouted with impunity and there is a serious non-reporting on the issue.

An attempt to encourage the 'two-child' norm is further aggravating female infanticide. In their efforts to control the population some states have formulated strategies that defeat the efforts to combat the skewed sex ratios. Disincentives like exclusion of people having more than two children are dangerously self-defeating.

In 1971 the Indian Council of Medical Research (ICMR) undertook a study of the use of amniocentesis and reported that it was a potent technology for sex detection and thus useful for population control. Thereafter, the amniocentesis test was made available in government health centers. Some years later the All India Institute for Medical Sciences (AIIMS) made a sample survey of 11,000 pregnant women and found that sex detection motivated women to opt for sex selective abortion. India's Health Ministry then banned the use of amniocentesis and other tests in government hospitals and clinics for sex determination.

The private sector meanwhile has gone to town marketing and providing the detection technology and the abortions. The advent of ultrasound testing has made action more affordable. The causality of this type of attitude is the mental and physical torture of fair sex. This is the social behavior, which is unethical immoral practice. That's why causing death of a living foetus is being made a crime in IPC. Sections 312-314 of the IPC deal with miscarriage subsequently the Medical Termination Pregnancy Act was passed to check this problem. Recently, the Pre-Natal Diagnostic Techniques (Prevention of Misuse and Regulation) Act, 1994 (PNDT) was passed and amended in 2003. It is a problem of social attitude rather than legal one. If society starts preferring girl child then only the problem shall be solved.

It is not desirable to ban the amniocentesis per see as it is an important clinical procedure highly to trace genetic disorders. What is required is to ban sex determination with determination and political will.

The Pre-Natal Diagnostic Techniques (Prevention of Misuse and Regulation) Act, 1994 (PNDT) has failed to arrest sex selective abortions though there are strong provisions for convicting doctors found eliminating foetuses selectively. The Act has also been unable to deal with emerging techniques to select the sex of the child prior to conception. The struggle to combat declining sex ratios in the country has been a long one and is on-going because of the numerous hurdles in implementing the PNDT Act. The infrastructure put in place to address the issue has been inadequate to implement existing laws.

The Pre-Natal Diagnostic Techniques Act stipulates that ultrasound and other techniques be used only to detect foetal abnormalities. In the hands of the right people it means safer childbirth safer. But the Act has been widely misused. Doctors simply put up a notice that sex determination is banned and then continue to do it. Government efforts to set-up state advocacy commissions various committees at the state and district level and tighten the implementation of the PNDT Act has proved inadequate.

Although section 27 of the PNDT Act, 1994 declares that any offence under the Act would be cognizable, non-bailable and non-compoundable, but section 28 provides that no court shall take cognizance of the offence under the Act except on a complaint made by appropriate Authorities or by a person, who has given notice of at least 15 days of his intentions.

Thus Police is debarred from registering First Information report directly and to submit its report to the court under section 173 Cr. P.C. Under these provisions, it has become very difficult to initiate criminal proceedings against the offender. This contradiction needs to be settled.

Professional fraternity of medical practitioners is a big hurdle in the implementation of the Act. The members of the Appropriate Authority are mainly doctors and the practicing doctor has connection with other doctors at professional and social level. In these situations, it is very difficult to initiate criminal proceedings against an offender, who is fellow Medical Practitioner, because of fellow feeling of the members of appropriate authority.

It is suggested that all state governments should make an effective and prompt implementation of the Pre-natal Diagnostics Techniques (Regulation and Prevention of Misuse) Act in its true spirit.

In order to check the menance of female foeticide, the district health department of Haryana has made inspection of ultrasound clinics mandatory after every three months. According to Officials, every hospital which is providing ultra-sound facilities should be registered with the civil surgeon's office. Besides that, hospitals should also register the details of every woman undergoing ultrasound.

Government and its enforcement machinery should ensure compliance of all laws relating to medical termination of pregnancy and implement strict measures to curb corruption, enforce accountability, transparency and sever punishment for the corrupt and the law-breakers. Unnecessary harassment of Medical practitioners should be avoided but the element of corruption, which has crept into the system in the name of inspection of genetic laboratories and clinics, should be tackled strictly.

The enforcement agency should be a different body of professionals consisting of Police, social workers and doctors of high morals. The Indian Medical Association, a professional body of practicing Doctors, should come forward and implement a 'No Sex Determination Code' for Doctors. The

Doctors need to be reminded of their sacred duty of protecting human life in any form rather than becoming a party in destruction of human foetus, especially female foetus in the womb. License to practice medicine of those Doctors, who are found guilty under the PNDT Act 1994 or the MTP Act 1971, should be cancelled and they should be debarred from practicing medicine.

Sex detection and sex selection have spread like a contagious disease in the country despite the legislations and directions given by the Apex Court of India. The following remedial efforts may be taken to get rid of this problem.

The Central Government and the State Government have to take implementation of the Pre-Natal Diagnostic Techniques Act seriously and ensure that the Central Supervisory Board, State Supervisory Boards, Union Territory Supervisor Boards, Appropriate Authorities and Advisory Committee in each State and Union Territory are promptly set-up and function properly.

While selecting members of the Boards, Appropriate Authorities and Advisory Committees, the Government has to ensure that only those who are sensitive to the issue, have sufficient time to spare for the cause and rare serious in their endeavor to ensure the implementation of the Act are appointed as members of these agencies.

The functioning of the enforcement machinery has to be periodically and effectively monitored. District administration of every district in the country has to be geared up to ensure that:

- Provisions of the Act are widely publicized in the district
- Banning promotion of sex selection procedures.
- Workshops are periodically conducted to educate all those involved in the pre-conceptual and pre-natal diagnostic procedures about the seriousness of the problem of female foeticide and the role they can play in controlling the misuse of the techniques periodically.
- Steps are taken to obtain information periodically from the companies supplying Pre-natal diagnostic techniques equipment regarding the genetic

counseling centers, genetic laboratories or genetic clinics to which they supply the equipment.

- Steps are taken to maintain a list of genetic counseling centers, genetic laboratories or genetic clinics involved in pre-natal diagnostic techniques and inspect their records periodically regarding violation of the provisions of the Act.
- Decoy agents, i.e. persons acting like pregnant women or persons related to pregnant women, can be periodically deputed by district administration to check whether sex determination service are offered by any clinics laboratories and counseling centers in their area.
- Prompt legal action is taken against any of the provisions of the Act and wide publicity is given of cases where penalties are imposed and licenses are suspended or cancelled.

The members of Parliament and the Sate Legislatures have to take the responsibility of monitoring the implementation of the provisions of the Act on priorities in their respective constituencies. The progress report on the implementation of provisions of the Act has to be reviewed by the Parliament and the State Legislatures in every session so as to ensure that provisions of the enactment are taken seriously by the enforcement machinery. Medical professionals, on account of their position of strength and repute, should counsel their patients and their families on the importance of the girl child and the impact of the skewed sex ratio on society.

The units/centers should comply with the requirements laid down under the PNDT Act. This would save them from troubles like suspension of licenses, prosecution, etc. Further, in this way; they will assist in making the monitoring of the Act easier. The Act should not be seen as an attempt to stifle the medical profession but rather as a regulatory effort in which the contribution and co-operation of the medical professionals is of vital importance.

The companies dealing in manufacturing and sale ultrasound machines/imaging machines/scanners, etc. that are capable of detecting the sex of the foetus, should take special care to sell these machines only to registered units or any other person registered under the PNDT Act. They should also fulfil other requirements of the PNDT Act.

The functions of the appropriate authority are extremely vital for the proper implementation of the Act. The authority is required to be diligent and vigilant. There should not be unnecessary delay and harassment in the granting of registration, as it might deter the units from seeking registration or losing sensitivity towards the issue of sex determination. The association of radiologists is begging for simplified and transparent registration procedures.

The hospitals/clinics with a high percentage of male child births should be placed under close watch. In villages, intermediaries like Anganwari workers have to be targeted because they are the nodal people who keep health records of all mothers and children and know the people intimately.

The measures taken for the implementation of the PNDT Act are mostly on paper. There is little interface between the public and enforcing authorities. It is vital that the public must know who the enforcing officers and how they can be accessed on the telephone, by fax, by SMS or through publicly notified post box numbers.

If enforcing authorities are headed by doctors, there is a little chance of an independent and impartial investigation and that ultimately accounts for very low prosecution. As a result of that the fate of the complaints filed under the Act remains unknown to the public.

There is a need to make the Act stronger. For instance, the penal provisions under the Act should be given more teeth. The present fine of Rs. 1 lakh and imprisonment up to five years should be increased substantially to act as a proper deterrent. The recent national surveillance cell is expected to give more teeth to the Act.

Persons in need of undergoing the use of pre-conception or pre-natal diagnostic techniques must first make an application, in the manner to be prescribed by the appropriate authority, seeking grant of permission which should include, *inter alia* the name address and specialization of the doctor/

hospital/diagnostic centre/clinic/laboratory where that person is going to have such a treatment.

No doctor/hospital/diagnostic centre/clinic/laboratory, etc. shall undertake any such use of pre-conception or pre-natal techniques without the production of the certificate of grant or approval for so undergoing issued by the appropriate authority under the Act.

Before granting or issuing any of the said certificate, the appropriate authority can take expert advice so as to verify genuinely in the requirement of such grant or approval.

A deeming provision empowering the court to presume use of pre-natal or pre-conception technique, especially in respect of female persons up to the age of 20 years, as a cognizable offence within the meaning of the Act as against the doctor or hospital or diagnostic centre of clinic, as the case may be, where any such technique is used without the requisite grant by the appropriate authority.

Sex composition is an important indicator and a measure of the equity between males and females. In India, where the social status of women is low, their diminishing numbers has lowered their status further. An urgent "zero tolerance" approach is needed to end sex determination tests and elimination of female foetuses through sex selective abortions. It is suggested that to do away this problem following measures needs to be taken.

Today, information technology has changed the communication paradigm, making it no longer difficult to reach a large number of people more or less at the same time and that too enable them to respond, interact as well as obtain a copy of the information within a low-cost. Technology is being used in this country to fashion a future without women this trend should be immediately reversed through stringent mapping and monitoring of ultrasound facilities in India.

Information Communication Technologies (ICTs) apart from sensitizing people against this heinous crime and helping them in general to change their opinion about a girl child, can also play a highly interventionist role by proactively pursuing cases against erring doctors, booking them under the law of the land and helplines for women need to be established. Girl children need both preventive and corrective protection.

To rein the malaise, the first step that needs to be taken is to end all discrimination and violence against women. The view that men are superior and women are subordinate to them must be demolished. Women need to be given equal rights, opportunities and the freedom to formulate their choices. Social discrimination, patriarchy, consumerism, technology, and violence against women, the cycle is only getting more vicious.

A multitude of organizations, networks and individuals need to come forward to advocate on these issues. There is a need to alter community attitudes and practices that endorse discrimination and violence against women to correct the dip in sex ratios. It must be recognized and publicized that gender inequality and dipping sex ratios is as much a loss to women as it is for men. Independence and assertiveness of women and the parent's concern for their daughters might initiate a new beginning for the girl child in India. The situation will improve only when mothers themselves treat their children with equality.

The Dowry Prohibition Act should be implemented more rigorously and stringently to ensure the parents that daughters are not a liability on the family. The Supreme Court has recently directed the Centre and the States to consider framing of rules to compel men seeking government employment to furnish information whether they had taken dowry if so whether the dowry had been made over to the wife as contemplated under the act. The rules could also seek such information from those already in government service.

The efforts would not yield desired results unless the people especially the women are educated and sensitized enough not to go for female foeticide or sex selection tests. Girls from poorer families generally drop out by high school. Girls who are educated are also likely to marry later and to have smaller, healthier families. Education helps girls to know their rights and claim them, for themselves and their families. As educated citizens, girls would be able to intervene more forcefully and positively on social issues to bring in a chain of social change. It is also essential to educate boys at school to respect, consider and even protect girls and women. Thus, students in schools and colleges need to be sensitized on this issue, and made aware of the far reaching impact of sex selective abortions at both micro and macro-level.

Mechanisms are essential to provide shelter, counseling, and possibility of foster or alternate placement, re-entry into schooling or development programs and for any prosecution of offenders.

An intense, awareness-raising cum advocacy national campaign on declining sex ratios must be formulated; it is important to involve both men and woman in the endeavor. There should be debate and dialogue on the pros and cons of the skewed sex ratio in India.

Needless to say, what is needed is change in the attitude of the society towards the female species and educating the public on the XY/XX chromosomes, which come from the father and are responsible for determining the sex of the child. Probably a mass awareness programme may change the social attitude which along with legislation can curb the evil sought to be protected by the Law. "A son is a son until the wife comes, while a daughter is always a daughter." The father's role in determining the sex of the male child must be emphasized to prevent unnecessary blaming mother.

One way to restore the gender imbalance is by making reservation in jobs for women, both in private and public sectors. Political empowerment is not enough without economic empowerment.

In Hindus, where male child is preferred for religious, cultural, social and inheritance purposes, situation will not likely to improve, unless the woman is given equal rights in family property and females are allowed to perform all the religious ceremonies, which a male can perform. It would require a lot of efforts and constant social engineering for decades.

The Hindu Succession (Amendment) Act, 2005, is a step in that direction. The parliament in its wisdom amended the Hindu Succession Act, 1956 by which a daughter is made coparcener and given equal status with the son. The amendment does give women equal rights in inheriting coparcenary property. But she can do so only in respect of ancestral (undivided) family property, and not the father's self-acquired property. The bulk of property and wealth at least in urban areas falls outside joint family property addressed by the law. However, what it will achieve is only a marginal improvement on the existing state of affairs.

Since the bias against the girl child is biased on economic considerations, the solution too will have to be economic. Turning the girl child from an economic liability into an economic asset is the most effective way of tackling the problem. The government should incentivise having a girl child through free education, extra PDS ration, perhaps even tax concessions for parents of girl children.

Thus, educational, financial and economic incentives should be given to girl child. Intensive efforts are needed to address the gender differentials in literacy, health care, land rights and work opportunities. Parents who have a daughter and no son should be rewarded. Mumbai launched a 'Ladli' campaign to save the girl child and the government recently announced educational incentives for 'single girl child.'

The Ministry of Human Resources Development, Government of India, has come up with a generous scheme providing free ships at graduate level. All single girl children will be eligible for free education from Class VI onwards (in case of two girls, a fee concession of 50%), and scholarships ranging from Rs. 550 to Rs. 2000 for graduate and post-graduate studies. The scheme would apply to all government-aided or affiliated schools and colleges in the country.

A system of financial penalties and incentives can be evolved. People who have a son and no daughter, and people who have sought female selective abortion (FSA), should pay more tax. The revenue from this tax would be used to support high quality care for orphan girls, their education, career placement, and trust funds.

Despite having a legal personality, an unborn child is generally considered in India as having no separate existence from the mother. Such right of an unborn child should also be expressly made a fundamental right. This will result in an enhancement of the status of an unborn child. When the parents themselves want to get rid of an unborn child, the state acting as parent can claim such right on behalf of the unborn child.

A 'reproductive rights regime' need to be evolved and should be considered in a theory of right to gender equality. The reproductive rights should focus on the value of the girl child and to make the girl child in difficult circumstances aware of her own potential; educate her about the rights to health guaranteed to her under all international human rights instruments, including the Constitution and Convention on the Rights of the Child, legislation enacted for her and the various measures undertaken by government. Child protection services at the local level must exercise special vigilance on the situation of girl children in every community. They will need to devise special needed approaches to serve girl children at all stages of childhood.

Strengthening of demographic records through monitoring sex ratios from birth, maintaining records of pregnancies and births and registration of births and marriages must be ensured. Registration of pregnant mothers should make compulsory like marriages, birth and death.

Registration of pregnancies should be notifiable under the law. If notification of a pregnancy is made mandatory at the time of the visit to doctor when a pregnancy is first confirmed and parents and doctors are asked to notify a local municipal authority, the creation of a record may act as a deterrent against sex selective abortion.

Medical Ethics and Humanities could be made part of the medical curriculum so we don't produce doctors who are technologically sound and morally corrupt.

Private hospitals at the district level are to be registered and their functioning to be brought under government guidelines. This is proposed in a Bill to amend the Medical Council Act. Medical ethics cannot be an option; medical malpractices need to be seen and punished as an offence.

The institutions which are given licenses for pre-natal diagnostic tests should be closely monitored and those who violate the law should be severely punished. A Medical Professional has responsibility to give correct information to his clients, and assist them in making the right decision. He can help the campaign immensely by:

- not carrying out sex determination tests,
- not revealing the sex of the foetus to parents or family,
- not performing abortions beyond the permitted time limits under the law,
- not providing assistance in pre-conception sex selection, and.
- reporting any such instances or doctors practicing any of the above to the concerned legal authority.

Thus, a medical professional can help us by realizing the important role in improving the sex ratio in the country. Social scientist in Indian universities and research institutions should give high priority to field studies and research to understand the deep-rooted son complex in Indian society. The University Grants Commission (UGC) and the Indian Council for Social Science Research (ICSSR) should likewise give the highest priority to such research while giving grants to scholars. Similar should be the case with economic, medical and legal research.

If apex religious organizations take stern action against those who violate their dictates a radical social change could come about. Gujarat has made a beginning with the health commissioner involving religious leaders and MLAs to implement the save girl child campaign. In Punjab too, religious leaders are participating in awareness campaigns. In Guatemala, the church had been approached to tackle reproductive health issues. United Nations has recently taken an unusual step by roping in religious organizations for the cause.

Sensitization on the issue is required for various groups. Young people, students, universities, corporate bodies, medical fraternity, media, elected representatives, religious leaders and lawyers. Students and teachers can share views and perceptions with other people in the community (like parents and neighbors) to identify common concerns as well as differences and discuss the problem as a human right and development issue and not purely as a women's issue and can mobilize political, cultural, administrative and community support for campaigning against SDT. Padyatras need to be organized in the districts which have been most adversely affected. Celebrities should go to villages to spread awareness. Steps should be taken to prepare girls to participate actively, effectively and equally with boys at all levels of social, economic, political and cultural leadership.

A student can join as a volunteer and contribute to its various activities. A citizen can help in disseminating information on the issue of SDT and participate in different activities that the campaign organizes from time to time and report cases of SDT to the appropriate authority in concern local area.

A teacher can become a member of campaign and provide valuable information to students about the issue and encourage them to join as volunteers. A mother can make an invaluable contribution by not differentiating between a son and a daughter. The safety of the child is a matter of supreme concern to a mother. If a mother is under any pressure from her family to 'give' them a son, and then resist it, and if necessary, report to the concerned legal authority, she can encourage gender equality at home. She should not seek medical intervention to conceive a boy child.

A father can help by not putting pressure on his wife for a son. He can support his wife, if the family and relatives are pressurizing her to undergo foetal sex-determination. He should not force her to determine the sex of the foetus and undergo abortion if it is a female child, or coerce her into going in for pre-conception sex selection. The decision to have a child (not a son or a daughter) should be taken together keeping in mind your wife's health. He can make a big difference by not differentiating between a son and a daughter. He should not seek medical interventions to conceive a boy child.

A family member or relative should not put pressure on women in the family to undergo pre-natal sex-determination or pre-conception sex determination. They should support her if other people in the family are insisting on sex-determination

A media Person should not publish advertisements offering sex determination facilities. Instead, make a positive contribution by publishing articles in his magazine or newspaper to generate awareness about the heinous proactive of PBEF, the law prohibiting it and difficulties in the implementation of the law. Support the cause of the girl child through your writing, photographs, films, documentaries or any other medium.

Government must also work to improve the existing infrastructure to ensure better access of women to education, health and economic resources. Social security measures need to be strengthened so as to reduce the dependence of parents on son during old age. Community services/pension schemes need to be strengthened in that direction. Recently, a Bill to protect old persons has been tabled in the parliament; the Bill makes it obligatory on the part of the children to provide support to their parents in the old age. The government might think of creating "dowry-free villages" where marriages are to be performed without the acceptance of dowry. A nation-wide movement with the help of local bodies and NGOs should be launched in this respect.

There is a need to reconsider introducing the two-child norm with serious disincentives attached for violators as its unintended fall-out could is lowering the count of girls. Instituting 'Balika Bodh Diwas' and 'Girl's Week' every year will help. Panchayati Raj institutions could be productively harnessed for awareness generation on the issue.

To keep a tab on the female foeticide, there is a need for a mass movement. The concerted efforts by the government and the people's bodies like the Panchayati Raj Institutions (PRIs), Village Education Development Committees (VEDCs), Parents Teachers Association (PTAs), Mothers Teachers Association (PTAs) and Mahila Mandals can help root out this problem from our society.

The Federation of Obstetrics and Gynaecological Society of India (FOGSI) which is a national body of gynaecologists had in 2009-10 formed 202 Dosst (Doctors Opposing Sex Selective Termination) cells across the country to check sex selective abortions and demanded maximum punishment for doctors doing foetal sex determination tests.

Some of the organizations actively working on this issue in Delhi are CAPF (Campaign Against Pre-Birth Elimination of Females), CWDS (Centre for Women's Development Studies), Deepalaya, Human Rights Law Network, Population

Foundation of India, National Foundation of India, Christian Medical Association of India, Action Aid, Jagori, Action India, PLAN India, etc. District level committees on violence against women need to monitor the clinics and activities of radiologists scrupulously.

Some initiatives developed by NGOs and governments to fight against female foeticide and girl infanticide include:

- Mass campaigns and rallies for awareness;
- Workshops, lectures, video spots, advertising and publication of articles;
- Piloting of conditional cash transfer schemes to support the survival and development of the girl child;
- Universal birth registration; Registration of pregnancies; Registration of ultrasound clinics;
- Collecting data on the status of the girl child, on still-born sex ratios and aborted foetuses sex ratio; and
- Constitution of vigil communities/task forces.

Exemplary work done by the members of public NGOs, doctors or officials should be highlighted. For e.g. there is a need to exemplifying examples of people who have adopted a girl child giving their reasons for doing so. It is heartening to note that in recent years, adoption of girl child have shown an encouraging response. These days many homes are urging childless couples to adopt girls with the one liner; "Take home a female child takes home emotional security". Parents who opt to stay with their married daughters should be applauded along with their sons in law. Highlighting cases of his kind would help to break the stereotypes.

The government needs to be pro-active in implementing the PNDT Act. A strong political will and honesty in the enforcement of such a law is needed for its success. There is a need to create public awareness against the practice of pre-natal sex determination of sex and female foeticide. Effective implementation of the existing legislation, existence of penalty and punishment, legal and policy reforms, advocating for women and gender-sensitive data collection, development of projects that improve women's health and expand their choices in life are also necessary.

Legal provisions need to be given more teeth. There is need for a clear and significant role of the police in implementing the Act. There should be elaboration of the process for filing a legal case, specifying the qualifications of officers and the conditions under which the power to search and seize records are delegated to such officers by the appropriate authority.

All States shall take effective measures, including legislative measures, to prevent and preclude the utilization of scientific and technological achievements to the detriment of human rights and fundamental freedoms and the dignity of the human person and to promote human rights and fundamental freedoms without any discrimination of religion, race, sex, language or cast.

All States shall take appropriate measures to prevent the use of scientific and technological developments, particularly by the State organs, to limit or interfere with the enjoyment of the human rights and fundamental freedoms of the individual as enshrined in the Universal Declaration of Human Rights, the International Covenants on Human Rights and other relevant international instruments and to satisfy the material and spiritual needs of all sectors of the population.

All States shall take measures to extend the benefits of science and technology to all strata of the population and to protect them, both socially and materially, from possible harmful effects of the misuse of scientific and technological developments, including their misuse to infringe upon the rights of the individual or of the group, particularly with regard to respect for privacy and the protection of the human personality and its physical and intellectual integrity.

All States shall promote international co-operation to ensure that the results of scientific and technological developments are used for the purpose of the economic and social development of peoples and the realization of human rights and freedoms in accordance with the Charter of the United Nations.

Science and technological development can benefit greatly by global cooperation and collaboration. Common goals can be effectively addressed by pooling both material and intellectual resources. International collaborative programmes especially those contributing directly to our scientific development and security objectives, will be encouraged between academic institutions and national laboratories in India and their counterparts in all parts of the world, including participation in mega science projects as equal partners. Special emphasis will be placed on collaborations with other developing countries, and particularly neighbouring countries, with which India shares many common problems.

To build a new and resurgent India that continues to maintain its strong democratic and spiritual traditions, that remains secure not only militarily but also socially and economically, it is important to draw on the many unique civilizational qualities that define the inner strength of India; this has been intrinsically based on an integrated and holistic view of nature and of life. The Science and Technology Policy 2003 will be implemented so as to be in harmony with our world view of the larger human family all around. It will ensure that science and technology truly uplifts the Indian people and indeed all of humanity.

These measures are more likely to have the desired result than sting operations against sex determination clinics that the government has just announced. In the end, one may feel the heart rending sentiment of an unborn female child addressed to her mother who is about to terminate the pregnancy.

To conclude, pre-natal sex selection has emerged as a serious problem in our country. Although the national law has brought all pre-natal testing (public and private) under legal regulations, it is full of loopholes. Forceful implementation of penal provisions (like imprisonment, fine and license revocation) is important, but the basic need is to improve the status of women substantially. Policies and programmes affirming and increasing the value of women are more important than governmental legislation to curb sex selective abortion.

If we are to take sex selective abortion seriously, we must place it high on the policy agenda. Effective control requires vision and long-term commitment to implement changes in the status of women that are truly comprehensive in scope.

A greater effort to engage the medical profession in taking a stand against genetic testing must be made both at national and international levels. In conclusion, the problem of sex selective abortion is just one more area in which medical professional women's organizations, social activists and policy-makers need to join forces to analyze the problem and seek a solution to this social problem.

Though the constructive side of development of science is concerned, it is of great significance, yet we can not ignore the other destructive side also. In fact, there is nothing wrong in science itself, but it is there in human being, who has exploited scientific developments for his vested interests. He has forgotten that scientific developments are not only meant for him, but also for the common good of the society.

Every coin has two sides, on one hand the progress of science and technology strengthened the human rights movement but on another hand the blind race of science and technology affected the human life adversely. It has become a major destructive tool for the human dignity. The excessive exploitation of natural resources and technological development has polluted the environment, created danger to public health and imbalanced the ecological balance in the world.

List of Cases

Olga Tellis *v.* Bombay Municipal Corporation, AIR 1986 SC 180; (1985) 3 SCC 545. 191
Pathuma *v.* State of Kerala (1978) 2 SCC1. 191
Paton *v.* United Kingdom (1980) 3 EHRR 408.
Parmananda Katara *v.* Union of India AIR, 1989 SC 2039.
Planned Parenthood of South Eastern Pennsylvania *v.* Casey, 1992 120 L.Ed 2nd 674. 164, 271
Paschim Bang Khet Mazdoor Samiti *v.* State of W.B (1996) 4 SCC 37.
P *v.* P (1965) 2 All ER 456. 271
Queen *v.* Arunja Bewa (1873) 19 W.R. (Cr.) 32. 227
Queen Empress *v.* Ademma, (1886) ILR 9 Mad 360. 185, 270
R *v.* Lobell (1957) 1 All E.R. 734. 168
Rex *v.* Bourne [1938] 3 AII E. R. 615-21. 167, 229, 270
Royal College of Nursing *v.* Department of Health and Social Security, [1981] 1 All E.R. 545 (H.L).
R *v.* Smith, [1974] 1 All E.R. 376. 229
Rosen *v.* La. State Board of Medical Examiners 380 F. Supp. 1217 (ED La 1970). 162
R. *v.* Tait (1989) 3 WLR 891. 162
Roe *v.* Wade (1972) 35 L Ed 2D 147. 160, 194
R. *v.* Cooper (1969) 1 All E.R. 615.
Royal College of Nursing of the United Kingdom *v.* Department of Health and Social Security (1981) 1 All E.R. 545. 170, 229
Ratlam Municipality *v.* Vardhi Chand, AIR 1980 SC 1622. 51
R. Rajagopal *v.* State of Tamil Nadu (1994) 6 SCC 632.
R *v.* Mc Donald (2002) N1 54.
Rance *v.* Mid-Downs HA (1991) 1 All E.R. 801.
R *v.* Collins & Others, Exparte S TLR May 8 1998.
Smt. Satya *v.* Shri Ram, AIR 1983 P & H 252. 137, 143, 270
Sushil Kumar *v.* Usha, AIR 1987 Del 86. 142, 143, 239, 271
State of Haryana *v.* Santra (2000) 5 SCC 182. 259
Sunil Batra *v.* Delhi Administration, AIR 1978 SC 1675.
Shri Bhagwan Katariya and others *v.* State of M.P., 2000.
Suman Kapur *v.* Sudhir Kapur (Nov. 7, 2008).
Subhash Kumar *v.* State of Bihar, AIR 1991 SC 420. 51
State of Maharashtra *v.* Madhulkar Narain, AIR SC 207.
State of Punjab *v.* Mohinder Singh Chawla, AIR 1997 SC 1225.

Sarinattudnga *v.* Government of Mysore (1935) 13 May L.J. 69. 226
TMA Pai Foundation *v.* State of Karnataka, AIR 2003 SC 355.
Unni Krishnan *v.* State of A.P., (1993) 1 SCC 645. 192
Vinod Soni *v.* Union of India, 2005 Cr. LJ 3408 (Bombay).
Vishaka *v.* State of Rajasthan (1997) 6 SCC 241. 157
William *v.* Marion Rapid Transit Inc, 87 NE 2d 334 (1949).
Walker *v.* Great Northern Rly. of Ireland (1890) 28 LR Ire. 176
Wilmington *v.* D.P.P. (1935) A.C. 402. 168
White *v.* White [2001] 1 A.C. 596. 142
Webster *v.* Reproductive Health Services, 492 US 490 (1989).
Yunghanns *v.* Candoora No. 19 Pty. Ltd. (No. 1) (1999-2000) 2 I.T E.L.R 589.

Bibliography

Agarwal, H.O., Human Rights (2005), Central Law Publications

Awasthi, S.K. and Kataria R.P., Law Relating to Protection of Human Rights (2000), Orient Publishing Company, Allahabad.

Alcorn, P., Social Issues in Technology—A Format for Investigation (1986), Prentice-Hall, Englewood-Ciffs, N.J.

Bakshi, P.M. and Singh Jaswant, The Constitution of India (1991), Vol. I, *Madras Law Journal Office*, Madras.

Baxi Upendra, Future of Human Rights (2002), Oxford University Press, New Delhi.

Ben Emerson and Andrew Ashworth, Human Rights and Criminal Justice (2001), Sweet and Maxwell Publications.

Bell, D., Fine Coming of Post-industrial Society—A Venture in Social forecasting (1976), Basic Books, New York.

Basu, D.D., Human Rights in Constitutional Law (2003), 2nd Edition, Wadhwa and Company, Nagpur.

Basu, Dr. (Justice) D.D., Human Rights in Constitutional Laws (1994), Prentice Hall of India Pvt. Ltd., New Delhi.

Basu, Dr. (Justice) D.D., Shorter Constitution of India 11th Edition, Prentice Hall of India Pvt. Ltd., New Delhi.

Chandra, U., Human Rights (1999), Allahabad Law Agency Publications.

Corillon, C., Science and Human Rights (1988), National Academy Press, Washington.

Donnelly Jack, Universal Human Rights in Theory and Practice (2003), 2nd Ed., Cornell University Press.

Doniger, Wendy and Smith, Brain K., The Law of Manu (2000), Penguin Boo India (P) Ltd., New Delhi.

Doniger, Wendy and Smith, Brain K., The Law of Manu (2000), Penguin Boo India (P) Ltd., New Delhi

Ellerman David, Helping People Help Themselves: An Alternative Philosophy of Development (2005), University of Michigan Press.

Ellul, J., The Technological *Society* (1965), Alfred A. Knopf, New York.

Forsythe, David P., Human Rights in International Relations (2000), Cambridge University Press.

Francis and Grootings, P., New Technologies and Work-Capitalist and Socialist Perspectives (1989), Rutledge, London/New York.

Goonesekere, Savitri, Children Law and Justice (2000), Allahabad Law Agency.

Gaur, K.D., The Indian Penal Code (2004), Universal Law Publishing Co., Delhi.

Handbook on PNDT Act, 1994 and Amendments (Revised Edition) (2003), Department of Family Welfare, Government of India, New Delhi.

Hauck, Vern E., Arbitrating Sex Discrimination Grievances (1998), Quorum Books

Hudson, Carl, Human Rights: A Compilation of International Instruments (1988), New York Press.

Haarscher, G., *Philosophie des droits de l'homme* (1987), Editions de l'Université de Bruxelles.

Hawrylyszyn, B., Road Maps to the Future Human Rights of Disadvantaged Groups (1980), Oxford Printing Press.

Havilland, William A., Anthropology: The Human Challenge (2005), 10th edition, Thomson Wadsworth Printing Press London.

Jain, Ashok K., The Saga of Female Foeticide in India, Socio Legal Offshoots (2006), Ascent Publications, Delhi.

Jaswal, Paramjit S. and Jaswal, Nishtha: Human Rights and the Law (1996), APH Publishing Corporation, Delhi.

Johnston and Sasson, A., New Technologies and Development: Science and Technology as Factors of Change: Impact of Recent and Foreseeable Scientific and Technological Progress on the Evolution of Societies, Especially in the Developing Countries (1986), UNESCO, Paris.

Jain, M.P., Indian Constitutional Law (2005), 5th Edition Wadhwa and Company, Nagpur.

Jaising (Ed.), Pre-Conception and Pre Natal Diagnostic Techniques Act, A Users Guide to the Law (2004), Universal Law Publishing Co., Delhi.

Kerr, C., The Future of Industrial Societies—Convergence or Continuing Diversity (1983), Harvard University Press, Cambridge, Mass./London.

Khosla Justice G.D., Our Judicial System (1992), The University Book Agency, Allahabad.

Klitou Demetrius, The Friends and Foes of Human Rights (1989), Manchester University Press.

Kochler Hans, The Principles of International Law and Human Rights (2006), A Mukherji and Co., Calcutta.

Kohen, In Defense of Human Rights: A Non-Religious Grounding in a Pluralistic World (2007), Oxford University Press.

Kamat, Vikas, India's Arranged Marriages (2003), Penguin Printing Press, New Delhi.

Littman, David, Universal Human Rights (1999), St. Martin's Press, Oxford Printing Press, 1980.

Latour, B., Science in Action (1987), Open University Press.

Murphy, J.W. and Pardeck, T., Introduction to J.W. Murphy and D. Pardeck, eds., Technology and Human Productivity—Challenges for the Future (1986); Quorum Books, New York.

Mehta, P.L. and Verma, Neena, Human Rights under the Indian Constitution (1999), Deep and Deep Publications, New Delhi.

M.P. Tandon, Public International Law (1996), 13th Edition, Allahabad Law Agency, Allahabad.

Machowski, J., Freedom to Disadvantaged group and Human Right (1989), Polish Printing Press.

Michael, D., Human Rights of Vulnerable Groups (2006), Princeton University Press, London.

Nirmal, C.J., Human Rights in India (2004), Modern Law Publications.

Nirmal, C.J., Human Rights In India (2000), Oxford University Press, USA.

Ogburn, W.F., On Culture and Social Change (1964), University of Chicago Press, Chicago/London.

Prendergast, William E., Treating Sex Offenders (2004), 2nd Edition, Haworth Press.

Registrar General India Census of India, 2001, Series 1, India, Provisional Population Totals, Paper 1 of 2001, (2001), Controller of Publications, New Delhi.

Singh, D.P., Female Foeticide in Punjab—Causes and Consequences (2007), Paragon International Publishers, New Delhi.

Saxena Priti, Preventive Detention and Human Rights (2007), Deep and Deep Publications, New Delhi.

Seervai, H.M., Constitutional Law of India—A Critical Commentary (1975), Vol. I, 2nd Edition, N.M. Tripathi Pvt. Ltd Company, Bombay.

Sen, Amartya, Human Rights and Asian Values (2004), Vikash Publications Pvt. Ltd.

Saxena, K.P., Human Rights perspective and challenges (In 1900's and beyond), World Congress on Human Rights, 1995 Re-Print, Lancers Books, New Delhi.

Siemienski, F., Constitutional Law (1976), Warsaw, Steiner J. and Alston Philip: International Human Rights in Context: Law, Politics, Morals (1996), Oxford: Clarendon Press.

T.K. Tope, Constitutional Law of India, 2nd Edition, Eastern Book Company, Lucknow.

Tittle, Carol K., What to do about Sex Bias in Testing (1979), WEECN.

The Indian Penal Code, 1860 (2005), Universal Law Publishing Co., Delhi.

The Medical Termination of Pregnancy Act, 1971 (2004), Universal Law Publishing Co., Delhi.

The Pre-Conception and Pre-Natal Diagnostic Techniques (Prohibition of Sex Selection), Act, 1994 (2005), Universal Law Publishing Co., Delhi.

Universal Declaration of Human Rights, The International Bill of Human Rights (United Nations, New York, 197X).

Weeramantry, C.G., Human Rights and Scientific and Technological Development (1990), United Nations University, Tokyo.

Wiedza, Civil Rights and Protection (1989), Warsaw Publications

Wolicki, K. and Marx Karl, The Emancipation of Humanity and Individual Freedom (1984), *New York Review of Books*, No. 4.

Weeramantry, C.G., The Slumbering Sentinels; Law and Human Rights in the Wake of Technology (1983), Penguin Books Australia.

Wisniewski, L., Safeguards of Fundamental Rights and Freedoms of the Citizens of the Polish People's Republic (1981), Wroclaw (In Polish).

Journals and Articles

Ahmad, "Pre Natal Diagnostic Techniques: A Source of Gender Bias", *Kashmir University Law Review-X* (2003).

Abortion Act, 1967 (as amended by Sec. 37, Human Fertilisation and Embryology Act, 1990).

All India Reporters, New Delhi.

Baxi, "Gender and Reproductive Rights in India: Problems and Prospects for the New Millennium", A Report by UNFPA, New Delhi (2001).

B. Joerges, "Technology in Everyday Life: Conceptual Queries", *Journal for the Theory of Social Behaviour*, Vol. 18, No. 2 (1988).

Bhagat, "Technology to the Rescue of Girl Child", *The Times of India*, New Delhi, December 11 (2005).

Chatterjee, "A Century of Social Reform for Women's Status", *Indian Journal of Social Work*, Vol. XLI, No. 3, October (1980).

Chandra, "Female Foeticide: Causes, Laws and Preventive Strategies", Paper presented at a Symposium held at New Delhi, July (2005).

Congenital Disability (Civil Liability) Act, 1976.

Human Right Annual Journal.

Indian Journal of Legal Studies, JNVU, Jodhpur.

International and Comparative Law Quarterly.

International Covenant on Civil and Political Rights, 1966.

Kishwar, When Daughters are unwanted: Sex Determination Tests in India (1995), Manushi 86:1522.
Mehta and J. Kothari, "Pre-Natal Sex Selection and Law", *Lawyers Collective,* November (2001).
Offences Against The Person Act, 1861.
"Pre-Natal Diagnostic and Female Foeticide", *Unreported Judgments Journal* (2002) (1).
Protection of Human Rights Act, 1993.
Reddy, G.B., "Role of Judiciary in Protection of Human Rights of Women", AIR 1999 Journal 148.
Supreme Court Cases published by NHRC.
The Employment News, New Delhi.
The Hindu, Newspaper.
UNFPA, "Sex Selective Abortions and Fertility Decline: The Case of Haryana and Punjab", New Delhi (2001).
Universal Declaration of Human Rights, 1948.
Violation of Human Right Cases.
World Health Organization Manual.

Web Sites Visited

Female Foeticide: Need for Effective Advocacy and Communication (2005), available at http://www.indiafemalefoeticide.org.
Handbook on PNDT Act, 1994 (2005), available at http://www.indiafemalefoeticide.org.
http://www.savegirlchild.org.
www.girlsrights.org
http://www.savethechildren.net.
http://www.indianchild.com.
Murthy, Sex Selection: Getting Down to Business (2005), available at http://infochangeindia.org.
www.lawindia.com.
www.unicef.org
www.findlaw.com
www.unesco.org
www.cehat.org
www.epw.org.in
www.un.org/womenwatch

Index